90 0890321 4

KW-491-929

University of Plymouth
Charles Seale Hayne Library
Subject to status this item may be renewed
via your Voyager account

http://voyager.plymouth.ac.uk
Tel: (01752) 232323

POLITEXT

Ricard Marí
Álvaro Librán

Safety and Security on passenger ships

EDICIONS UPC

GOBIERNO
DE ESPAÑA

MINISTERIO
DE FOMENTO

Publication sponsored by the Ministry of Public Works (2009)

First edition: September 2009

© Ricard Marí Sagarra, 2009

© Edicions UPC, 2009
Edicions de la Universitat Politècnica de Catalunya, SL
Jordi Girona Salgado 1-3, 08034 Barcelona
Tel.: 934 137 540   Fax: 934 137 541
Edicions Virtuals: www.edicionsupc.es
E-mail: edicions-upc@upc.edu

Production: LIGHTNING SOURCE

Legal deposit: B-36523-2009
ISBN: 978-84-9880-373-0

Prologue

Transporting cargo by sea has always been considered somewhat of an adventure due to the influence of atmospheric and oceanographic conditions that are capable of causing delays in the crossing, the breakdown of the ship, damage to the goods, maritime accidents and injury of crew members.

Concerns regarding safety at sea appeared with the very emergence of the art of sailing itself. Such concerns were, however, mainly limited to merchant transport. In a sector which has historically suffered deep-rooted marginalisation, it is only in recent times that a new social concern for anything regarding the sea, the people who make their living from it and the passenger transport service, has arisen. Repercussions from recent maritime accidents with passenger fatalities, coupled with worrying land-based terrorist activity, have led to certain incidents (considered crisis situations because they may affect a large number of people, passengers and crew members) being more readily identified, dealt with and resolved from a public perspective.

Until recently, the term *security* was only really applied to situations relevant to the actual operating of the ship itself and to the geographical maritime environment it was sailing through. Nowadays it includes incidents caused by human error and everything related to coexistence on board a passenger ship. It covers a broad range of possibilities from a simple complaint or non-compliance with regulations to gang violence on board or vandalism carried out by unhappy or rude individuals, and reaching as far as crimes committed by organised criminals and hostage taking.

The purpose of this publication is to provide information about the causes of crisis situations on board passenger ships, the peaceful procedures to be followed by crew members for controlling the situation with negotiation, how intervention plans should be carried out as a supplement to the official ship's security plans, and how parameters which can lead to shock and panic among passengers can be controlled. By doing so, it aims to ensure the majority of people involved in the situation are evacuated safely and efficiently.

By including the subject of public safety on board ship, we bring the topic of comprehensive maritime transport safety full circle. In doing so, we believe that this book will help professionals accept the aforementioned parameters both on board ship and in port facilities.

THE AUTHORS

Index

1 Introduction

1.1 General aspects

The expression *'crisis situation*' has always been applied to extremely serious incidents affecting a large number of people, and which need resolving or controlling in accordance with agreements adopted by high ranking officials in the field concerned (political, governmental, ministerial, managerial, etc.). However, when the incident takes place aboard ship, especially a passenger ship, it should be resolved, first and foremost, by the Captain, his officers and, in more serious or far-reaching incidents, with external help whenever possible. In both cases, the crisis situation will be brought under control using strategies agreed by the respective crisis cabinets or by the immediate application of specific, well-practised procedures.

A crisis can be defined as any situation created by a threat which could result in serious injury or death, damage to goods, to interests or to image. This publication will show how breaking with the ship's routine activity in any way can cause a crisis situation, whatever the real nature or seriousness of the original situation.

Aboard merchant ships, so-called *maritime accidents* are classified as emergencies when they affect the ship and its crew entirely or partially: fires and explosions, leaks, running aground, excessive listing and others which seafarers are well-acquainted with and are generally accepted as part of the maritime adventure, such as inherent vice and any danger associated with the merchandise being transported.

All ships, but especially passenger ships, are also vulnerable to incidents intentionally provoked by human beings, whether through intentional wrongdoing or the involuntary degeneration of a situation between persons. In all situations, the resulting breakdown does not only require the application of well-structured technical measures befitting the level of aggression, but it also requires a correct treatment of the human factors involved in the incident and, consequently, a specific approach towards personal attitudes of both individuals and groups, in an aim to control the situation. This is, of course, always done with the objective of not aggravating the crisis situation which could lead to uncontrollable levels of seriousness and dire consequences, and assuming that the problem will quite likely be solved in a different manner to that generally seen in the aforementioned accident or emergency crisis situations.

The common denominator for all the crisis situations dealt with in this publication is the variability of the human factor in regards to responses and attitudes shown by both the perpetrators, considered instigators of the situation, and persons affected when attempting to oppose the aggression. Unexpected and very different responses can result from the emotional state of both parties and, in most cases, these are only provoked by the tone or loudness of the voice used in communication, hand gestures, body movements or any other interpretation of the passive or active reaction of people.

There are not many publications dedicated to the treatment and control of crisis situations with a focus on prevention, protection and intervention in each case in point. Our objective, therefore, is to begin to fill this void in the maritime field whilst, at the same time, providing a supporting document meeting the criteria indicated for the courses in *Basic passenger ship training* and, especially, the *Ro-ro passenger ships and passenger ships other than ro-ro vessels training*, in accordance with BOE (Spanish Official Gazette) n° 226 of 20/09/02 which annuls the contents of the BOE n° 200 dated 20/08/1992. It further develops the criteria incorporated by the IMO regarding the rigorous, well-thought out and forward planning in anticipation of conditions and circumstances surrounding all events and types of accidents, especially those classified as maritime accidents, which fully define the expression *gestión de planes de emergencia* (crisis plan management). This is found in the different sections of the texts in Resolutions: MSC 66 and 67 (68)[1], A.865 (20)[2] and A.852 (20)[3], which constitute courses given in line with the STCW, such as:

> *Basic passenger ship course* for captains, bridge officers and engine officers, sailors and any other person having responsibility for the safety of passengers in emergency situations on passenger ships with a gross tonnage over 100 and less than 500 GT or which are authorised to transport more than 50 and fewer than 300 passengers.

> The course content elaborates on the regulations regarding competence in paragraphs 1, 2, 3 and 5 of both regulations of Section A-V/2 of the Training Code and, respectively, on crowd management, familiarisation and safety for all personnel providing a direct service to passengers in passenger spaces.

> *Course for ro-ro ships and passenger ships other than ro-ro vessels* for captains, bridge officers and engine officers, sailors and any other person having responsibility for the safety of passengers in emergency situations on passenger ships, including both roll-on roll-off (ro-ro) and conventional ships with a tonnage of over 500 GT or which are authorised to transport more than 300 passengers.

> The course content elaborates on the regulations in paragraphs 1 and 5 of the regulations in Section A-V/2 and A-V/3 of the Training Code on passenger safety, cargo and hull integrity, and crisis management and human behaviour, respectively.

---

[1] Approval of amendments to the amended International Convention STCW/78, both dated 04/06/97

[2] Knowledge required by personnel designated to aid passengers in emergency situations.

[3] Knowledge required by officers who must manage a comprehensive emergency plan system aboard [Resolution A.852 (20) of the 27.11.97], especially taking into consideration *Illegal acts which pose a threat to the security of the ship, to the passengers or to the crew.*

> ➢ *Evacuation, abandoning ship, crowd and panic management,* corresponding to regulation V/3 of the STCW, established on 01.01.99.

However, given the evolutionary nature of prevention in the area of public safety, every one of the principles put forward could be applied to any kind of vessel (cargo, passenger, recreational or fishing vessels) and to all shipping company managers, passenger port managers, heads of Civil Defence, State Security Forces, paramedic services and the fire service, all of whom may be involved in a crisis situation on board a passenger ship, either on a management level or taking part in the intervention itself. This is, of course, providing they do not already have an objective, effective and easy-to-use tool to deal with the security problems specific to our century. As the will to do wrong will always exist and people will strive to achieve notoriety through illegal acts or to get rich through crime, there is a need to have specific plans of action in place to reduce risk and to regain control of the situation.

1.2 Structure

The contents of this publication have been divided into blocks as follows:

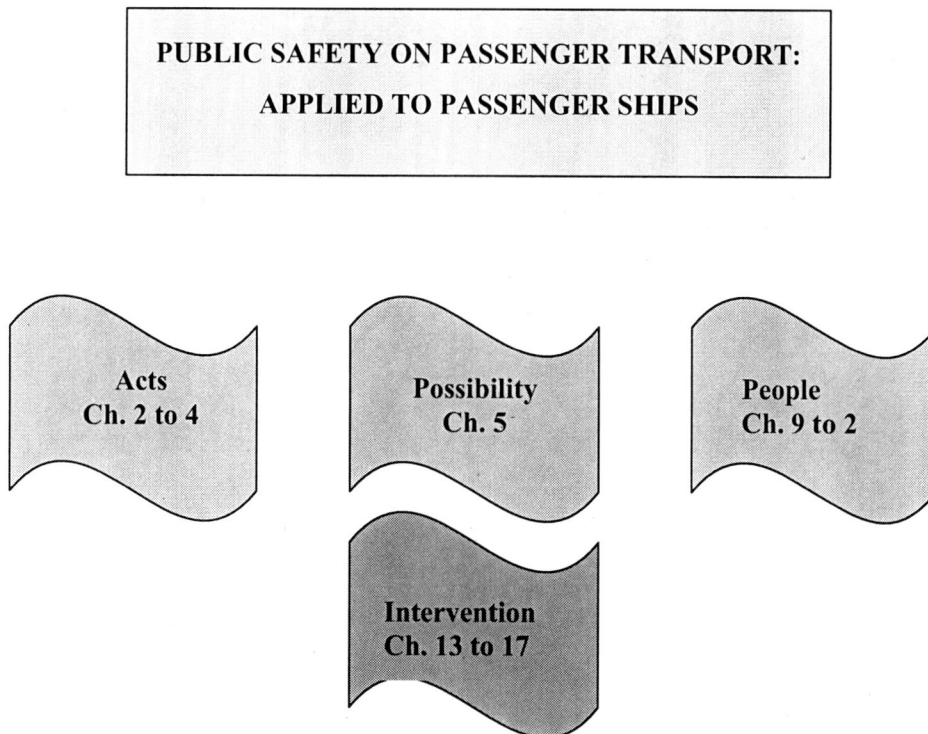

PUBLIC SAFETY ON PASSENGER TRANSPORT:

APPLIED TO PASSENGER SHIPS

Acts
Ch. 2 to 4

Possibility
Ch. 5

People
Ch. 9 to 2

Intervention
Ch. 13 to 17

2 Illegal acts

2.1 Piracy

The current international law against piracy, introduced as a result of the 1958 Convention on the High Seas, and reinforced in the 1982 United Nations Convention on the Law of the Sea, defines piracy in article 101 as: "any illegal acts of violence or detention, or any act of depredation, committed for private ends by the crew or the passengers of a private ship or a private aircraft, and directed:

    a.   On the high seas, against another ship or aircraft, or against persons or property on board such ship or aircraft.

    b.   Against a ship, aircraft, persons or property in a place outside the jurisdiction of any State.

    c.   Any act of voluntary participation in the operation of a ship or of an aircraft with knowledge of facts making it a pirate ship or aircraft".

Maritime commerce and piracy run almost parallel with each other, as the practice of seizing a ship's cargo was widespread throughout history. From the era of the Phoenicians to Greek and Roman times, particularly intense periods of pirate activity were recorded. During the Middle Ages, piracy in Europe was linked mainly to Viking and Arab conquests and led to true pirate states being established under the aegis of the Ottoman Empire. Known as Barbary States, these survived until the 14th century.

The discovery of the New World and the impressive flow of merchant traffic carrying valuable cargo from America to Spain led to the creation of a powerful pirate fleet, with the Golden Age of piracy being more or less between 1690 and 1720. For a long time the Caribbean was a paradise for pirates, but in 1689 England and Spain joined forces temporarily and, for a short time, they put a stop to the impunity of pirates in the area. In the main it was the English who plundered Spanish ships. They then turned their sights to the Indian Ocean and established bases in North American ports where influential individuals were willing to give economic support to the capture missions in return for a percentage of the profits. This also provided them with superficial legal cover, granting them worthless authorisation, quite unlike the *privateer patent.*

The latter, issued on behalf of the Crown or government, authorised a private, armed vessel (privateer) to operate in wartime with a license to attack and capture enemy merchant ships, while establishing the limits of the power that could be exercised. The first "privateer patent" was granted in England in 1293, but it was not until the end of the 16th century that the system of taking prize at sea became an institution. According to this system, the Crown received 10% of the value of the cargo whilst the rest belonged to the privateer. Other countries adopted the same system and it was used until 1856 when it was abolished by the Paris Declaration.

Piracy still exists today. Although pirates do not have quite the same notoriety as those of the days of sail, their attacks are still just as cruel. On a global scale, theft at sea continues to be a cause for concern for both national and international authorities. Often the criminals target passengers on board boats with expensive instrumentation and electronic equipment, plus they can expect to find enough cash to make the attack thoroughly worthwhile. However, such passengers are not the only people in danger; any vessel, from a simple boat to a large petrol tanker, can fall victim to pirates. Piracy can be any violent act, including the theft or hijack of a ship, its sinking, the taking of hostages on board, contraband and even privateering.

There are two kinds of pirates operating on the high seas, one is the professional pirate and the other what we could call an amateur or "casual pirate". The objectives of these two pirates are entirely different, the first seeking regular income and the latter looking to make the most of an opportunity to steal cash and items which will be easy to sell on. Both groups of pirates aim for a quick hit allowing them an easy escape and as little fuss as possible. In this manner, a thief at sea is no different from a land-based one.

Over the last twenty years certain changes have been observed in types of piracy around the world, though these have made them no less illegal. Twenty years ago the main driving force behind piracy was drug trafficking. The traffickers would hijack comfortable and well-equipped yachts to transport drugs from South America to the Caribbean and even the United States without being detected.

Today, drug trafficking has become just another of the motives for casual piracy where theft is the main objective. Professional pirates on the other hand continue to assault small vessels as much as large ships, and their actions encompass everything from the simple theft of money, personal effects and equipment, to the hijacking of the ship itself and the stealing of its cargo.

The places where pirates have been operating in recent years, or where acts of piracy have been most frequently reported are:

- The Caribbean, where the main motivation is drug trafficking.
- The South China Sea, especially in the area of the Thousand Islands.
- The Malacca Strait and the Singapore Strait.
- The Philippines, especially the Sulu Sea and the Mindanao coast.
- Ports in Brazil (especially Port of Santos), and in Ecuador, Columbia and Venezuela.
- Many ports on the Western coast of Africa, particularly in Nigeria.
- In India, Bangladesh and, more commonly, in the anchorage belonging to the Port of Colombo.
- To a lesser extent, the Gulf of Aden.

Acts of piracy are generally carried out at night and are classified into several groups:

A) Attacks made whilst the ship is docked or at anchor by pirates which climb up the mooring ropes, the anchor chain, or the sides of the ship from small boats. In some cases the thieves can enter the ship via the gangplank, or via the doors used for taking on fuel or provisions.

B) Attacks made whilst the ship is in motion. Making the most of the darkness the pirates approach the ship in small, fast boats with six to eight people on board. They pull up to the stern or alongside and board the ship by throwing a grappling hook on a rope over the railings or climbing up a bamboo pole with a hook at the top.

C) Another system uses a large "mother ship" which then releases several small boats linked by a rope measuring more than forty metres in length. These smaller boats position themselves in front of the ship which then runs into the rope thereby pulling the dinghies into their desired position and allowing the pirates to climb aboard using ropes or bamboo poles.

Pirate attacks on moving ships are very frequent in the waters around South East Asia. They are particularly common to the south of China where many nations converge, or where there are nations made up of many small islands, as these help pirates act with total impunity. These pirates do not seem to be organised and have no allegiance to anyone but themselves. They operate close to the borders with international waters and in territorial waters, ensuring they have rapid access to a safe port in case they are chased by a foreign, armed patrol. They do occasionally operate away from the coast, but rarely on the high seas.

The bridge is their first objective, given that it is the control and management centre. In the meantime, other pirates spread out all over the ship, intimidating the crew. It is advisable not to put up any resistance to the pirates. They are most often armed with knives and machetes, but on occasion will carry firearms. The most dangerous even have automatic weapons, normally AK-47s which are readily available on the arms market, especially in the Far East.

The frightening part of the operation carried out by pirates who attack a moving ship is the fact they often tie up the crew and abandon the moving ship leaving it with the automatic pilot working. In such busy shipping lanes as the Malacca Strait, this creates a potentially dangerous collision situation or the possibility of an ecological disaster. The ship may also be hijacked and sailed into a "friendly" port where the cargo is then sold and the ship is later freed. In some more dramatic cases, pirates have taken over the ship completely, stolen the cargo, murdered the crew and later sold the ship itself.

The recent case of the "Anna Sierra" is a good example of this type of act[1]

To show the developments in piracy since the events of the 11th September, the following short news articles have been collected from specialist sources over this period, and summarised to keep them brief.

2.1.1 News items relating to piracy

1. The project to open a canal through the Kra isthmus, in Thailand, is currently being reconsidered, not only to create a shipping lane between China and Japan, but also to open further routes from South East Asia and Australia, as pirates would then find it more difficult to take the ships to the north of Kra, assuming the anchorage was considered safe. *13/09/2001 – Fairplay International Shipping Weekly*

2. The United States Maritime Administration issued a terrorist threat warning to all shipping agents flying the U.S. flag and to patrol boats, in which it explained that hostile action directed towards merchant ships is a real and growing problem. These hostile acts include piracy, theft and terrorism. *17/09/2001 13:41:55 – Fairplay Daily News.*

3. Three days after the attacks, the U.S. Congress has approved $40bn to cover all damage. A large part of the total sum, $600m, will be spent immediately on port and maritime security. The aim is to ensure the Coast Guard has a full picture of everything related to a ship before it enters any U.S. port. *20/09/2001 – Fairplay international Shipping Weekly.*

4. The participants in an international conference in Tokyo reached the conclusion that in the fight against piracy a multilateral regional cooperation is an absolute must, and that Asian countries must take the initiative and adopt anti-piracy measures in Asia. *05/10/2001 11:38:10 – Fairplay Daily News.*

---

[1] This case came to light when the crew were rescued after having been abandoned on a raft and a pontoon. "Saga of the Anna Sierra". Planed pirac/ Fairplay, 30th November 1995.

5. In relation to the increase in piracy-related incidents in South East Asian waters, the heads of INTERTANKO have requested protection for oil tankers in the Malacca Straits, as they do not agree with crew members having access to weapons on board. 05/10/2001 12:44:18 – *Fairplay Daily News.*

6. BIMCO has written to the United Nations General Secretary, Kofi Annan (with a copy sent to Hill O'Neil), warning of the maritime transport security problems, and with the hope that fear of a floating bomb will make people fully aware of pirate attacks. 18/10/2001 – *Fairplay International Shipping Weekly.*

7. According to the International Maritime Bureau (IMB) in Kuala Lumpur, the number of pirate attacks on merchant ships has decreased, registering only 253 attacks in 9 months compared with 294 attacks during the same period in the previous year. However, the Bureau still considers the waters close to ports and anchorage in Indonesia dangerous. Increased surveillance by the authorities in Bangladesh has resulted in attacks being reduced from 32 to 19. In waters to the south of India, however, and in Chennai, Kochi Kakinada and Kandla in the north, the same amount of attacks as last year are still taking place. The pirates are asking for a ransom in exchange for releasing the crew of the hijacked vessel. 18/10/2001 09:24:59 – *Fairplay Daily News.*

8. Members of the Coast Guard from both the Philippines and Japan took part in a joint exercise on the 31st October to determine their potential to fighting piracy, both in ports and at sea. 18/10/2001 13:56:24 – *Fairplay Daily News.*

9. In the future, ships transporting nuclear fuel must be escorted by armed patrols as protection against terrorist acts. After the September the 11th attacks, the possibility of a terrorist attack on a ship carrying radioactive material in the Pacific Ocean has increased tenfold. An exclusion zone will need to be established at 5 to 10 miles around the ship. 31/10/2001 10:04:42 – *Fairplay Daily News.*

10. The vulnerability of maritime transport to terrorist attack has been highlighted. This is especially true of ships transporting radioactive material rather than ships transporting standard cargo. 15/112001 – *Fairplay International Shipping Weekly.*

11. Consignees in the Dominican Republic say private security guards are needed in the port of Río Haina as protection against pirate attacks and stowaways. In two separate incidents in April and August, armed pirates boarded oil tankers in the anchorage there. Local authorities say theft is infrequent, but stowaways are a serious problem, especially on ships bound for the United States. 29/11/2001 – *Fairplay Internacional Shipping Weekly.*

12. In the 22nd session of the IMO General Assembly, held yesterday in London, decisions were made regarding piracy and the treatment of persons rescued at sea. In order to fight against piracy, the delegates urged governments to sign the 1988 Rome Convention and to establish strict security measures in port and terminal areas, including those found at sea. 30/11/2001 13:13:47 – *Fairplay Daily News.*

13. Maritime sources in Ecuador have urged ship owners to pay careful attention to reports of pirate attacks in the commercial port of Guayaquil. In an event which took place on the 6th December, 7 pirates armed with pistols and knives boarded a moving container ship. The alarms sounded and the crew went straight to the bridge. In the meantime, the pirates accessed the containers on the ship, stole part of the cargo and escaped on a speedboat. Several acts of piracy have taken place this year and thirteen were reported in 2000. 03/01/2002 - *Fairplay International Shipping Weekly.*

14. The state of Sabah, in Malaysia, has given instructions to all ships planning to enter or leave its waters. Under new rules, no firearms are allowed on board, and the flag of a ship's home port, or country must be flown when sailing in their waters during the day. 15/01/2002 09:53:42 – *Fairplay Daily News.*

15. Many ships using the port of Mongla, the second port serving Bangladesh, on a regular basis are reaching the limit of their tolerance regarding port security levels due to the increase in acts of piracy there. 16/01/2002 09:31:39 – *Fairplay Daily News.*

16. Although pirate attacks in the Malacca Strait are decreasing, the International Maritime Bureau has issued a warning regarding the ransoms demanded in exchange for kidnapped crews. The amounts demanded by the pirates are known not to be excessive and ship owners are paying them to avoid problems. 04/02/2002 11:04:58 – *Fairplay Daily News.*

17. Korea's maritime minister has established communication with countries in South East Asia and has had GPS installed in 100 merchant ships as part of the measures he is taking to prevent pirate attacks in the Malacca Straits. 20/02/2002 10:04:57 - *Fairplay Daily News.*

18. Ship owners and ship's captains are loath to report pirate attacks for fear of their ships being investigated as a result. In the wake of the September 11th attacks, both the industry and governments are aware of a possible relationship between terrorist groups and armed attacks on ships. A possible scenario is that terrorist groups will hijack large petrol tankers to use on suicide missions. 22/02/2002 10:14:57 – *Fairplay Daily News.*

19. Twenty-one seafarers were killed by pirates in 2001. Although the equivalent number for 2000 is sixty, this number is not accurate because of the inclusion of two terrorist incidents in the final figures. The violence used in attacks on crew has escalated as has the number of attacks made by pirates carrying firearms. Attacks using knives were more numerous in 2001 (105 compared to 73 with firearms), but the tendency is towards the greater use of firearms. 21/02/2002 – *Fairplay International Shipping Weekly.*

20. After talks lasting five days, the Navigation Section of the Maritime Safety Division has been restructured to form the Navigational Safety Section and the Maritime Security Section. 21/02/2002 – *Fairplay International Shipping Weekly.*

21. Piracy in Guayaquil, the largest port in Ecuador, has become so commonplace that armed patrols have been placed along an 81 km stretch starting from the entrance canal. General Management of the Merchant Marina and the Maritime Chamber of Commerce have declared a crisis situation after five ships were attacked last month. Patrol boats patrol the canal constantly and helicopters equipped with infrared detectors operate at night in areas most prone to pirate attacks. 08/05/2002 09:19:46 – *Fairplay Daily News.*

22. The oil tanker Han Wei, which was hijacked by Thai pirates in March, has been found in Thailand. The thirteen crew members are safe and have returned home. The ship was discovered at anchor five miles out of Sriracha by a Thai naval helicopter. 15/05/2002 08:15:09 – *Fairplay Daily News.*

We can draw the conclusion here that, as far as piracy is concerned, concepts for dealing with the problem have evolved considerably. In addition, recognition and interest in the problem are much keener and procedures have been significantly improved since the tragic events of the 11th September. The main objective has been to create a solid and general block against all illegal acts perpetrated against anyone in our global society.

Areas suffering frequent, high intensity, aggressive attacks showing a complete lack of respect for the lives of crew members still exist. Substantial funds have been designated to make safe the maritime areas most frequented and most at risk, and cooperation agreements in the fight against piracy have been strengthened in affected countries. Pirates set up their criminal procedures with a focus on the crew whom they kidnap and demand a ransom for.

Special shipments of dangerous cargo are identified and targeted by pirates to be later used in terrorist attacks. Maritime countries create safety zones around their ports and control them with sophisticated equipment. As a political measure on an international scale, the Navigation Section of the Maritime Safety Division has been restructured to provide two main bodies of action, the Navigational Safety Section and the Maritime Security Section.

2.2 Terrorism

It is clear that strict measures should be taken against terrorism in all areas, but without giving in to the temptation of suspecting and criminalising entire ethnic groups. A clear distinction must be made between politically motivated terrorist threats and other forms of violent threats. One has to realise, however, that there is an infinite number of basic criminal acts which have been carried out, and are still carried out, by political extremists in support of their cause.

Regarding international rules and regulations, Spain ratified the convention and protocol, dated 10th March, 1988[2], for the suppression of unlawful acts against the safety of maritime navigation and of fixed platforms on the continental shelf. Of all the articles, article 3 stands out as it gives a definition of what is understood by aggression against safety in navigation which is very similar to that of terrorism.

Broadly speaking, a person is committing such a crime if they intentionally seize a ship or take control of it through the use of violence or any other form of intimidation; if they commit acts of violence against persons on board, providing those acts risk put the ship in danger; if they destroy or cause damage to a ship or its cargo; if, by any means, they place, or have placed, a device or substance which may destroy or damage the ship or its cargo and place the ship in danger; if they destroy or cause damage to the maritime navigation facilities or services, or seriously impede their correct functioning; if they give out information they know to be false, thereby putting a ship in danger; or, in relation to all these acts, if they kill or injure any person. Any attempt to commit these crimes, to incite them, or any complicity in them is also considered an offence, as is any threat made.

Within the internal organisation, these acts would be sanctioned in the main (although not entirely) in accordance with Organic Law 10/95 of the Penal Code, dated 23rd November, as crimes of destruction, a term with similar connotations to sabotage.

Article 346 states that those who cause destruction are any persons who cause damage to airports, ports, collective means of transport, among others, by causing explosions or similar, or who sink a ship or cause it to run aground. Terrorism is covered by article 571 and the following articles of the Penal Code which define terrorists as those who belong to, serve or collaborate with armed gangs, organisations or groups whose objective is to subvert constitutional order or seriously breach the peace, commit crimes of destruction or fire-realated crimes as described in articles 346 and 351[3]... (art. 571). It is also a crime to store weapons or ammunition, or to possess or store explosive, inflammable, incendiary or asphyxiating substances or artifacts (or their components) as well as to manufacture, deal in, transport or supply them in any way, and to simply place or use such substances,

---

[2] According to document 15th June 1989, published in the BOE, number 99, 24th April 1992.

[3] Article 351. Any person causing a fire which puts the life or physical safety in danger, will be punished with a prison sentence of ten to twenty years. Judges or Courts may pass a more lenient sentence if the resulting danger and other circumstances are of a lesser degree.

instruments or artifacts… (art. 573). Any person who makes an attack on private or public assets with the aim of supplying money to the aforementioned terrorist groups, or for supporting their cause, is considered a terrorist… (art. 575), as are those who carry out, claim or facilitate any act of collaboration in the activities or aims of a terrorist group.

Collaboration refers to information provided on (or the surveillance of) people, goods or facilities, and the construction, fitting out, provision or use of lodgings or storage areas; the hiding or transfer of persons linked to armed terrorist gangs, organisations or groups; the organisation or attendance of training sessions, and any similar activity.

The following acts are also considered acts of terrorism. Any acts carried out by persons who, not belonging to terrorist groups, but with the intention of subverting constitutional order or seriously breaching the peace, commit homicide, cause certain injuries[4], or illegally detain, kidnap, threaten or coerce others, or who cause fires, carry out sabotage or possess, deal in or store weapons or ammunition (art. 577). For crimes related to the activity of terrorist organisations, the sentence of a foreign judge or court shall for purposes of imposing sentence on repeat offenders be deemed equivalent to the verdicts of Spanish judges or courts. (art. 580).

Based on the current situation, we can say that sabotage is related to terrorism in as much as it can, and often is, an instrument for terrorism itself. State Security Forces and Bodies (plus any police forces belonging to the autonomous communities of Spain which have taken on new responsibilities in this area) must investigate terrorist elements or groups which, due to the characteristics of their organisation and the violent methods and procedures they use to have their demands met or to reach their goals, have the wherewithal to carry out any of the aforementioned acts.

It is for this reason that any suspicions must be reported to the police. Sometimes just reporting a sighting of a person taking notes surreptitiously in a port or near a boat can help stop a terrorist attack. In Spain it is the National High Court which gives pre-trial hearings and ultimately tries terrorist crimes.

Persons on board ship are more in danger of becoming victims during a terrorist attack than they are of any other criminal act. However, they are not always affected. When the Provisional IRA boarded and subsequently sank the M/V "Neille M" and the M/V "St. Bedan" (in February 1981 and February 1982 respectively), they did so with no intention of harming the persons on board. In fact, they did everything within their power to ensure the crew reached the coast safely. Such actions illustrate the fact that politically motivated terrorist groups employ different tactics in different situations for a variety of different reasons. They occasionally commit crimes for purely material reasons, often without harming anyone as it would not be in their interest. It would be unwise, therefore, to apply clear and distinct patterns as this might lead to an inadequate response to the main threat.

A terrorist is flexible, as is a pirate. Their tactics are adjusted to adapt to each new situation, and the same should be done in any reponse carried out to prevent or combat a violent situation at sea, however insignificant it may seem, and whatever the motivation behind it. From a maritime transport point of view, there is practically no difference between piracy and maritime terrorism. It is of no concern to the captain whether his ship has been hijacked by political terrorists or by financially motivated pirates, the end result is very similar (and pirates can be just as ruthless as their terrorist counterparts).

---

[4] Those described in articles 149 and 150 of the Penal Code.

Statistics also reflect that, up until now, the number of politically motivated terrorist incidents involving ships has been very low compared with other types of violence. A ship is much more likely to have to make use of its fire-fighting systems in the engine room, or to have to deploy its lifeboats after a collision, than it is to have to deal with a terrorist incident. Alarm bells have started to ring, however, after the tragic events of September 11th, 2001.

2.2.1 Case studies of terrorist attacks

Fortunately, although there have been some cases of criminal acts at sea and of piracy (and although these are increasing in number), apart from the sinking of the Greek cruise ship "Sanya" in 1973 after she hit a mine planted by the Black September terrorist organisation in Beirut, there have only been three main terrorist acts committed at sea: those against the "Santa María" in 1962, the "Achille Lauro" in 1985 and the "City of Poros" in 1989. It is interesting to note that none of the objectives were achieved by the perpetrators of these attacks. All three cases showed military incompetence and were total failures from a professional point of view. They did, however, achieve publicity on a worldwide scale, not so surprising when you consider that the sea provides the perfect backdrop for a terrorist drama.

The case of the SS "Santa María"

On the 22nd January, 1962, when the body of the third officer and an injured crew member were brought off the Portuguese-flag liner SS "Santa María" at St. Lucia, Portugal requested international collaboration for the capture of the perpetrators of this act of "piracy".

When it was made known that there were 42 American citizens on board, American and English naval ships on manoeuvres in the waters of Puerto Rico were quickly deployed for a rescue mission in what seemed to be a clear case of hijack and murder. To everyone's surprise, when contact was made with the "Santa María", the "pirate" Captain Henrique Galvão declared that he and his group of sixty one Portuguese and Spanish collaborators were not committing a criminal act, but were carrying out political action with the aim of bringing down the Portuguese dictatorship of Antonio Salazar.

The British and American governments then changed tack and, instead of taking up arms against the "pirates", to the annoyance of the Portuguese government, they began negotiations. Now, with no intention of taking the ship by force, the warships simply followed it to Recife where they were ordered to withdraw.

The incident made the headlines around the world and several attempts were made to get an "exclusive", with some journalists even trying to parachute on board.

As often happens with terrorist incidents, things finally became confused as several different countries tried to have some influence on the outcome. Brazil, in a tacit agreement with the U.S. government, offered Captain Galvão and his crew political asylum and the passengers disembarked safely.

The events in this case panned out in a very similar way to those in the case of the "Achille Lauro". A ship was taken by force, murder was committed, passengers were intimidated, political demands were made and then the perpetrators negotiated their freedom. In the case of the "Santa María", no trial was held over the death of the third officer.

The case of the SS "Achille Lauro"

On the 1st October, 1985, Israeli commandos raided the headquarters of the Palestinian Liberation Organisation (PLO) in Tunisia. During the operation several militants were killed and the PLO were quick to declare that their Arab comrades would be avenged.

Earlier in 1985 Abu Abbas, a member of the Palestinian Liberation Front, had boarded the "Achille Lauro" using a Greek passport to examine the security system on board. His report made reference to how easy it would be to take weapons on board and explained that the ship made a stop in the holiday resort of Ashdod. From where the ship was moored, it would be possible to kill many people sunbathing on the beach.

The terrorists decided to carry out this attractive plan, as the tough security measures in place in Israel made it impossible to enter the country with weapons. This plan also met other necessary requirements of their terrorist objective: their aim was to kill innocent people, and the ship guaranteed them excellent access. Plus, if they were able to take Amercian hostages they would get worldwide publicity and have an ace up their sleeve for negotiating their retreat.

Four men were selected for the operation and one of them went to the cruise ship's main office in Geneva to purchase the four tickets. He had to go to the office twice as the receptionist was reluctant to give him the tickets because it was a very late booking. After some insistance, however, the man was able to persuade her to take his money and to book them a four-bed cabin.

All the terroristas had false passports. They held Norweigan passports and neither the photographs nor the details had been changed. In their hand luggage, which was visibly excessive, they carried folding machine guns, revolvers and hand grenades.

During the voyage they kept themselves to themselves and mainly used room service for their meals. It was this fact which initially led staff to suspect them, one Italian attendant making his suspicions known by saying "if you're Norwegian, I'm African". None of the crew, however, informed the Captain of their suspicions.

On the 7th October, around half past one in the afternoon and just after leaving the port of Alexandria, a steward entered the cabin without warning, thinking its occupants had gone to lunch. To his surprise, instead of finding the cabin empty, he found its four occupants busy cleaning their automatic weapons. The terrorists were equally surprised, but immediately agreed on an alternative plan. Instead of going to Ashdod to kill Israelis, they would take control of the ship and make the most of the situation as it unfolded.

The four burst into the restaurant where the majority of the passengers were having lunch and began shouting and firing into the air. Once all the passengers and staff had been moved to the back of the restaurant, one of the terrorists went up to the bridge and another down to the engine room. The one who entered the engine control room shouted that the engineers should obey all orders coming from the bridge and then left. None of the terrorists returned to the engine room after that. On the bridge the Captain and the navigation officers were threatened and ordered to alter their course. Acting under duress, the Captain made an announcement saying that everyone should "go to the restaurant, remain calm and nobody would get hurt".

Six English dancers were sunbathing on the Lido deck when they heard the shots. After a quick discussion with one of the officers, they went to a cabin belonging to crew members and they locked themselves in. When they heard the Captain's announcement, however, they too headed for the restaurant. The terrorists looked for an interpreter and then asked all Israelis, English and Germans among the passengers to step forward.

The terrorists moved around constantly, frequently relieving each other from their posts, so neither the crew nor the passengers were ever sure of exactly how many there were aboard. In spite of the heat in the room, when a girl asked if she could go to the toilet, she was told to take a dish from the buffet and squat behind the counter. The men had to urinate on the carpet. To keep the pressure up, the terrorists said they had placed explosive charges all around the ship and they made the crew bring them plastic containers full of fuel which they then placed around the passengers. The thirteen American passengers and the six English dancers were then separated from the others and taken outside to an area under the bridgewings, and they were also surrounded by fuel tanks.

Some of the younger deck officers suggested to the Captain that they could get the rifles used for clay pigeon shooting and launch an attack to rescue the ship. The Captian was against the idea, however, and the guns were handed over to the terrorists.

In the afternoon, one of the passengers, Mr. Klinghoffer, an elderly, disabled Jew was taken out of the dining room and shot. Two crew members were then made to throw the body and the wheelchair overboard. The passengers were told nothing of the incident, but the Captian was informed of the killing and was told that the next person to be killed would be the American passenger Mr. Hodes. The Captain offered himself instead of Mr. Hodes, suggesting his death would have greater impact, but his offer was rejected.

After forty-eight hours, in which four men had been able to capture a large passenger liner, control 400 people, kill an American citizen and grab the attention of the whole world, the ship arrived outside Port Said. The terrorist "leader" Abu Abbas managed to reach an agreement through negotiations and the four terrorists abandoned the ship as free men. They would have remained free as well if it had not been for the audacity and skill of the United States air force which managed to identify and intercept the Egypt Air flight carrying the terrorists and their supporters, forcing the plane to land in Sardinia where special forces were waiting to arrest them and everyone else involved.

From the terrorists' point of view, this had been a well-executed operation that had led to widespread publicity of their cause. Their mistake was to believe the United States Government would respect international laws and would not force a plane from another country to land when it was in international air space.

The case of the M/V "City of Poros"

Throughout 1989, America was putting a lot of pressure on the Greek government for the extradition of a Palestinian man, alleging he was implicated in the placing of a bomb on a TWA plane. In March 1989 the United States warship USS "Vincennes" made a mistake in the identification of a civil aeroplane, Iran Air flight 655, and shot it down leaving no survivors.

Two weeks later a Palestinian was tried in Athens after having been arrested while trying to board a ferry to Israel in a vehicle loaded with weapons and explosives.

At the beginning of July the American defense attaché in Greece, Captain Mordeen, was killed. Three hours beforehand, whilst the Greek ferry M/V "City of Poros" was waiting to dock in Paleen Faliron, a car bomb had suddenly exploded close to the port. Inside the car the dismembered bodies of an Arab man and woman were found, along with evidence of a large amount of explosive and documents relating to terrorism.

The 540 passengers on board the "City of Poros" were enjoying the end of a nice day's sailing when, without warning, a group of Arabs suddenly appeared among them and began to kill men, women, children, officers and crew indiscriminately with automatic pistols and hand grenades. Within minutes nine people had died and 46 had been injured. On the ship the explosions started an intense fire and terrified the passengers; the English girls from Worthing Convent School jumped overboard into the water below. The two or three men and women who carried out the slaughter managed to escape among the victims by making the most of the reigning confusion.

Yet again there are similarities with the "Achille Lauro". A passenger ship is taken by a group of Arab terrorists, innocent people are killed and a political statement is made regarding the extradition of an imprisoned Palestinian. The difference, however, in this case is that the authorities were not able to arrest the terrorists.

Other acts of terrorism carried out on ships have been: a bomb placed on the yacht belonging to Lord Mountbatten (the last governor of India) by the IRA; the state terrorism carried out by French forces on a Greenpeace boat; the attack against a ship belonging to the U.S. Navy in the Yemen using rubber dinghies loaded with explosives.

2.2.2 News items related to terrorism

To follow the evolution of terrorism since the events of the 11th September, the following news items have been selected:

1. Preparations are being made for war on the high seas. Orders have been given for three tankers carrying diesel and jet fuel to be directed to two military bases in the United States (the Indian Ocean and Spain). In the meantime, a fleet of cargo and ro-ro ships are located in different ports ready to enter into action within a period of five and fifteen days. 17/09/2001 13:41:55 – *Fairplay Daily News*

2. Cruise ships have always been vulnerable. Just as with luxury items, many people consider they carry too much of a risk. Fear of terrorism is not good for tourism and many bookings are being cancelled. 20/09/2001 – *Fairplay International Shipping Weekly*

3. With delegates still confused over the recent terrorist attacks in the United States, the Port Risk Management Forum 2001 opened on a gloomy note in Sheveningen on the 17th September. However, the message conveyed in the conference was a positive one, with many delegates believing European ports are now better equipped to achieve security standards comparable to those of American ports. 27/09/2001 – *Fairplay International Shipping Weekly*

4. Before the events of the 11th September, the general view held by the maritime industry was that security was a dead investment. The majority believed that the hijack of the "Achille Lauro" in 1985 was the only incident relative to maritime terrorism, but the increase in the number of cases in recent years must be made known. For example, members of Tamil Elam in Sri Lanks have carried out several terrorist attacks against the navy and merchant ships. Abu Sayyaf's radical Islamic separatist group regularly attacked ferries in the south Philippines, and the Chechens have hijacked a ferry. ETA, the Basque separatists, placed a bomb on board the Santander/Plymouth ferry, although the attack fell through at the last minute. In Aden, a boat belonging to Bin Laden's suicide group is suspected of carrying out an attack last October on the SS "Cole" in which seventeen American sailors died. 27/09/2001 – *Fairplay International Shipping Weekly*

5. Military action in Afghanistan is having negative effects on Indian commerce. The anti-terrorist campaign is causing serious transport delays resulting in a drop in tea exports from 206m kg to 195m kg in the current financial year. The textile business may also suffer a loss of between 15% and 20%. 15/10/2001 11:47:06 – *Fairplay Daily News*

6. Royal Caribbean, the second largest cruise line, has stated that the loss of 500 jobs marks the end of its programme of cutbacks. The order for the cutbacks was given to help reduce costs and keep a balance in the face of a fall in bookings as a result of the fear generated in America after the September 11th attacks. 18/10/2001 – *Fairplay International Shipping Weekly*

7. Both India and Pakistan are resisting enforced war risk insurance quotas in the maritime sector. They describe the measure as unjustified given that the situation at sea is normal and all ships destined for Pakistan are accompanied by the Navy. 18/10/2001 – *Fairplay International Shipping Weekly*

8. Maersk Sealand has declined to comment on the incident involving the "Gioia Tauro" when a man of Egyptian origin was found in one of its containers and subsequently arrested by Italian police. On the 18th October, Rigk Amid Farid, a Canadian passport holder, was found in a container on dry land when noises were heard coming from inside. The container itself had been equipped with a bed, a wash basin, a portable heater and enough water for the three week journey to Canada. Farid was found to be carrying a mobile phone, a satellite telephone, a computer, a camera, identity documents, an aeronautical chart, air security passes and an airline mechanic's certificate. 08/11/2001 – *Fairplay International Shipping Weekly*

9. Shipping companies in the Philippines are worried at the increased restrictions on coastal shipping due to it being opened up to foreign companies, making the country more vulnerable to terrorist attack. 09/11/2001 12:15:24 – *Fairplay Daily News*

10. In light of the evaluation of Alaska's vulnerability to terrorist attack after the events of the 11th September, the security package put together for the state includes security cameras in Whittier and Seward docks, training and the provision of equipment for dealing with dangerous materials in Juneau, Valdez and Fairbanks, security and emergency personnel in the security offices, etc. 14/11/2001 10:20:04 – *Fairplay Daily News*

11. The Caribbean maritime industry urgently needs to revise its security procedures if it wants to avoid the financial guarantees required by the U.S. which will cause delays for cargo and containers arriving from that area. Adopting poor security measures could mean delays for ships entering the United States. This can be avoided by carrying out ship inspections in the port of origin, thereby, allowing ease of passage into the United States. 29/11/2001 – *Fairplay International Shipping Weekly*

12. The U.S. Coast Guard will be granted the authority to board and inspect foreign ships more than 12 miles out, four times the territorial limit of 3 miles. Emphasis has been placed on the importance of stepping up inspections to include the 45,000 containers which are being moved daily in U.S. ports. Technology will be used to detect what exactly there is in these containers, meaning terrorists will no longer find it easy to ship biological or nuclear weapons in a container without being detected. 13/12/2001 – *Fairplay International Shipping Weekly*

13. The U.S. Congress has asked the Navy about the possibility of buying two of the American Classic Voyages cruise ships to use as hospitals or control centres in the war against terrorism. 08/01/2002 14:15:31 – *Fairplay Daily News*

14. The port of Cochin took unprecedented security measures after an anonymous bomb threat was issued for the 39,860 DWT oil tanker "Iona" flying the flag of Hong Kong. The threat was made in a letter declaring explosives had been placed on the ship carrying 12,000 tonnes of kerosene from Bahrain. The ship was stopped in open water and a search operation was carried out by the Indian Navy. No explosives were found. The ship later docked at in a coal dock at a safe distance from other vessels, and its cargo was unloaded safely. 10/01/2002 13:45:32 – *Fairplay Daily News*

15. At the IMO, government and industry officials are analysing the use of automatic ship identification systems, the need for security plans on board ship, in ports and in off-shore terminals, verification of the identity of crew members and container security from their port of origin to their destination. 11/02/2002 10:10:21 – *Fairplay Daily News*

16. The Israeli shipping company, ZIM, has reduced the war risk surcharge in the Mediterranean from 100 dollars to 35 per container. This reduction has been made in response to complaints from Israeli manufacturers who were being hit hard by the high insurance costs. ZIM clients, however, are aware they will have to keep paying more than 130,000 dollars a day for war risk. 25/02/2002 08:54:38 – *Fairplay Daily News*

17. Meetings of the IMO Maritime Security work group have resulted in a number of proposals which will have a greater impact on ports, but many of which are also directed at ships and their operating procedures. The proposals recommend that AIS systems should be implemented in ships of more than 500 GT on international journeys as soon as possible, thereby creating transparency with regards to shipowners and introducing crew identity documents as an urgent measure. 07/03/2002 – *Solutions and Newbuildings*

18. The U.S. transport committee is to present its version of the port security document for ports, shipping companies and foreign crews. The 2002 Maritime Transport Act requires cargo ship operators to provide the U.S. authorities with lists of passengers and crew electronically 96 hours before their entry into U.S. ports. Since September 11th, this information has been sent by fax and is, more often than not, illegible. 20/03/2002 14:22:05 – *Fairplay Daily News*

19. It was a bright afternoon in Le Havre and the editor of Fairplay had a few hours to spare before he had to catch the ferry home. The conditions were perfect for a spot of photography. Quite unintentionally, he suddenly discovered a side entrance which led directly to the container storage area and the docks. There was no gate, no barrier and no surveillance. It was a photographer's dream. The editor is an honest person, but others may be less scrupulous and carry more dangerous things than a camera, and undoubtedly coming away with more interesting things than photographs. 16/05/2002 – *Fairplay International Shipping Weekly*

20. Greece has rejected a request form the U.S. Navy to intercept ships in its territorial waters as part of the fight againt terrorism. The initial response of the Greek government was to discuss such action with other EU countries, Italy, France and Spain which have received similar proposals. 30/05/2002 16:23:26 – *Fairplay Daily News*

21. Security officers and security plans will be requirements both on board and in port facilities. The deadline for the obligatory implementation of the automatic identification system (AIS), the identity documents for seafarers and the container inspection system has been brought forward. At least ten drafts will be looked at in an IMO session in September before they are finally included in the 11th annexe of SOLAS. This seems the best vehicle for a security code rather than the plan of inserting the new measures in the ISM Code proposed by Japan. The ILO has been assigned the task of developing the seafares' ID card to be ready for June 2003. The World Customs Organisation will reach an agreement with the IMO regarding container inspection. 06/06/2002 – *Fairplay International Shipping Weekly*

22. Singapore is the first port outside the U.S. to take on board the Container Security Initiative (CSI). This is a counter-terrorist measure to prevent terrorists using containers to transport weapons of mass destruction. 06/06/2002 06:58:01 – *Fairplay Daily News*

23. U.S. Customs administration has confirmed talks are underway with France to have inspectors placed in the port of Le Havre as part of their global anti-terrorist plan, an initiative already shown in the CSI. The American authorities see the port at Le Havre as critical in their plan as many ships leave there bound for the United States. Le Havre will be the first European port to accept the U.S. customs inspectors who will be checking high-risk containers. Singapore is the first port to have taken part in the initiative. Canada and Hong Kong have also agreed to a similar proposal. 14/06/2002 05:32:17 – *Fairplay Daily News*

24. The International Chamber of Shipping (ICS) and the International Shipping Federation (ISF) are urging governments not to ignore the problem of piracy and just concentrate on terrorism. 18/06/2002 09:04:12 – *Fairplay Daily News*

In this section we can also see a series of tendencies developed over this period. Passenger ships and cruise liners are likely to be the new targets for terrorist attacks, due to their greater vulnerability and the large numbers of persons using their services. This situation results in a negative trend in this type of activity. The regulations established for the control of cargo, especially that transported in containers, creates serious problems for countries with fewer means. On an international level, procedures have been established to control ships, their crew, their cargo and procedures in ports.

2.3 Other forms of criminal violence at sea (security)

Ships, as a means of transporting human beings or goods, can also fall victim to all the other kinds of crime and criminal damage which occur on land. Whether for economic reasons or justified as a means to an end, ships sometimes find themselves caught up in violent acts such as extorsion, vandalism, fighting, affray, sabotage, work-related tension, etc.

According to the Diccionario de la Real Academia (the Spanish language regulating body), sabotage refers to all damage or deterioration of facilities, products, etc. which is inflicted in a conflict with the owners, with the state, or with the occupying forces in social or political conflicts. Also, figuratively, it is the hidden opposition or obstruction of projects, orders, decisions and ideas, etc.

In the maritime field, sabotage refers to a situation where a ship, its cargo or passengers are victims of illegal aggression from either external or internal sources with the aim of causing damage which will put the ship out of operation, destroy its cargo or cause personal harm to the crew or passengers. This normally takes place in the context of an intentional attack by members of a gang or terrorist group. It can also mean control is taken of the ship itself by a terrorist group for use against a strategic position or to help them board another ship to cause a great degree of material damage and/or harm to persons.

2.3.1 Extortion

The idea of extortion in relation to passenger ships no doubt stems from the success achieved with similar tactics used against companies and aeroplanes.

Whether the method used is an active or a passive one (the latter via anonymous threats), the extorter is always seeking financial gain. However, it is obvious that in a case of direct action, for example a hijacking, the truth and urgency of the matter is much greater than in the case of an anonymous bomb threat.

There are several examples of a ransom being demanded using the threat of a bomb placed on a passenger ship. One such example dates back to 1973 when American citizen Gerry Priddy demanded $ 250,000 from Princess Cruise Lines after he threatened to blow up their ship "Island Princess", alleging to have planted a bomb aboard. At the time the ship was at sea with 850 people aboard.

In this particular case it proved to be a false alarm. Having been informed of the problem, the Captain carried out a discreet search for explosives aboard and only two brown paper packages, the size of cigarette packets, were found. They continued on their journey without incident and, in the meantime, the FBI arrested Priddy where the handover of the money was supposed to take place. He was locked up and sentenced to nine months in prison.

There have also attempts to hijack ships for financial reasons. One case, in 1978, saw four individuals arrested by an undercover officer pretending to be an arms dealer. The four were planning to take over the "Emerald Seas", a ship belonging to Eastern Steamship Lines, and sail from Miami to South America with both passengers and crew, demanding a ransom of six million dollars.

2.3.2 Sabotage

Although cases of sabotage are infrequent, they can be unpredictable as the vessel is, quite literally, in the hands of its crew.

In 1982 an incident of this kind took place on board a boat belonging to the United States Coast Guard, meaning it received more publicity than many other similar cases.

Whilst it was patrolling the Gulf of Alaska, the "Boutwell" patrol boat captured the "Orea", a 39 foot yacht, which was carrying 1240 kilos of marihuana. On the return journey to Kodiac with the captured yacht in tow, the "Boutwell" began to experience several mechanical failures which were eventually identified as sabotage. A 19-year-old coast guard was formally charged on two counts of damage to machinery, one count of damage to military property, one count of conspiring to endanger a patrol vessel and one count of attempted theft of the yacht. The conspirators planned to immobilise the "Boutwell", put protective suits on and flee with the "Orea" and its cargo. Another member of the crew was involved, whilst a third, who was found drowned in his diving suit, may also have been implicated.

2.3.3 Hijacking of yachts and other violent attacks on small boats

Many people and vessels continue to disappear from areas where, poverty and a lack of protection at sea, or small time drug trafficking, make sailing for pleasure a risky pastime.

It is not likely that professional pirates will bother to attack small vessels but, as with street crime, wherever you are in the world there will always be an opportunist looking to increase his income.

A case in point for a pirate attack on a leisure boat is the case of the 36-foot yacht "Tara" which took place in the South China Sea in 1994. On its journey from Fremantle to Hong Kong, the yacht left Singapore and, off the coast of Vietnam, was persued relentlessly by several local fishing boats until finally, after two hours of persecution, a freezer ship appeared on the horizon and the pirates preferred to back off than be identified. These were obviously amateur pirates with theft as their main motivation.

In August 1974, the "Kamalii" was boarded and taken over by two Vietnam veterans, (Mark Maynard, age 27, and Kerry Bryant, age 25) and an ex-member of the Coast Guard (Michael Melton, age 24) in Honolulu port. The three gagged and bound the real crew members on board (Bob Weshkeit, age 49, Frank Power, age 57, and John Freitas, age 52) and set off for Thailand to collect some drugs. Two days into the journey, in spite of their pleading, the original crew was ordered to jump into the Pacific Ocean. The hijackers only stopped to throw them a life raft. Although they were not in any of the main shipping lanes, the castaways were picked up five hours later by the Italian freezer ship "Benadir". The incident was reported to the Honolulu Coast Guard and, after being chased by the patrol boat "Point Corwin", the "Kamalii" was reached and the hijackers arrested.

There are countless cases: for example, the possible hijack of the "Tecumseh" and the "Kat Mei", both well-equipped boats which disappeared after leaving ports in the Caribbean where they had taken on crew.

The "Lupita", hired by two American couples in Mexico, was later found stripped on the island of San José. It is believed that the hired crew killed the Americans who had hired the boat and then used it for transporting drugs.

The "Peregrine" had been booked for a journey from Acapulco, through the Panama Canal to Grand Cayman island, so it took on six crew members from the south of California. The boat disappeared without a trace, but investigators discovered extra provisions had been taken on board before its departure. Yet again the suspicions are drug-related.

Perhaps the most curious cases are the ones concerning the "Puerto Limón" and the "Como No". The first left Houston for Costa Rica after drug dealers had been spotted aboard. The ship and its twelve crew members never reached port and, even more surprisingly, its radio beacons (which would be activated on contact with water) did not indicate any position. Federal agents put the disappearance down to a drugs-related hijacking. The "Como No" was supposed to be being taken by a retired couple from Fort Lauderdale, Florida, through the Panama Canal to their home on the west coast. In Nassau they hired a German to work on board and, on his recommendation, they added an Indian to the crew when they reached Barbados.The boat stopped in Venezuela and in the canal itself, and the letters sent home by the wife from these ports expressed her increasing concern regarding the crew. The "Como No" never reached port. An investigation revealed the crew's ID was fake and it was suggested that the boat may have been hijacked for drugs-related purposes.

Some cases have even made it onto our tv screens, including the disappearance of the ketch "Sea Wind" from where it was anchored at the island of Palmyra, in the Pacific Ocean. At anchor, the owners of the ketch did not make a scheduled radio broadcast to a radio buff in Hilo, Hawaii. In previous broadcasts the couple had expressed their suspicions regarding a couple aboard the yacht "Iola". After three weeks of waiting for a call, the radio buff finally reported the disappearance of the "Sea Wind" to the Coast Guard. At the end of October an off duty coast guard found a boat in Honolulu which coincided with the description of the "Sea Wind", the "Lokahi". He requested the "Lokahi" be investigated. When Coast Guard officers and FBI agents drew close to the boat, a man jumped overboard and swam for shore. They did manage to arrest a woman, Stephanie Sterns, who they charged with drug smuggling. The man, arrested later, was Buck Duane Walker (alias Roy Allen), who was a fugitive bank robber and drug dealer on the run from a federal prison. Regarding the hijack of the yacht, both were charged with grand theft and, some years later, when the bones of Mrs. Graham surfaced, Walker was charged with murder.

Although it may seem that yachts only need worry about their inflatable rafts or outboard motors being stolen, physical violence is actually quite common among sailors and is, therefore, a topic to be considered when discussing security at sea.

2.3.4 Work-related problems

Other violent acts similar to piracy may arise from underlying tensions behind arguments at work or expressions of unhappiness or unease caused by unsatisfactory living conditions on board.

In 1980 two incidents occurred which were very representative of this kind of act.

The first took place on the 12th January of that year aboard the "Easy Rider" whilst it was at anchor approximately 25 miles to the south west of Morgan City, Louisiana. While they were in this situation a member of the crew, Robin Stansbury, suddenly decided he wanted to go home immediately, stating it was regarding an urgent matter that could not be resolved over the radio. Armed with a pistol and a rifle, he forced Captain Jack Walker to raise the anchor and head for Brownsville, the latter managing to report he was doing so at gunpoint.

The Captain and another crew member were locked in a storeroom throughout the night while the ship was chased by the Coast Guard in a light aircraft and patrol boat "Point Noel". Finally, after having shot at his persecutors, Stansbury gave himself up and the crew regained control of the boat.

The second incident lasted longer and involved several of the crew, making it a true mutiny. The Liberian-flagged motor tanker "Ypapanti" was denied entrance to the port of Philidelphia for reasons relating to security and pollution, so it anchored in international waters close to Delaware Bay, whilst the ship's owners negotiated its entry to the port.

On the 23rd May, with negotiations underway, the crew (headed by the boatswain and the first officer) mutinied, demanding their pay and condemning the terrible state the ship was in. The Coast Guard decided not to interfere at that time, as it posed no threat to shipping, and the United States government contacted the Liberian government to request their help in negotiations with the crew. However, after several days of talks between the ship owner's lawyers, the Liberian government and the mutineers' representatives, there seemed to be no possibility of reaching an agreement.

On the 25th May the Captian of the "Ypapanti" warned the Coast Guard that the mutineers had taken hostages and were threatening to flood the engine room with fuel and set the ship on fire. This was confirmed by a crew member who managed to escape by swimming to the Coast Guard patrol boat "Alert", which arrived at the scene on the 29th May and remained in contact with the ship until the end of the mutiny.

Over the next few days, the Liberian government formally requested the intervention of the United States and an assault plan was formulated by the FBI. After one final attempt at negotiating, and without reaching an agreement, the "Ypapanti" was finally stormed on the 22nd June by a team made up of members of the Coast Guard and the FBI. The two organisations combined their forces to carry out the first significant maritime rescue of hostages in modern history.

2.3.5 Violence related to emigration

Attacks on persons trying to enter a country illegally from the sea are frequent, often happening even before they have reached their objective. Although this refers to illegal acts, the violence takes place on board boats. No matter whether they are large or small, they are all still vessels.

It is sometimes difficult to establish after the fact, whether the crime was committed in international or territorial waters, and this creates jurisdiction problems. In other cases there are no witnesses to the crimes or, as in the majority of cases, the witnesses refuse to speak for fear of being discovered as illegal immigrants or suffering the consequences.

However, even if it is not possible to prove the guilt of the perpetrators, the facts are fully recognised by the authorities. In August 1979, the owner of a speedboat bringing illegal immigrants into Florida from Haiti forced 18 passengers to jump into the water at gunpoint. In this incident a mother and her five children drowned.

In July 1980, the crew of the "Dieu Qui Donne" threw a refugee overboard because they believed him to be possessed by evil spirits.

The "Jesula" left Haiti in July 1981 with a total of between 200 and 250 persons on board. The skipper demanded money for food and water, and those who could not pay went hungry and thirsty. Anyone who complained about the running of the ship was hacked to death with machetes, stabbed to death or strangled. According to eyewitnesses, 16 people died after having protested and dozens were thrown overboard when they died of hunger and thirst. However, the FBI was unable to prove anything as the vessel, its crew and its passengers, being Haitian. Very little cooperation was offered by the authorities in that country.

2.3.6 News items related to the term security

Short news items appearing since the 11th September, 2001 have been selected:

1. The Argentinian Coast Guard is making a concerted effort to keep standards of service up and introduce new security measures for international cruise liners which visit ports in Argentina after the 11th September. 31/01/2002 – *Fairplay International Shipping Weekly*

2. The U.S. Coastguard has announced the creation of new security zones around cruise liners, tankers and military ships for the ports of South Carolina, Hawaii, California and Florida. These zones, which apply to both stationary and moving vessels, range from 90 to 450 metres, and may only be entered with express permission from the ports Captain. These security areas are deemed necessary to protect people, ships and facilities from sabotage or other subversive acts, accidents or any other incident of a similar nature during operations. 01/02/2002 14:27:13 – *Fairplay Daily News*

3. Taxes for passengers arriving in the U.S. by ship or plane are now between 5 and 11 dollars per passenger. This increase is to cover the rising cost of Customs services in the U.S. Cruise liners have additional taxes of 1.75 to 2 dollars. 05/02/2002 14:12:42 – *Fairplay Daily News*

4. Now that security for air travel is so much more effective, it is obvious that any destruction in the U.S. will be done by ship. It is estimated that half the world's merchant fleet visits the U.S. each year. This is probably somewhat of an exaggeration, but it does clearly show the scale of the security issue currently worrying the United States. 14/02/2002 – *Fairplay International Shipping Weekly*

5. In order to avoid an attack on a catastrophic scale whilst taking into account globalisation, international transport security and logistics systems have to be fine tuned to reduce the risk of importers, exporters, freighters and transporters becoming channels which criminals and terrorists may use. 14/02/2002 – *Fairplay International Shipping Weekly*

6. Countries should take steps to ensure that their ships do not represent a security risk to the United States. Countries such as Panama, Liberia and the Marshall Islands must make sure that they are fully aware of all their ships operations and that the ships pose no threat to our nation. 28/02/2002 – *Fairplay International Shipping Weekly*

7. The deterioration in levels of security due to the war between Isreal and Palestine has meant an all time low for the tourist industry in Israel this year. Eleven passengers disembarked in the port of Haifa in February, all of them arriving on cargo vessels. As cruise liners visiting the port are known about well in advance, tour operators have written 2002 off as a loss-making year. 05/03/2002 09:35:17 – *Fairplay Daily News*

8. X-ray detectors have been installed in the ports of Kobe and Osaka in Japan to check containers in a hope to prevent trafficking of arms, drugs and other items. Japanese customs officials say that their equipment which is able to detect merchandise in chasis has reduced the old 2 to 10 hour inspection process to 20 minutes. X-ray equipment was first installed in Yokohama in March 2001, and will be in use in Tokyo, Nagoya and Hakata before the end of March 2003. 15/03/2002 15:07:47 – *Fairplay Daily News*

9. An electronic passport for seafarers was one of the proposals put forward by the IMO as an answer to the problem of the abundance of counterfeit certificates. The idea is to provide all seaferers with an ingenious card containing a microchip, to replace the current international card which is easily lost. This could reduce red tape for both sailors and Port State Control, thereby improving security on board. 21/03/2002 – *Fairplay International Shipping Weekly*

10. Panama Canal authorities will be imposing a new security tax as from the 1st June, 2002, for all ships using the canal. This is to cover the heavy investment made in monitoring, follow-

up and protection systems for their operations. The tax will be 400 dollars for ships of more than 3000 PC/UMS, and 50 dollars for all those under that tonnage. 17/04/2002 06:52:54 – *Fairplay Daily News*

11. Twenty five Islamic extremists have illegally entered the United States since March as stowaways on cargo ships via the ports of Miami, Savannah and Long Beach. The reports, recognised as official and confirmed by the Washington Times, say the terrorists planned to attack a nuclear power plant on the 4th July. 14/05/2002 06:49:32 – *Fairplay Daily News*

12. More details have been released about the Islamic extremists who entered ports in the U.S. in recent months. Some of them wore protective clothing normally worn by dock workers, including hard hats, so they would blend in. 30/05/2002 – *Fairplay International Shipping Weekly*

It should also be noted that in applying the term "security" to everything, whatever its actual importance, a new wave of rejection has been created by the adopting of measures serving as deterrents. These include measures of prevention such as establishing security zones around special or highly-vulnerable ships, extensive and sophisticated systems for controlling the cargo inside containers in a quick and effective way which will ensure shipping and the maritime business survives. These measures are, in part, covered by the taxes imposed by the countries on persons and merchandise, and this creates many problems regarding prices and competetiveness between shipping companies. There is a general opinion expressed by everyone: these measures will only be effective if they are adopted by a large number of countries.

3 Crime

All kinds of crimes can be, and are, committed on merchant ships, especially on passenger liners. Of course, a case of fraud will have less of a chance of succeeding and be less of a threat on board than if it were committed in a shopping centre or a company on dry land, but the type of people who go on international trips or cruises, do attract opportunist fraudsters and involve the ship directly. For this reason we will evaluate all the risks posed by criminal activity as well as the extent to which a ship is vulnerable to it. This information should then be helpful when decisions are to be made regarding measures of prevention and protection.

3.1 Crime factors

These factors result from circumstances surrounding an individual and which can then lead that person to commit illegal acts or which may increase the possibility of them committing illegal acts.

Such factors constantly bombard a person with their negative aspects, thereby leading them to commit crimes. However, it does depend on the personality of an individual and their strength of character as to whether these factors influence their social behaviour in a negative way, or not.

The main factors are perhaps:
- Urban development of rural areas, leading to the creation of slums on the outskirts where the feeling of rootlessness is strong and there are high levels of marginalisation. Such areas are fertile ground for crime among non-integrated individuals.
- Prolonged and recurring economic crises coupled with a continual rise in unemployment and the subsequent creation of pockets of high unemployment. This, in turn, produces a drop in the purchasing power of the population. Members of a certain section of the population then try to satisfy their needs by any means possible.
- A sharp increase in drug abuse that creates an overwhelming need for money, sometimes resulting in all manner of crimes being committed to help pay for the habit.
- The negative situations caused by alcoholism, overcrowding, personal indifference and begging are a permanent breeding ground for crime.
- Prostitution and all the illicit activity it generates can occasionally lead to murder as well as a wide range of crimes committed against individuals.

- Psychological factors which can produce deviate or antisocial behaviour.
- The ever more demanding consumer society which uses a barrage of publicity to encourage people to spend. The resulting desire to have everything leads to some people using any available method to achieve this.

3.2 Age and crime

It has been suggested that the probability of marginalisation decreases with age. For a young person social control takes priority, whereas an adult is generally ruled by self-control. Young people are starting criminal activity at an increasingly younger age, even before puberty.

In general, the total number of young people arrested in recent years by Spanish police has accounted for 40% of all arrests. Of this 40%, 30% are youngsters between 18 and 20 years of age, 30% between 16 and 18, and the remaining 40% under 16.

The most common first crime committed by a young person is theft of a motor vehicle, a crime almost exclusively attributed to young people. This crime, although a grave offence in its own right, often becomes the catalyst for committing other more serious crimes.

Among other factors, it is currently drugs that drive young people headlong into a life of crime. In today's society, 80% of crimes committed by young people are crimes against property, with most of them being theft with intimidation committed by under 20's carrying either knives or firearms. These take place in banks, jeweller's, chemists and business or leisure premises, and young people of this age group are leaders in the statistics for committing such crimes.

Recently, ordinary fights between young people resulting in slight injury have taken an alarming turn towards attacks by specific groups known as *street gangs*, which can end in homicide.

3.3 Alcohol and drugs

Alcohol is the most predominant drug because it is both the most widely consumed and readily available (including in our current society), and the most addictive, causing more health and psychosocial problems than any other. It is also the principal drug that leads to and encourages the taking of other drugs.

As we have already seen, the use of all other substances defined as drugs is currently one of the most important factors contributing to crime. They go hand in hand with marginalisation, lack of socio-professional expectations and the breakdown of the family, etc.

It is important to point out the different ways these two factors generally influence crime. In crimes where alcohol is detected it is always a contributing factor in the crime being committed, but never the reason for it. Drugs, however, are usually the cause of a crime. An inebriated person feels uninhibited and may commit a crime against property or an individual which is something that, sober, he or she would probably not do.

On the other hand, a person will steal and even kill to get money to buy other, more inaccessible, drugs. The need for these drugs is motive enough for these more serious crimes to be committed.

3.4 Female delinquency

Crimes committed by females are frequently influenced by psychosocial phenomena. However, in line with modern society, women are now generally regarded as equal to men in all areas, including, in a negative way, criminal activity.

Nevertheless, there are still major differences which must be mentioned:

- As women are generally less physically strong, they are more likely to participate in crimes such as: fraud, criminal deception, slander, libel, false accusation, perjury, procuring, concealment of offenders, arson and theft.
- Women are generally less aggressive than men, although, it is important to remember that in certain crimes committed by women with deviate personalities, the aggression shown may be far greater than that shown by men. When compared with the average for their sex, truly unimaginable levels of aggression can be reached by these women. This has been seen clearly in cases of subversive activity or terrorism.
- Women often try to use their sex to their advantage, both to make the crime easier to commit and to avoid arrest (or at least make it more difficult) by trying to get the public's sympathy or accusing the arresting officer of abuse. In these circumstances, women tend to insult and be violent towards the person arresting them.

It is important not to forget the additional problems surrounding the frisking and searching of women, which must always be done by female personnel. This can make the situation difficult if there are no female officers present at the moment of arrest.

3.5 Socialisation

The term 'socialisation' refers to the process of integrating individuals into the social system. Several factors contribute to the process, the most important of which are a person's family, local community, school, workplace and circle of friends, as well as certain associations and the State.

Depending on how individuals act or behave with regards to society's norms, they will be fully integrated, or not, into the social system, and we can say they are socialised to a greater or lesser extent.

Those who are less socialised (because they do not comply with the established norms) are kept out of the social group and known as social "deviates".

It can be said there are different degrees of socialisation, and these depend on the social and economic opportunities which present themselves throughout a person's life. Generally, the older a person is, the less likely they are to be marginalised or deviant in behaviour.

It is possible for social deviation to appear in very socialised individuals later in life (white collar crime).

Deviate behaviour can be caused by any of the following:

-   Inefficiency of social controls.
-   Insufficient self-control.
-   The basic needs of an individual not being met.

Certain factors influence deviant behaviour.

Age. There are several stages in a person's life and these, in turn, can be subdivided (childhood, youth, adulthood and old age). As an individual moves from one stage to the next, their social position changes and this brings about changes in behaviour. Social control predominates in young people and self-control in adults. At each stage, the individual has different needs which must be satisfied in different ways.

Family. The better educated a woman is, the better equipped her home and the fewer children she has. This, among other factors, means she has more free time and, along with the need to meet the family's consumer needs, has contributed greatly to women entering the workforce. Today, the family is nuclear (father, mother and one or two children) and symmetrical (both the man and the woman work and the division of chores according to sex is less distinct). Not only has the social control exerted by the extended family (parents, grandparents, uncles, aunts and cousins) been lost, but the control by the nuclear family is becoming less intense.

Level of education. The goal of the education system is to ensure an individual enters the world of work, and enjoys both a social and political life. In theory, the longer a person spends in education, the better his/her job.

Economic activity and the job market. The law of supply and demand dominates the job market. The system by which employees are contracted generates competition to secure jobs with higher remuneration and requiring greater degrees of self-control and responsibility but which make higher levels of spending possible, thus boosting the consumer index.

A young person's world is characterised by the following:

-   Young people socialise outside institutions and away from socialising agents.
-   They enter the workforce late and have more free time.
-   They are easily influenced by the media.
-   They belong to a youth culture and socialise at their meeting places (disco-bars, pubs, bars, night clubs, etc.)

For a child, social control is applied via the family. As we have seen, in an adult that social control is self-control. A young person may escape both self-control and responsibility.

3.5.1 Marginalisation

Society excludes people who, for different reasons, do not fit in with what is considered the norm, the established order, with what is lawful or permissible, etc. When criteria are applied to define marginalisation, and the risk factors are considered, concepts such as poverty, insecurity and exclusion appear. On this level they are the cause of:

a. Physical and sensory deficiencies.
b. Deviance resulting from incomplete socialisation due to drug addiction or delinquency.
c. Lack of education, measured by failure both academically and at work.

Such circumstances make it difficult to get a job (resulting in unemployment), to establish social relationships (resulting in deviant behaviour), and to have a social life (resulting in self-rejection).

The following are contributing factors which must also be taken into account:

- Poverty generates areas of poor housing and marginalisation where deviant behaviour in individuals is reinforced by the groups they belong to.
- Unemployment mainly affects less well-educated people and social change causes peripheral jobs to disappear, resulting in crime and drug addiction, etc.
- The role played by the parents within the family is deteriorating.

3.5.2 Types of crime and how they are most frequently committed

A. Common single or isolated crimes

Common crimes referred to as single are defined as *criminal activity carried out by an individual or a small group of people who attack other people, their belongings or their estate.*

'Criminal activity' can be used as an umbrella term to cover the majority of the crimes described in the Penal Code. However, those that cause the greatest concern are crimes against property, against persons and crimes of a sexual nature.

Crimes against property:

a. Appropriation and Theft: These refer to the illegal gain of another's property by surreptitious action.
b. Robbery: The illegal gain of another's property with the use of violence or intimidation, or with the use of force against property.
c. Fraud: This also involves illegal gain, but it is mainly characterised by cheating.

Among the crimes against property, there is a variety of theft with violence known as bag-snatching, which may, and does, lead to injury (knocking a person down) and damage (ripped clothing).

Crimes against persons: Personal injury, homicide.

Crimes of a sexual nature: Aggression, sexual abuse and other, modern day, offences such as "sexual harassment" and "mobbing".

B. Organised crime

This kind of collective criminal activity can be described as the joint objective of a large, or small, group who are dedicated to committing crime. Members of such groups also have certain characteristics in common.

- They are well-organised. They usually act on the orders of a head or boss (leader) and they commit a wide range of crimes.
- These groups tend to be interrelated; in fact, it has even been proven that criminals of different nationalities collaborate. Criminals from other countries have been found to be in possession of art and jewellery stolen in Spain.
- The groups are normally made up of individuals between 30 and 50 years old who have surprising knowledge in technical and specialist fields. In addition to this they are exceptionally meticulous when they commit a crime, carrying out a thorough investigation and a detailed analysis prior to the event. They affect a very normal social life which, along with frequent moving from place to place, makes it difficult to identify and control them.
- Such groups also use other people (normally people with businesses in industry or the service industry) to launder part of their money for them. They also occasionally do this by investing in property using the names of third parties or false companies.

Characteristics

- Subordination and respect for the boss' orders.
- Perfectly synchronised organisation. All members know their place within the group.
- Each member specialises in something. They use the latest technology to help carry out their crimes with the greatest of precision.
- Ages range from 30 to 50 years.

Crime typologies

The types of criminal activity associated with these groups include:

- Counterfeiting money
- Illegal traffic of motor vehicles
- Drug trafficking
- Human trafficking
- Trafficking of illegal credit documents (traveller's cheques, credit cards)
- Illegal arms trafficking
- Illegal trafficking of art, jewellery, etc.
- Illegal trafficking of national and foreign identity documents

C. Violent crime

This type of crime is characterised by violence and is, almost exclusively, crime against property.

- Robbery in commercial, industrial, financial establishments, etc.
- Attacks on the aforementioned establishments
- Attacks on armoured vehicles used for transporting money

Characteristics

These criminals collect a large amount of information on their objective, and can sometimes count on the collaboration of unfaithful employees working on the inside of the companies targeted by the criminals.

They carry weapons to allow them to deal with any contingency arising from alarms being activated, the presence of security personnel or police, or any members of the public or employees trying o take action, etc.

Knowledge of technology: map reading, use of sophisticated systems for attack including blowtorches, explosives (dynamite, nitro-glycerine, plastic, gunpowder), electronics expertise.

Technological expertise regarding printing systems for counterfeiting money and credit documents.

Knowledge of laboratory techniques (production of psycho-tropic drugs).

Knowledge of commercial documents. The last three characteristics are more closely associated with organised crime.

In attacks on commercial premises to collect money and valuables, the criminals tend to trick their way into the establishment or act violently towards people or equipment to force their way in.

However, the criminals do need prior information regarding the location of the safe, and the positioning of any sensors and alarm systems. They also need to know if there are security guards on duty, etc. They usually choose to act during times when people are absent from the business, thereby giving themselves more time to carry out the crime.

3.6 Identification of suspects

Describing means transmitting observations to others so that they may get as good an idea as possible of the facts.

The description may be: verbal, written, or mixed: with visual support, drawings, etc. Thus it is communication between people using the spoken word, writing, or both at the same time.

Of these three types of communication, the most solid is the written form (as in a report) as it can be said that *spoken words are gone with the wind, but the written word forever remains*. It is for this reason everything related to communication, particularly written communication (reports), is so important.

Descriptions are based on observation, this being the first link in an observation-description-identification-communication chain.

A good observer should, therefore, not only have a general idea of events, but also memorise all the details, however insignificant they may seem, which would not be seen by the untrained eye.

Description refers to:

- People: physical description, demeanour, etc.
- Objects: vehicles, weapons, places, etc.
- Events: what happens, in what order does it happen, etc.

3.6.1 Describing people

To be able to describe people, their main characteristics need to be noted: gait, mannerisms, etc., as well as any other particular traits which can be used to identify and differentiate the person from others with similar characteristics.

Personal descriptions contain the following information:

a) Personal information

NAME:	Full name, including surname(s)
NICKNAMES:	All known aliases
ADDRESS:	Current and previous (if known)
ID DOCUMENT Nº:	Or passport number, for foreigners
NATIONALITY:	Original and adopted
OCCUPATION:	List all
MARITAL STATUS:	If married, name of spouse also

b) Physical description

SEX:	Male, female
ETHNIC APPEARANCE:	White, black, gypsy, mixed race, African, Asian, etc.
APPROXIMATE AGE:	Less than 20, between 20 and 40, over 40
HEIGHT:	Less than 1.60 m, between 1.60 and 1.80 m, more than 1.80 m, etc.
PHYSICAL SIZE:	Slim, normal, plump, etc.
WEIGHT:	Approximate
POSTURE:	Normal, straight-backed, hunched, round-shouldered, etc.
DISTINGUISHING FEATURES:	Scars, freckles, warts, moles, etc.
DISABILITIES:	Broken limb, badly-mended injury, missing limb, deafness, bad eyesight, etc.
PECULIARITIES:	Tics, bad habits, way of laughing or smiling, s/he licks his lips when s/he speaks, etc.
VOICE:	Soft, deep or harsh, high-pitched, etc.
WAY OF SPEAKING:	Slow, fast, clear, confused, uses strange expressions, foreign accent, regional accent, etc.
WAY OF WALKING:	Striding, agile, heavy, with difficulty, large or small steps, knock-kneed, with a limp, etc.
HABITS:	Clean or dirty, smoker (type and make of tobacco), drinker (type and make of alcohol), drug addict (type of drugs), hobbies, places frequented, etc.

c) Physical characteristics

HEAD:	Normal, large or small, round or partly round, square or partly square, pointed, etc.
FACE:	Round, square, rectangular, wide, long and thin, etc.
COMPLEXION:	White, brown, ruddy, sallow, pallid, freckles or birthmarks, etc.

EARS:	Normal, square or round, triangular, large or small, flat to the head or sticking out, etc.
FOREHEAD:	Low or high brow, normal, large or small, wrinkled, etc.
EYEBROWS:	Short or long, thin or bushy, arched, straight
EYES:	Normal, protruding or sunken, with bags underneath, slanting, cross-eyed, wall-eyed, etc.
NOSE:	Straight or Greek, sunken, aquiline, wide or narrow, bent tip, normal, long or short, pinched or flared nostrils, etc.
MOUTH:	Large or small, pinched, upturned corners, downturned corners, etc.
LIPS:	Normal, thin, full, hair-lip, etc.
TEETH:	Large or small, sticking out or prominent, even or uneven, broken or chipped, false or gold, etc.
CHIN:	Pointed, square, with a groove or dimple, etc.
HAIR:	Straight, wavy, curly, receding in a triangular or rectangular pattern, partial or total baldness, etc.
BEARD:	Short, ending in a point, rounded, bushy, etc.
MOUSTACHE:	Long or short, trimmed, drooping or curling up, pointed
SIDEBURNS:	No sideburns, large, gypsy-style, etc.
NECK:	Long or short, thick or thin, wrinkly, prominent Adam's apple, etc.
SHOULDERS:	Broad or narrow, square or rounded, sloping, one lower than the other, etc.
STOMACH:	Flat or prominent, firm or floppy, etc.
HANDS:	Large or small, long or short fingers, missing fingers, nicotine stains, etc.

d) Clothes

CLOTHES:	Well-cared for, not cared for, loud, work clothes, business attire, expensive or cheap, etc.
TYPE, SHAPE & COLOUR OF:	Jacket, jumper, shirt, tie, trousers, shoes, etc.
HEADWEAR:	Hat, beret, cap, headband, hood, hard hat, etc.
WAY OF WEARING IT:	Carried in the hand or worn on the head, pulled down as far as the eyes, at an angle
OTHER OBJECTS:	Jewellery, watch, objects carried, etc.

4 Vandalism

The identification and classification of people or groups by their appearance carries the risk of error when the same style of clothing and accessories are currently considered fashionable. Although the individuals wearing these clothes may outwardly appear to have the same tendencies and share the same philosophies, they are, in fact, people who have no affinity to the origins of the group and who simply enjoy looking like they belong to it rather than actually behaving like its true members. These individuals do not share the ideals of the members of the group they are emulating, although they may sympathise with them to a certain extent.

4.1 Acts of vandalism

Vandalism is defined as a desire to destroy with respect for nothing; a definition that tells us vandalism is an attitude.

The common assumption is that vandalism is exclusive to young people who, acting in groups, damage property with destruction as their only objective. Such acts are considered pointless violence and, as a result, require a more flexible approach than that mentioned previously. There is generally a distinction made between acts of vandalism and of hooliganism. Hooligans can be identified by their anti-social attitudes and behaviour. They are a nuisance and can damage property, although generally not severely.

In line with these concepts, we can define an act of vandalism as an act carried out by one or more individuals, resulting in the damage of public and/or private property, and with no other motivation than the actual destruction itself. There are generally two types of vandalism: the one-off, opportunist kind and the organised variety.

4.1.1 Opportunist vandalism

This is spontaneous vandalism. There is no particular reason for it other than as a means of escape and diversion. In this case, members of the group have not normally made any prior plans for destruction, they simply improvise as the situation develops.

The group does not get together with the preconceived idea of carrying out specific acts of vandalism; these just arise as each particular situation presents itself (encounters with other groups, concerts, sports events, etc.).

4.1.2 Organised vandalism

The members of this group already have an idea of the acts of vandalism they are going to commit and they are well-prepared, generally carrying the tools they need to do the job. They usually act at specific events (football matches, concerts, political rallies, etc). These groups generally have leadership of a sort and an ideology which may be of their own creation, or may be taken from elsewhere and adapted to suit their requirements.

These groups do not hesitate to take part indiscriminately in any type of vandalism. Their motivation is simply the turn of events at any given time.

Material objectives of vandals

The frequency of acts of vandalism depends on the objective of the vandals, who usually make the most of a situation and explore all possibilities for destruction that an object presents. The acts of vandalism usually committed are the following:

- Breaking windows

- Breaking objects

- Putting locks and equipment out of use

- Arson

- Graffiti

- Using firecrackers

It is usually public property that is targeted. If we regard acts of vandalism as demonstrations of protest, it seems safe to say that perpetrators target objects which are somehow symbolic or are used regularly by the general public.

People who commit acts of vandalism

Acts of vandalism cannot be attributed to one particular age group or to a particular social group. Anyone can carry out wanton destruction of an object; although it is true to say that young people or adolescents do commit a high percentage of such acts.

Acts of vandalism are usually carried out by groups of people. It is very rare to find individuals carrying out such attacks by themselves. The groups usually comprise three to seven members, although, depending on the event, there may be more.

Ages range from 14 to 23 years old, with the younger ones forming larger groups.

Groups of vandals can be identified as members of so-called urban tribes. In fact, some of these tribes see acts of vandalism as a means of expression or protest. This does not mean to say, however, that there are not groups of young people who commit crimes even though they do not belong to these tribes. Cases of the latter are, however, few and far between. Little damage is caused and they tend to result as a consequence of the accumulation of several circumstances. It has been noted that, depending on the ideology professed, the violent aspect of the crime is more or less acute.

4.2 Urban tribes

The term 'urban tribes' is used to describe certain groups which generate a following based on strict rules of conduct, image and beliefs. These factors allow them to be clearly identified and for any preventative or protective action to be taken before any incidents occur.

On their own, these urban tribes may be totally inoffensive for the general public but, at a critical juncture, they can also generate situations which make other passengers uncomfortable, create an intolerable amount of trouble, cause incidents which pose an unacceptable risk, and provoke violent clashes between different tribal groups.

Below, in data sheet format, is a list of the most prominent urban tribes from the last few decades. Information is provided about their look and the basis for their behaviour.

a.   Skaters or the hardcore

Origin: California (U.S.A.), 1960's. Due to a lack of wind the surfers move on to skateboards or roller skates. They arrive in Spain in the eighties.

Attitude: healthy mind, healthy body. Prolonged childhood.

Interests: alternating between surfing and snowboarding, playing the Nintendo, decorating their skateboard and listening to hardcore and rap music.

Dress: baggy jeans and t-shirts with skateboard logos in luminous colours. Flat-soled trainers or army boots, hooded sweatshirts, baseball caps worn back-to-front, bum-bags.

b.   Squatters

Origin: England in the 1960's. A break-off group from the mods and hippies.

Attitude: anti-military, anti-fascist, anti-racist; in general they are against all established systems. They are only violent o occasion, for example, when they are being evicted or at certain demonstrations.

Interests: all types of cultural activity, their favourite music is anything that has protest as a theme, such as Barricada, La Polla Records, etc.

Dress: scruffy, dark colours.

c.   Cyberpunks

Origin: in 1984 William Gibson published *Neuromancer*, a book envisaging a society dominated by microprocessors with information as the main form of currency.

Attitude: they want to bring down all hierarchies and the establishment via use of digital information. Technology will be the only bond in the future. The body will be a shell, and the mind will roam freely and happily through computer networks. They are rebels who do not respect traditional values.

Interests: they are Internet addicts. They know all about the latest in cybernetics thanks to the magazines *Mondo 2000*, *Wired*, and *2600*. They listen to techno music (Cosmic Baby, Jim Clark, etc.), and attend cyber-parties and multimedia parties where they drink "intelligent" drinks containing vitamins and amino acids.

Dress: A cross between *Blade Runner* and *Mad Max*. Like punks, their costumes are very much DIY.

Industrial-style accessories: electrical circuit boards, floppy disks, silicone, gas masks, welder's glasses.

d. Flamenco youth

Origin: descendents of the big flamenco families, mostly of gypsy ethnicity. They have modernised the traditional flamenco "jondo" music with a mixture of rock, jazz, blues and salsa. True ethnic beauties with jet-black hair, the flamenco youth are the latest sensation in the nightclubs.

Attitude: good-looking, fun-loving hedonists. They fight for integration and to adapt "gypsy" law to modern times.

Interests: clothes shopping, make-up and spending the night in pubs and flamenco bars. They live for their art and their people: Ketama, José Soto, Aurora, Potito.

Dress: long hair, polka dot scarves, brightly-coloured silk shirts, hoop earrings, tattoos, heavy gold chains and bangles. The girls wear very tight fitting clothing with very low-cut necklines. They wear Lycra outfits and are heavily made up.

e. Bikers

Origin: U.S.A. in the eighties.

Attitude: they are not violent unless provoked by other urban tribes.

Interests: riding their motorbikes for miles with their group. They drink a lot of beer and like motorbike rallies and exhibitions.

Dress: Leather jackets and trousers, or denim jackets with their group's logo on the back, old-fashioned helmets and lots of tattoos.

f. Cyber hippies

Origin: a branch of Cyberpunk, a combination of cybernetics.

Attitude: they strive to achieve an inner void to reach a vegetative and impenetrable state.

Interests: keeping their body and mind absolutely pure. Loyal supporters of bio-culture fairs, alternative medicines, whole foods and energy drinks. They are fascinated by the cosmos.

Dress: they are regulars in second-hand shops and recycle their clothes and other objects. They wear clothes with a lot of silver vinyl printing and Latex as well as t-shirts with holograms on them.

g. Hell's Angels-style bikers

Origin: these bikers are Harley-Davidson fans. Their group has existed ever since these bikes first appeared.

Attitude: travelling the world on their bikes, always on the edge of the law. They proclaim themselves nomads, saying they have no home but their bike.

Interests: cleaning and tinkering with their Harleys. Listening to country music, playing pool, drinking beer and surrounding themselves with women.

Dress: the typical California 'Hell's Angel' style: long hair, beard and a beer belly. They have pointed sideburns and wear leather jackets and trousers. They also wear an earring in one ear, pointed boots and scarves tied round their necks.

h.   Mods

Origin: they first appeared in the jazz clubs of London in the sixties, when Quadrophenia was released.

Attitude: to always be elegant in appearance. They have a bright and colourful outlook on life. Their way of life is dominated by aesthetics and fun.

Interests: the film they identify with is Quadrophenia (the life of urban tribes and their encounters). The music groups they listen to are The Who, Los Sencillos and Los Flechazos. They ride scooters covered in mirrors. They love pop music. They drink beer and take amphetamines.

Dress: bowl haircuts. Four-button suits with narrow lapels and badges of their favourite groups. Green Parkas.

i.   Grunge kids

Origin: this group appeared at the end of the eighties with a new, hard style of rock music.

Attitude: neo-hippy scruffiness. They reject consumer society and the Establishment. They are cynical and conformist. They are atheists.

Interests: vegging out in front of the TV. They love Beavis and Butthead. They take drugs and go to concerts to dance.

Dress: old clothes, wearing t-shirts on top of long-sleeved shirts, long, greasy hair, lumberjack shirts and ski hats.

j.   Goths

Origin: born of a rejection of the decadence of punk in which their roots lie.

Attitude: to absolutely reject all punk beliefs. They are fascinated by aliens, magic and fantasy worlds. They are also pessimists.

Interests: horror films, like Dracula or The Crow and gore films. They love role-play games, cemeteries, the Middle Ages and dragons. Their favourite music groups are Christian, Death, and The Mission, among others.

Dress: favourite colour: black. Pale faces, dyed and back-combed hair and long, black nails. Floaty and medieval-style dresses, netting, crucifix pendants.

k.   Rockers

Origin: U.S.A. in the 1950's. They were young people who worshipped their king, Elvis Presley, as well as Marlon Brando.

Attitude: romantic and chauvinistic. They are known troublemakers and love to dance. They stick together in groups and each group has a leader.

Interests: they collect, and dance to, rock and roll records, they drink bourbon or beer. Their dream is to own a motorbike (especially a Harley-Davidson) and to visit the Elvis museum.

Dress: The most important thing for a boy is to have a good quiff. They use Brill cream and wear frock coats, embroidered shirts, string or bow ties, boogie shoes (platforms) or pointed boots. The girls wear can-can skirts. Their day to day outfits are rolled-up Levi's or Lois jeans with white socks and ballroom-type shoes, and leather jackets.

l. *Bakaladeros*

Origin: this group originated when the repetitive, electronic music of the late eighties reached Spain from Germany, Belgium and Holland.

Attitude: they spend their weekends in a catatonic state, dancing to the frenetic rhythm of 'techno' music which is widespread in Spain.

Interests: they take designer drugs and do not drink alcohol. The DJ is their idol.

Dress: childlike. T-shirts and sweatshirts with printed pictures. Number 2 cut hair with a 'Woody Woodpecker' fringe. The girls have the back of their neck shaved and wear the rest of their hair in a ponytail.

m. *Nacionalbakaladeros*

Origin: this group appeared in the nineties, coinciding with the boom of "rave" and "techno" music. They mainly gather in the large nightclubs on the eastern coast of Spain.

Attitude: they act violently towards young people who are not part of their gang.

Interests: they live to spend their weekends in a catatonic state, dancing to the frenetic rhythm of techno music.

Dress: T-shirts and sweatshirts with printed pictures. Short hair and an earring in one ear or in their nose. The girls wear miniskirts and leather boots.

n. **SHARPs or Redskins**

Origin: the SHARPs appeared in the nineties as an offshoot of the Redskins (skinheads with extreme left wing ideologies). Their objective is to achieve race equality.

Attitude: they belong to the ultra-left and their main enemies are the skinheads and the nacionalbakaladeros, who they have violent confrontations with.

Interests: they relate well to squatters and participate in activities held in the squats.

Dress: camouflage trousers with hiking boots or baseball boots and a 'Keffiyeh' (Palestinian scarf).

Things have changed a lot in the five years leading up to the writing of this document. Where there was once a bright array of urban tribes, this has more or less been reduced to four main groups; although some of the old groups do still remain. Many of the groups, who some years ago were fighting for their own identity, have now become integrated into the four remaining groups. What's more, it is now only their free time that they dedicate to the group and its activities, it is no longer their life. An example of this is the music listened to. Whereas before each group identified itself with a specific type of music, nowadays all groups listen to all kinds of music. A factor all these groups have in common is their rejection of established society, and they are confronting it with new values, a new look and new ways of having fun.

Their way of dressing and their gestures are aggressive, meaning all security staff responsible for an event or place will be alerted to the possibility of violent behaviour as soon as they see members of an urban tribe.

The fact that they provoke such a reaction actually fulfils one of the objectives of the group, to instil fear into others. This can sometimes lead to violence and aggression used simply to confirm they were right to be afraid. It must be noted, however, that not all groups are violent to the same degree.

- **Heavy metallers**

In Barcelona members of this group tend to be from the outskirts of the city and are not particularly active. They are avid concert-goers, to be a 'metaller' is to live for heavy metal music. They do not generally use hard drugs, but are quite tolerant of those who do. The use of hashish is common.

Their groups do not normally have leaders and they get on reasonably well with the punks. They do not normally commit acts of vandalism, although they are very noisy.

Origin: they first appeared in the sixties when hard rock was popular. In the eighties, several *heavy metal* groups were formed in the UK and attracted an army of followers.

Attitude: they feel their music very intensely and it is what brings them together. They also feel they are social outcasts, chauvinists and high-spirited individuals.

Interests: they buy magazines dedicated to their favourite music. Their favourite music groups are Iron Maiden, AC/DC, Scorpions, Metallica, Los Suaves, etc. They go to all the concerts. They love comics. They are nonconformist and against police repression. They drink beer and use soft drugs.

Fig 4.1

Dress: tight, faded jeans, trainers. Long hair. T-shirts showing their favourite music groups, leather jackets, denim jackets or similar.

- **B-Boys**

They usually wear their hair short or have the sides of their heads shaven. They wear baggy, tracksuit-style trousers and shorts in the summer. They wear boot-type trainers, big, baggy t-shirts and usually a cap.

They love rap music which is protest music combined with expression of life experiences. They also like funk music and their favourite drink is Coca-cola.

They are great fans of graffiti; almost all of them carry spray cans or, at least, thick marker pens so they can leave their 'tags' (personalised signatures) or pictures everywhere they have been.

Their graffiti is an act of hooliganism and vandalism which needs no provocation. Skaters (skateboard fans) have their origins in this group, with members generally being individualists. Their activity is focused on the dangerous use of a skateboard and, to a lesser extent, on graffiti. The breakages and damage they cause are due to the use of the skateboard

Origin: they first appeared in the U.S.A. at the end of the seventies. Their roots are in the Bronx area of New York where their influence was rap music.

Attitude: anger at the system and marginalisation. They do not take drugs.

Interests: graffitiing walls, dodging the police and breakdancing. Their music idols are Public Enemy and Master Ace. In Spain they are groups such as Madrid Rap and Poetas Violentos, T-7.

Dress: Baggy, bright-coloured clothing, Bermuda shorts, caps, gold chains around their necks with logos on them, rings, goatee beards or soul patches and afro hairstyles.

Fig. 4.2

- **Punks**

This urban tribe is, perhaps, the most easy to recognise by appearance. Members characteristically dye or spray their hair bright colours, and the most radical ones shave the sides of their head and create a Mohican with the rest of their hair. They usually wear army boots and some army clothing, they wear belts with big buckles, bracelets or studded wristbands and chains.

In the early days of punk, members used hard drugs. Nowadays however, they only smoke hashish and drink beer. They love hard rock, something they share with the heavy metallers. They normally dance in a very aggressive way, and to onlookers it may seem they are attacking each other.

The punk movement originated in the United Kingdom. Punks consider themselves anarchists and are antiestablishment. Rules have no meaning for them.

When they first appeared in Spain they were very violent, although, today, that gratuitous violence has been eradicated. However, if they feel threatened they will respond very violently, and it is precisely in such moments that they will commit acts of vandalism. Once they are in that frame of mind, nothing is safe and they will not hesitate to attack using chains or any other potential weapon they have at hand.

They are the archenemies of the *skinheads*, and a chance encounter between the two groups will almost always lead to trouble.

Origin: they first appeared in mid-seventies London as a movement that rebelled against society and used its image as its primary weapon.

Fig 4.3

Attitude: they see themselves as the culture of the dispossessed. They are anarchists, anti-social and tough. They are nonconformist and live in squats. They smoke marihuana, hashish and drink alcohol.

Interests: They juggle fire for money and listen to groups like the Sex Pistols.

Dress: Coloured Mohican, nose rings, earrings and piercing in their mouths. Clothes in a deplorable state, ripped t-shirts worn over other clothes, leather jackets, painted army boots with red laces.

- **Skinheads**

This is currently the only group which still abides by the ideals of an urban tribe, meaning they have an ideology, making them identifiable by adults and feared by all others. This urban tribe uses violence as one of its forms of expression.

This movement began in the United Kingdom in the sixties. It brought together neo-fascists and football hooligans.

Their look consists of shaven heads (number one cut), high top, steel toe-cap boots, bomber jackets (reversible: green outside, orange inside), brand-name jeans, short enough to show off their high top boots which are always kept very clean. When they are "at war" they will normally wear their reversible jackets with the orange on the outside.

They drink beer and, if they take drugs, it is usually hashish or amphetamines. They boast about not paying for their drinks anywhere.

They need no real motivation to vandalise property or become violent, the slightest excuse is enough. In groups of only two or three, they are not violent.

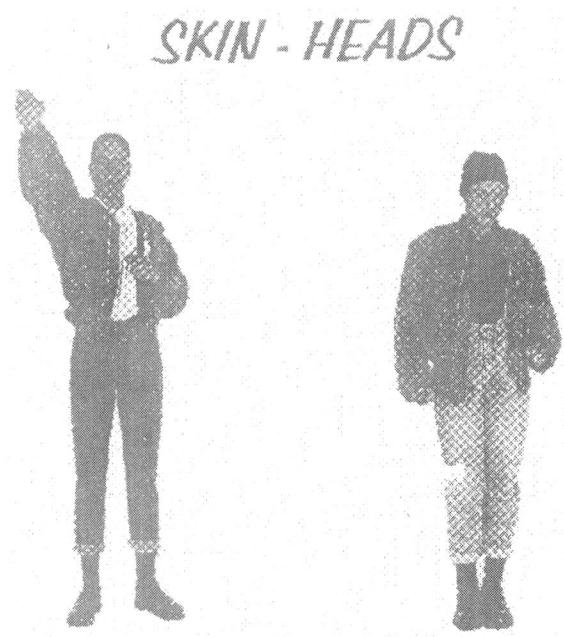

Fig. 4.4

They usually carry weapons, or objects that can be used as such (knives, sprays, carabiners, baseball bats, etc.). Once they have begun their vandalism spree, they move quickly, attacking indiscriminately.

It is important to remember that, with all these groups and skinheads in particular, there are fashions which emulate their look. In other words, the skinhead fashion means there are people who dress in the same way but who are not violent.

Origin: the sixties. They formed street gangs comprising young people between the ages of 16 and 23. The skinhead movement reached Spain in the eighties, becoming well-rooted in the larger cities between 1988 and 1991.

Attitude: they are the most violent of all the urban tribes, attacking homosexuals, transvestites, punks, prostitutes, etc.

Interests: they like beer, hashish and getting drunk at the weekends. They belong to extremist football supporters groups and always seek to fight the supporters of opposing teams.

Attire: shaven heads, green or black bomber jackets, braces, black jeans rolled-up to show off their steel toe cap Dr. Martens boots, scarves and balaclavas to cover their faces during acts of violence. The use the swastika and the Celtic cross symbols.

4.2.1 Places where acts of vandalism are carried out

On land, it is difficult to determine a specific place for acts of vandalism as there is always something to hand that can be destroyed. It can be said that opportunist acts of vandalism generally take place in quiet, less frequented places, whilst organised vandalism can take place in busy or quiet places.

The latter depends on the level of violence of the particular group as to whether they choose a busy or quiet place. On board ship, acts of vandalism can be committed anywhere groups are permitted to gather (dining areas, cafés, wide corridors, etc.) and where there is security equipment such as alarm buttons, etc.

Areas near bars or cafés where alcohol is sold, or corridors leading to them, are most prone to attack. It is a well-known fact that an area that has been attacked once will generally undergo more attacks on a regular basis if the damage is not repaired. It is almost as if the vandals feel less guilty about attacking an area that has already been damaged.

Vandalism usually takes place during the night and is frequently related to alcohol consumption. This is, of course, heavily affected by a ships departure and arrival times and the duration of the journey, as well as the characteristics of the ports of origin and destination.

4.2.2 Intervention when confronted with acts of vandalism

The best kind of intervention is, in fact, prevention. If no measures have been taken to prevent an incident, then any repressive action taken as intervention will be made more difficult.

Quite clearly the best way to prevent such incidents is to check passengers in the port before they board the ship, as is done for passengers boarding aircraft. Any individual showing signs of drunkenness, or aggressive or antisocial behaviour, should not be allowed to embark.

Once persons, who it is considered pose a risk, are aboard, the best way to prevent an incident is to allocate them an area where they can be more easily controlled and managed, and where they will bother other passengers less. In a case where there are members of more than one urban tribe on board, it is recommended the groups are kept apart, so they cannot enter into contact with each other. Doing this greatly reduces the chances of any incidents occurring.

Any preventative action should begin with a study of elements on board which, because of their fragility, location or symbolism, may be targeted by groups (décor on the ship), as well as a study of the relationships that exist between the groups that most frequently travel on that route and the reactions that can be expected from them.

Once such studies have been made, the question of how crimes can be prevented must be analysed. For example, lighting in areas at risk, using tougher materials or materials which are easier to replace, and increasing security at certain times and in certain places.

All crew members dealing with passengers must quickly identify any members of conflictive groups on board, as well as be aware of their "ideologies", ways of behaving, and what might provoke them to violence, so that they can try to avoid such incendiary situations arising. When acts of vandalism are already being committed, the best approach is to channel the violence into alternative ways of expression that pose less of a threat to the safety of the passengers and the ship's facilities. This will also create situations that are more easily controlled by the crew.

5 The vulnerability of ships

5.1 Prevention and protection

Prevention as a concept means action taken to avoid undesirable situations. Action programmes designed for public safety would be aimed at reaching a utopia in a world populated only by good, understanding people who believe in equality, bear no grudges, are not greedy or envious and are not bad in any way. One of the easiest ways to achieve this is the universal acceptance of knowledge, culture and education. Although the tendency is to move towards this, there is still a long way to go and, unfortunately, all humanity does not have the same goals nor does it follow the same course to achieve them. We can only imagine that tension and violence will be with us for some time to come.

Regarding ships, as well as any other means of transport which carries a large number of passengers, the best measure for prevention would be to screen passengers as they embark, and identify any who may be conflictive during the voyage. By doing so, the problem would remain on dry land where the correct preventive measures could be applied by qualified personnel.

In reference to the concept of protection, goods which must be protected will be anything of value that others wish to steal, damage, or destroy, or which may undergo an alteration in the aforementioned value by any other means.

The people who should be protected are those who have a high social standing, are high level politicians, are very affluent, are highly cultured, have expert technical knowledge, or are famous or very popular, thereby making them targets for threats. In a more general way, this is also extended to people who are inside any of the buildings, port facilities or ships which require protection.

Of course, differences of opinion leading to arguments can easily arise between two ordinary people as well as between conflictive individuals, thereby leading to a breach of the peace. In such cases, measures of protection ought to consist of the removal and physical separation of the individuals concerned. An escalation of violence would thus be avoided and the incident would not reach the second phase.

Such a course of action would ensure protection, the concept of which deals with the measures taken, or obstacles used, to prevent the situation becoming more serious or to deal with the person(s) causing the problem.

5.2 Threats and risks

'Threat' is defined as a qualifying or descriptive term given that it describes what can happen (theft, sabotage, destruction, fire, loss, copying and counterfeiting, etc.) to goods, as well as attacks, (kidnapping, hold-ups, intimidation, rape, accidents, etc.) on people.

Uncovering and describing possible threats aimed at goods and people is known as a "threat analysis". This is considered very important as if the cause of possible total or partial losses of goods or people is known, we can protect them better against such eventualities.

Logically, all these possible threats do not have the same probability of being carried out against a facility, property or a person. Because of the nature and circumstances surrounding these threats, there may be a greater probability of some rather than others of these threats being carried out. For this reason, the threat analysis comprises only a part of the hypothetical protection programme.

Another essential part of the programme is the calculating of this probability; in other words, the risk assessment or analysis which quantifies the level of probability of an incident or threatening situation occurring. It is, therefore, a measurement, not a description and can be high, medium, low or small.

Fundamentally, the difference between threat and risk lies in the fact that a threat describes "what could" happen, and risk describes "to what extent" it is likely that the threat is carried out in comparison with other threats, or in comparison with nothing happening.

In the field of security, threat analysis and risk assessment is used in the design, organising and installation of security systems specially adapted to protect property and people from identified threats that pose the greatest risk for said property and people.

The most likely possibility on board ship is premeditated violent crime against passengers or crew, or against the cargo.

However, the most dangerous possibility is still the threat of terrorist attack because, although terrorist groups use violence under the pretext of supposed ideals and seek the greatest impact from their actions, there is always a financial motive to the attack and terrorists will aim for both if they can.

5.3 Vulnerability

The term 'vulnerability' defines to what degree the preventive and protective measures established in the security programme are really invalid, both within the system itself and in the elements of the organisation which are still opposed to threats and risk.

When applied to security equipment, the term determines the quality of the element in relation to its reliability for resisting or detecting attempts at putting it out of use or sabotage.

Another important aspect is threat analysis and risk assessment, both of which should be accompanied by a vulnerability analysis.

Vulnerabilities can be quantified by looking at the result between the value assigned to the "risks" and that assigned to the "damages" produced once the threat has been carried out.

On a ship, it is the rigorous access control (both before boarding and once inside), the physical resistance of the elements making up the ship, the layout of the cabin areas, the distribution, location and number of crew members, the accessibility to the control centres, the efficiency of the localised or general means of communication, etc., among others, all constitute points which will provide vulnerability criteria, depending on their state and condition.

Regarding persons themselves, areas of vulnerability can be classified as:

a) Stimuli: greed, ambition/lust for power, desire to be famous, popularity.
b) Uncontrollable impulses: anger, hate, jealousy.
c) Premeditated action: revenge, spite, jealousy.
d) Of non-rational origin: drug addiction, drunkenness, madness.

Generally, by analysing the vulnerability of ships (especially passenger ships), and why they may be targets for attack, we reach the conclusion that they are particularly attractive because:

a) *of the impact* they create by generating fame, propaganda and popularity. All sensationalist incidents involving a ship reverberate in society. Aviation has not managed to put passenger ships in the corner totally as such ships still hold a traditional significance for most people. A little old fashioned, perhaps, but with a real romantic touch and a certain taste of adventure.

Groups of ecologists, political, separatist, religious and social groups and even terrorist organisations can all choose such a target with the absolute guarantee that the event itself, the name or acronym of the organisation, the objective, the names of the leaders and their demands, etc. will be in the newspaper headlines and will be talked about on radio and television, becoming the main topic for discussion.

It is, without a doubt, a very profitable objective in this sense. The most dangerous possibility, however, is certainly that the attacker is a terrorist organisation. Terrorist activity, whatever faction it comes from, does not exactly create many interesting anecdotes.

b) *they generate resources.* It should be taken into account the fact that greed is, perhaps, the most powerful and most frequent motive behind these attacks, and that a ship is a complex world of resources.

- It itself is property, as a ship with machinery, facilities, elements, materials and equipment of all kinds.
- Its cargo.
- It transports both qualified personnel and ordinary passengers.
- It can be used to apply an enormous amount of pressure when in the hands of people who will not hesitate (as experience has repeatedly shown us) to sacrifice human lives and property.

c) *of their structure*, referring to the enormous and complex skeleton of the ship. Its horizontal and vertical structure. The compartmentation. The many dead spaces. Once these, and other, structural characteristics have been studied in detail, it is easy to make the most of the advantages they offer for illegally entering, hiding and moving around inside, as well as being able to carry out other activities such as isolating areas, closing off thoroughfares, studying timetables, keeping a close watch on people's movements, etc.

If the target is the ship itself, a small group of motivated and well-trained men can easily take over and take control of it. If the target is someone or something on board, the attackers (lone individuals or very small groups) can use these structural characteristics to great effect.

d) *of their systems.* Whether the aim of the attack is destruction, or looting, the valuable and often sophisticated systems can be decisive in the success of the attack if used wisely.

Attacks on board ship present different problems when compared with other cases as a ship, when sailing, is moving. An attack can take place in the port, anchored out of the port, in a foreign port, or whilst sailing. Each type implies a different turn of events and different situations and, in each case, systems play an important role.

If it is not a terrorist attack, the navigational systems, etc will have to be used by the personnel responsible for them under the supervision (and threat) of the attackers as the latter will not (except in certain isolated cases) have the specialist knowledge required to be able to operate them.

e) *of their occupancy*. Passenger ships can be considered floating hotels. Such a name means they lose some of their romantic charm, but they do gain on the descriptive side... even if the comparison does not fully do it justice. In a hotel there is much greater movement in occupancy, and far less of a chance of the guests getting to know each other.

For a few hours, or days, a considerable number of people (alone, couples, groups, families) will share mealtimes, spaces, entertainment, walks, views and horizons.

They will ignore each other, watch each other or strike up conversation with each other. They will all get to know a little bit more about each other and some friendships will be made.

It is an unbeatable environment and provides the perfect opportunity for anybody wanting to carry out an attack. Mingling with the crowd, attackers can get on board, observe and study every little detail they need. They can prepare and carry out their operation, carefully choosing the most apt time and place.

f) *of the surroundings*. When a ship enters a port it becomes part of a complex organisation with irregular activity. There are ships of all types from all over the world, people and cargo being moved around, docking and departure operations, lorries, containers, cranes, forklift trucks, crews, onlookers, sales representatives, dock workers and many more.

Then there is the hustle and bustle of the loading and unloading, checking systems, maintenance work, restocking of provisions, fuel and other exchangeable goods, all of which employ outside contractors who may not be particularly strictly controlled, unless there is a comprehensive security plan in place, for both the port and the ship, which is fully complied with.

All these circumstances make it easier to observe the ship, to get information about it and to get near and actually access it. Such possibilities provide a wide range of opportunities for anyone who has chosen it as a target, or who is suggesting it as a possibility for anyone looking for an easy and profitable target.

Ships are certainly very vulnerable, and the mere fact of realising that and being aware of it is already something. In the field of security, being able to mentally picture yourself in a risk situation is one of the first and foremost measures of self-protection. The element of surprise is extremely valuable in any attack. Anything that can be done to avoid being surprised is very positive action.

However, more can be done, starting with the in-depth knowledge of the ship and taking into account the risk of attack via the aforementioned areas of vulnerability: impact, resources, structure, systems, occupancy and surroundings. Security is essentially logic and all good security measures result from observation which is then turned into an analysis, considered carefully to reach conclusions and then tested with practical experience.

5.4 Risks

The risks intrinsic to a ship (as a basic object of maritime transport) are due to its function and were identified long ago.

The most common risks, as well as being recognised for their frequency and the seriousness of their consequences, as included in the expression "maritime accidents", which may be classified in two main areas:

1) *Dangers associated with the sea*: leaks, running aground, collision.

2) *Dangers associated with transport*: fire, risks related to machinery, work-related risks, environmental contamination, plagues, risks related to the cargo.

In some cases, given the nature and special relevance they acquire when they appear in a ship at sea or on international journeys, a third block may be included:

3) *Medical/health*: infections, illnesses, extensive food poisoning.

Seafarers are fully aware of all these risks, and on board ship they know how to deal with such situations. They have procedures to follow (which they readily apply) to evaluate the level of risk and the corresponding measures to be taken. In such circumstances, a sailor knows how to evaluate his position in a situation by weighing up the disruption being experienced and looking at the alternatives available.

In any case, the severity of the consequences can only be counteracted by the ship's own means and resources designed to control the situation and return normality. The availability of such resources is limited and not always adequate for the handling of the situation in question. This means efficiency is greatly reduced, although any level of intervention is greatly appreciated.

During the 19th and 20th centuries, the aforementioned risks constituted the greater part of security concerns. Unfortunately, regarding the field of risk prevention, they were only able to apply corrective action after the event, with reference to previous cases.

Acts of piracy are generally considered to belong to the past and to have been eradicated. This, however, is a misconception as, not only have they progressively been reappearing, but they have taken on a new violence, becoming more frequent and having truly dire consequences. In addition to this, new forms of criminal activity and antisocial behaviour have also increased. The same can be said of other types of risk which take place on board more or less frequently depending on the type of ship (passenger or cargo), the waters sailed in (destination ports and countries), time of year (holiday season or not), public events (political, cultural, sporting, etc.). Such variables greatly affect the likelihood of the following occurring:

4) *Violent acts*: terrorism, guerrilla activity, hijacking, piracy, bomb threats.

5) *Antisocial risks*: robbery, petty theft, vandalism, hold-ups, fraud and criminal deception, attack, assault, sabotage, blackmail, extortion, data falsification, drug trafficking.

6) *Social problems*: illegal immigration.

Sections 1 to 3 are encompassed by the word 'safety', whilst those in sections 4 to 6 are covered by the word 'security'.

5.5 Different courses of action taken to combat the vulnerability of merchant ships

The type of ship criminals are most drawn to seems to be that referred to as a *cruise* ship. Up until the fateful 11th September, the cruise sector was the fastest expanding within the tourist industry. New York Cruise Lines International Association (CLIA) represents the world's main cruise lines which have their social base in the U.S., even if they do not fly the American flag. It is, therefore, in the United States where, for obvious reasons, there is the highest level of security. This fact is reflected in an article entitled 'Cruise Control' by Teresa Anderson[1], published prior to the 11th September, 2001:

"… In the 1990s, approximately 80 new cruise ships were built, and more than 52 are being planned for release before 2005…

Jurisdiction… Issues of jurisdiction can affect how security investigates crimes that occur at sea. "A crime can occur among two people of different nationalities on a ship from a third country that is sailing in the territorial waters of a fourth." Royal Caribbean reports most crimes to the FBI because it is the only federal agency that has jurisdiction outside the United States. In the waters of a foreign country, the crime is reported to the officials of that nation and to the embassies of the parties involved… For example, security is instructed to contact the FBI when in international waters and the state or local police when in the waters of a U.S. state. When in the Caribbean, incidents are reported to officials at the next port of call…

Personnel. To help mitigate security problems, all major cruise lines have both security managers and officers on each ship, which also typically has a central station from which security activities, such as CCTV monitoring and access control, are conducted. No standards govern the training of cruise line security personnel… For example, all Carnival security employees go through a new 40-hour training programme… Royal Caribbean selects security officers with experience in security and seafaring. Most of their security personnel are former British navy or marine officers with ship experience. Security for Renaissance Cruises also selects security employees from the British navy… On Renaissance, security officers oversee a team of security watchmen composed of former British Gurkha Regiment soldiers from Nepal. The Gurkhas are world-renowned soldiers and each must have a minimum of 15 years of military experience before being hired by the cruise line. Prior to being hired, they must also receive safety and fire-fighting training...

Cruise lines, and the security force that protects them, must meet regulations established in 1986 by the International Maritime Organization (IMO). These regulations outline specific security measures that ships must implement, including preparing security plans, restricting access to certain areas of the ship, establishing ID systems, and screening passengers and crew… Security has also increased the number of CCTV cameras in certain areas of the ship…

Since the training and other changes have not been fully implemented, complaints have remained stable at about two cases for every 100,000 passengers. However, Newhoff feels confident that the rate will decline over time.

At Royal Caribbean, a new system requires that a photo be taken of each passenger at the embarkation port. The photo ID, complete with bar code, must then be presented each time the person boards the ship. The system can determine whether the passenger is registered, whether

---

[1] Teresa Anderson is senior editor at Security Management.

the card has been used, and whether the total number of passengers on board tallies with the registry. Carnival has just completed the installation of a similar electronic access control system. The A-Pass system, designed by SISCO of Palm Beach Gardens, Florida, is used to track both passengers and crew.

Piracy… Most pirates operate in three areas, according to Newhoff: the Far East, the east coast of South America near Brazil, and the west coast of Africa. "Luckily, these are not major cruise ship operating areas," says Newhoff. "We don't find pirates in the major areas [where] we do business." Also, pirates are more likely to attack a commercial boat with a small crew, rather than a cruise ship… "Cruise ships are well-lit, fast, and hard to board," says Newhoff, making them a harder target. "But even though we present the wrong environment for pirates," says Newhoff, "we still prepare for them… At night, for example, security patrols are increased and crew members place fire hoses on the deck to repel anyone using grappling hooks. Royal Caribbean also works closely with the Piracy Centre in Kuala Lumpur. The centre serves as a clearinghouse for all marine vessels to report suspected piracy. If a suspicious activity is noted, the ship's captain places a report to the Piracy Centre on the main frequency so that the potential thieves can hear the report. After receiving a report, the centre sends immediate warning notices to all ships in the affected area and to coast guards and law enforcement agencies worldwide.

Terrorism. The hijacking of the Achille Lauro in the Mediterranean in 1985 proved that cruise ships can be vulnerable to acts of terrorism. In that incident, an American passenger was killed by the terrorists who took over the ship… But its victimization completely changed cruise industry security. Terrorism became a major industry concern overnight. Royal Caribbean, for example, hires contractors to keep an eye on activities in various ports. The contractors provide intelligence and help devise risk management strategies. Carnival conducts three-day terrorism awareness seminars for new employees and conducts security searches each week on every ship. And all cruise lines get monthly government briefings on terrorist activity…"

The insight given by this extract from the report shows us that security is not just a question for security forces: The maritime industry, as a private business, in the majority of cases, must tackle the subject seriously.

Regarding the current situation of ships in general, and merchant ships in particular, and focusing mainly on terrorist attacks which target them, these attacks may:

- Come from the outside: In port or At sea.
- Come from within the ship itself.
- Use the ship itself as a deadly weapon in a terrorist attack.

5.6 Attacks on a ship from the outside

A) In port

Any attack on a ship made from outside the hull will be aiming to sink or cripple the ship as well as causing the greatest possible number of victims to get as much national and international coverage as possible.

Preparation for the attack will include the compulsory transportation of a large amount of explosive material to the ship or its immediate vicinity. The amount of explosive needed will be calculated according to the destructive power needed to breach the barrier that the hull itself represents.

From experience, it is known the most frequently used methods are the following:

    a.   One or more terrorists, acting as frogmen, carry the explosives and attach them to weak areas of the hull below the water line. All conventional, as well as homemade, limpet bombs can be used.[2] If an attack is successful, it normally causes the sinking of the ship and casualties or fatalities among the crew and passengers.

    b.   Individuals on suicide missions steer smaller boats loaded with explosives into the side of the ship facing the sea. They aim for the point which will cause the most material damage and individual victims, depending on how the situation presents itself.[3]

    c.   Small, radio-controlled boats (or even planes), to minimise risk, are used to carry small amounts of explosive to a pre-determined spot where they are detonated. As the amount of explosive used is only small, they are generally used to attack specific targets and are activated by remote control.

    d.   Explosives placed between the dock and the ship.

B) At sea

This kind of attack is more difficult and complex to carry out, so the method will only be used by terrorist groups which have a strong infrastructure behind them (both human and material), and which are efficiently organised and adequately informed about the routes, stopovers and ships to be targeted.

With the use of divers ruled out as unlikely, the most likely form of attack seems to be that using suicide bombers on small boats loaded with explosive material. The ship would be at greatest risk when near a port, on entering or leaving.[4] This is because it is close to the coast, and is therefore easy to observe, which increases its chances of being attacked by terrorists.

To a lesser extent, it is possible to imagine an attack being carried out by radio-controlled boats or planes. It is also possible that the ship could be taken by terrorists boarding it.

---

[2] On 24th June, 1979, the French ship "Montlhery" was sunk whilst docked in the Port of Pasajes (Guipúzcoa). The terrorist attack was carried out by divers and blew two holes in the hull on the starboard side of the ship, at 2.20 m below the bilge keel. This ship was used to transport Ford motor cars built in Spain to England.

[3] On 12th October, 2000, there was a terrorist attack in Aden, Yemen. The target was the United States destroyer "USS Cole". The Cole was in the Yemeni port to refuel when a small boat loaded with explosives was detonated next to the ship, creating a large hole in the hull. 17 sailors were killed in the attack and 39 were injured. The two attackers, standing, crashed a rubber dinghy into the side of the ship.

[4] The departure of the ship is the most dangerous time as it is more easily predicted. Whilst it is docked it can be observed.

5.7 Attacks from within the ship itself

Any lack of preparation or security procedures on board will improve attackers' chances of success. Such attacks would also reflect some kind of failure in the screening of passengers accessing the ship. Groups will need to get as many terrorists and explosives on board as they need to carry out their planned criminal act. Occasionally the attackers will need the collaboration of a crew member. This individual will usually pass on information and help with the aforementioned objectives, although in some cases it is the crew member himself who will commit the crime surreptitiously.

Depending on the aim of the attack, the terrorists will carefully choose the place where the explosives are to be placed. It should not be forgotten that being inside, especially in cases of sabotage, means the nerve centres of the ship itself can be reached and acts can be committed against sensitive equipment or instruments without the need for explosives.

The objective of these acts may be to take over the ship to make demands,[5] to put it out of action, to sink it and to create victims.

Acts where the ship itself is instrumental in a terrorist attack.

The magnitude of the events of the 11th September, 2001 marked a qualitative and quantitative milestone in the history of the evils of terrorism. This criminal atrocity was a step towards a new and changing concept of war, or, at least, that is the spirit in which the attacks were committed and all responses are still being made. Commercial aeroplanes were used like giant missiles against financial and political nerve centres in the USA. An event like this puts us on alert and obliges us to study the possibilities of a merchant ship, a petrol tanker, a chemical tanker or a cruise ship, not only being used as a target in a terrorist attack, but actually being used as a weapon in one.

Due to the nature of the surroundings, the hypothetical scenario for such an attack planned and carried out by criminal minds aiming of causing as much damage as possible, would be a marina, a commercial port or a chemical or petrol terminal close to a large city.

Large ports are generally surrounded by densely populated cities and are, in fact, often the very heart of such cities.

In the worst case scenario, a cruise liner carrying several thousand people could be attacked. One lone ship can carry more people than all the victims killed in the attack on the Twin Towers. The enormous, fuel-filled bowels of the ship are a potential hazard and are kindling the unhealthy plotting by leaders of terrorist groups at the beginning of this millennium.

Just the idea of a ship of this type going full steam ahead towards a petrol or chemical terminal is terrifying. This hypothetical situation has been studied by analysts, and even revealed in the media, so it should definitely be taken into account in the study of responses to potential threats.

---

[5] On the 8th October, 1985, during a cruise between Alexandria and Port Said, the Achille Lauro was hijacked by Arab terrorists who made up a Palestinian terrorist cell belonging to Abu Abbas' group. A North American passenger was killed.

As far as possible, the prevention of such acts has to be a constant concern. Security measures have already been taken in airports, some of which could be used to draw up security plans for ships. In the maritime field each and every seafarer and port employee should be involved. Security plans should be designed for every shipping company, for every individual ship and for each port of call. Chemical and petrol terminals located in ports or on the coast should have security plans which reflect these possible threats and plans of action and necessary facilities to be able to try and neutralise them.

A criminal gang planning to carry out an attack of this kind would need to get a considerable number of fanatical terrorists on board. Phase two would be for the terrorists to take control of the ship and its crew and passengers. Due to the complexity of the superstructure of a ship of this kind, and the amount of crew and passengers on board, to carry out such a feat, once on board they would need to formulate a concrete plan regarding the strategies to be used in each of the different phases of the planned and premeditated violent attack. This requires contacts, comings and goings, etc. movement, in other words, suspects. The presence of security personnel inside the ship is fundamental and they should be specially trained and constantly vigilant to be able to detect these indications.

5.8 Counter terrorist measures

A. Against external attacks in ports

It is difficult to define police activity in ports without taking into account the different seafarers and port employees. The port and harbour authorities, sea captains, shipping companies, concessionaires running public areas within the port, etc., must take on the responsibility encompassed in a general concept of security to such an extent that security should now be part of everybody's job. This is especially true in Spain where maritime and port responsibilities are divided in such a way as to make coordination complicated.

The port and harbour authorities must take into account the fact that it is in the port where hypothetically the most dangerous and most likely attack situations will take place.

Using port police, a careful and effective screening of all the persons entering the port should be made. A second control point should be established for access to the area immediately surrounding the ship in question. As this area is not a permanent, established area defined by a fixed structure, on each occasion a temporary barrier should be erected.

Any anomaly or suspicion aroused at one of these control points should be reported to State security forces for evaluation.

The job and responsibilities of the port police should be detailed in the security plan for each port. The part of this plan which refers to the kind of risks analysed here, must be approved by both the Port Manager and the corresponding government official, who will listen to those responsible for both security at sea and public safety.

For vessels at a higher risk of being attacked, the docking areas should always remain the same. They must be fenced off and isolated as well as having access control points. They must be well-illuminated, be directly patrolled by the port police and, on certain occasions, depending on the circumstances surrounding the threat or risk, also be patrolled by officers and patrols belonging to State security forces or bodies.

If the port has a closed-circuit television and a surveillance system for monitoring, then it will be useful if the control room is also fitted with equipment which allows them to watch the perimeter fence with moving cameras and zoom feature. The person in charge of the control room must be able to decide if a patrol should be sent out whenever an anomaly is detected. This person will also be the link to the security forces.

When suspicions have proven to be justified, one or two hours before the expected arrival of the ship in the port a thorough check of the docks should be made. The relevant instructions should be followed and there should be close collaboration with the specialist teams belonging to the security forces, with the bomb-disposal experts and with the police dog handlers, whenever their use is deemed necessary.

During the time the ship remains in the port, it will be kept under surveillance by both ground and sea patrols. This way it will be insured that the ship's surroundings, including the hawsers[6] used for mooring, are secure. This measure may be replaced by, or used in addition to, direct surveillance of the perimeter of the ship itself from its entry in the port right through to its departure.

It is possible that, independently of the naval support from the security forces, the port and harbour authorities (especially those in ports which have a lot of cruise ships stopping over) may create teams of port police to work with general security and to carry out the surveillance needed from the sea within the service area of the port.

The port and harbour authorities will need to coordinate with the security managers on board. This is normally done via the shipping company before the ship reaches the port and then directly if necessary.

The port and harbour authorities will provide security in the dock and in the water:

- Efficient control of entrances to the port and the boarding area.
- Assigning a place for docking. As far as possible this should always be the same place so that all facilities and passive security measures can be fixed permanently to meet needs.
- Enclosure and control of an area measuring 50m from the bow and from the stern with physical, vertical barriers on the side of the ship facing the port.
- Although it poses many difficulties, an attempt should be made, as far as possible, to enclose and control an area identical to the aforementioned one on the sea side with floating barriers.
- Illumination of the outside of the ship and its immediate surroundings.
- A control point for cargo and passengers.
- Security within the confines of the port in collaboration with the security forces.
- Appointing of a security manager who will be in permanent contact with the security forces.

There must be a patrol of port police appointed to the boarding and loading areas within the port and communication must be maintained with the security forces. The port police who are recognised, albeit somewhat reservedly, as authority figures have, in recent times, been kept too much on the periphery of public safety both in real terms and in the eyes of the law. Public safety cannot and must not, however, be considered separate from port security.

---

[6] Rope with several functions which runs from one ship to another at anchor or to any fixed object.

The harbourmasters, under the Dirección General de Marina Mercante[7] (Merchant Navy General Management), in as far as their territory also covers ports of general interest, are required to establish procedures with the ship owners and shipping companies, and are in the privileged position of being able to obtain and provide information and advice to the police when necessary. For this reason they should be involved in all planning procedures regarding security issues, because the organisation and planning of the maritime security which involves them has large areas in common with port security and pubic safety.

Local and area centres of the Sociedad Estatal de Salvamento y Seguridad Marítima (State Society for Maritime Rescue and Safety) can also provide information of interest about ships, courses and ship owning companies.

The shipping company must provide the port police and maritime authorities with a list of passengers and crew members at least 96 hours before arrival so that their identities can be checked against the data base and a risk and threat analysis may be carried out.

The security forces must try to ensure that, where possible and according to the risk or threat implied by its nationality and other factors, the ship is accompanied by a patrol boat[8] from the port entrance to the mooring point. In the worst case scenario where the threats are considered imminent, the possibility of escorting the ships (and in this case potential targets) in territorial waters should be considered as well.

In exceptional cases, the arrival of the ship in the port should lead to a meeting being held between the representative of the security forces[9], the managers responsible for security on board the ship[10], and managers responsible for maritime[11] and port[12] security. An agreement will be sought on the communication channels to be opened, persons in charge, specific preventive measures to be taken in the port and on board ship. The services will also be decided on according to the threats made and level of risk.

In this meeting it should be explained which measures have been taken and which no, so that any security gaps may be covered by port security, ship security or private security if deemed necessary. Whatever the decision, defining which tasks are carried out and who carries them out is very important for the security plans of both the ship and the port. These limits are currently neither well defined nor identified.

The aforementioned will be agreed on for each port within a security protocol which can be designed to have different levels of response depending on the case in point.

Regarding the persons on board ship, their identities and their records should be checked if there any are grounds for suspicion. This goes for both passengers and crew members because certain terrorists, if they feel under pressure in the areas they use for training or their activity, may find themselves forced to use a boat (especially a merchant ship) to avoid border controls and reach other "safe

---

[7] Belonging to the Ministerio de Fomento (Ministry of Public Works)
[8] Surveillance of national waters corresponds to the maritime section of the Guardia Civil (Spanish Civil Guard).
[9] Guardia Civil (Spanish Civil Guard) and the National Police Force.
[10] Normally private security firms. Sometimes ex-military or ex-police.
[11] Personnel from the Harbour Master's office.
[12] Port police in Spain.

havens" where they will be welcomed, hidden and offered further support by other like-minded groups. They may be on board disguised as crew members if they have been given help, or simply as stowaways.

One year after the events of the 11th September, 15 Pakistanis with suspected links to Bin Laden's network were arrested. They were arrested on the 5th August, 2002, of the coast of Sicily in a merchant ship which was travelling from Morocco to Libya.

Nevertheless, the feeling of security and control is always an important card to hold as a preventive measure. Security measures taken to control the traffic of people should be no fewer than those used at border controls on land or in airports. Regarding this point, maritime controls have become too flexible in some cases and restrictions have been relaxed on the control of merchandise, which is actually clearly the main reason for the existence of ports.

The intelligence services belonging to the security forces must create lists of ships which, according to a risk analysis that takes into account nationality, resources, cargo, crew, course, ship owners and main areas of activity, could be used by terrorist groups to achieve their goals or which are really controlled by them via ship owners who act as intermediary companies and are registered in registers created for the purpose or which are substandard. These lists must be kept up-to-date and made available to the sections of customs, financial services and police concerned with security at sea and in ports.

If the ship in question were a cruise liner which represented a significant risk due to the nationality of the passengers or other factors and said passengers were due to disembark and stay in the city for a certain amount of time, then the local council would be involved so that security was stepped up in areas close to the port and in the commercial area of the city as far as possible with the available personnel. Shipping companies are fully aware of the importance of passengers' safety on land at each of the different stopovers.

Inspections of the keel, where necessary, must be carried out by divers from the security forces. They should always be made when there is a serious risk of attack. From a current perspective, and in routine cases only, there is no reason why this preventive measure should not be carried out by a private diving company as a specialised port security service, In any case, any doubts, incidents or suspicious packages will always ensure the security forces are mobilised.

It would be a good idea to provide the security forces with equipment which would allow them to detect traces of radiation during inspections of suspicious vessels. These traces would indicate radioactivity and point to any previous illegal activity.

At least one patrol belonging to the security forces must be on the alert within the service area of the port close to the dock, and should be in communication with the other security services via radio and be ready to act when confronted with any type of incident.

Due to the infrastructure of certain ports and cities, this latter goal can be difficult to achieve. However, it is important we persevere in that direction and take precautions in preparation for extreme situations of threat, as determined by the analyses carried out by the various parties involved in security.

These precautions would be the main lines aimed at public safety. The concept of security covers several areas, so the IMO[13] works with shipping companies and ship owners to ensure they take on the responsibility for establishing countermeasures to efficiently deal with threats.[14]

In recent times competition has taken precedence in the field of security. As a result, state control has been relaxed, boosting the privatisation of management and services which not long ago were considered state controlled. Ports have dived headlong into globalisation and are heading for privatisation, something which is favoured by their international elements: ships, cargo and crew.

This fact (to the extent that some ports are being moved away from the large cities) has forced ports to open themselves up to their surroundings, meaning the old concept of port/customs as a perfectly enclosed and safe place has little to do with today's ports. State control is now scarce and they have been moved (if they exist) from the area of the port to the ship itself, and not always permanently. It is, therefore, necessary and advisable to involve port operators, as well as the ever-increasing number of private security firms to be found in the port, in all aspects of port security.

When it is the shipping companies and private businesses that are the concessionaires of the docks and facilities in public maritime port areas[15] and which, therefore, intensely or exclusively occupy a specific marked area within the port, they must accept responsibility for its security in accordance with the terms described later in this document. This security must be demanded by the police and port authorities, be carried out at the cost of the company and must have some minimum requirements as a necessary part of taking control of:

- The entry of private vehicles to boarding/loading areas.
- The passengers
- The cargo
- The loading services and, especially, who the suppliers are.

The concessionaires should create lists of all the vehicles and individuals who have periodic authorised access to the cargo depot and the port services, and make the lists available to the port, police and customs authorities (Guardia Civil, customs, etc.).

This will allow employee details and information of interest to be checked.

An area of parking must be established at least 50 metres away from the active loading and boarding areas of the ship.

---

[13] International Maritime Organisation.

[14] The IMO has begun to have some affect with its resolutions regarding the security of ports, ships and cargo. By doing so it is surpassing its initial field of responsibility which was limited to the protection of the safety of human lives at sea and the fight against marine contamination. Resolution A. 872 (20) approved on 20/11/97, provides directives for the prevention and supression of the trafficking of drugs, psychotropical substances and precursor chemical products in ships dedicated to international maritime transport which are, definitively, those which enter general ports. In this study some of the directives have been adapted to terrorist threats, as they are considered to be useful.

[15] Although they are not specific to the case, they do follow, to a certain extent, IMO recommendations.

The duties will fall to the private security personnel who, in Spain, are obliged to assist the security forces.[16] These activities are not far from those of defending goods, interests and people which is the fundamental objective of their work.

Considering the relationship to security, the concessionaires and/or shipping companies should notify the police of any suspicious packages or unauthorised cargo discovered on board ship. These loads and packages must be kept under observation whilst the discovery is being reported. An area around the object should be cleared and cordoned off to avoid fatalities or injuries if an unexpected explosion should occur.

The shipping company must provide the police with all the relevant information on the contracted companies of dock workers who work on the ships in the ports, as well as on the companies which provide services.

Regarding personnel, the shipping company must only allow authorised and identified employees to have access to any information related to the boarding or loading of the ship.

Everyone with responsibilities related to ship security, both on board and on land, is essential for a security system to work, whether they are specifically dedicated to it, or not. These personnel will report to a manager who will be the link with the security forces.

The seriousness and the strictness of the measures adopted both on board and at the entrances to the ship, as well as the services which are offered on land, significantly affect security so the personnel must be aware of their function and of the importance of the threats. Preventive surveillance will help obtain information of interest and will make accessing the ship difficult, thus dissuading possible attackers.

Establishing restricted areas on land helps control and channel access to the ship and the cargo, improving security and increasing effectiveness. If access to the hold and cargo handling areas on land are controlled, the ship owner will be able to prevent the ship being used for illegal purposes in general, whilst at the same time avoiding sabotage and terrorism.

The passengers' luggage must be systematically checked, especially on cruise liners. On these pleasure cruises passengers always have all their large amounts of luggage available,[17] something which does not happen on an aeroplane where the luggage is stored in the hold. This fact means extreme precautions must be taken, especially at the port of departure.

Inspections of the perimeter of the ship must also be carried out by the security forces if a threat has been made or they consider it necessary, whenever a they have been informed of a risk or threats and terrorists have been observed, and when there is a suspicion regarding explosives or other devices which could cause damage.

In Spain there are no clear legal requirements, no code of conduct has been drawn up, and no sanctions have been defined, to oblige the captain, the ship owner and other shipping agents to keep

---

[16] Law 23/1992, regarding private security firms, dated 30.7.1992. (BOE 4.8.1992, no. 186.)
[17] These trips are usually two weeks, or even months, long. This means passengers carry luggage in direct proportion to the amount of time they are going to stay on board.

up levels of security in the access areas between the dock and the ship which will prevent merchandise being disembarked or introduced into the ship with a certain impunity.

Whenever possible and depending on the individual case in point, the ports and the concessionaires should erect physical barriers to prevent unauthorised access to the passenger boarding area and the cargo storage and handling areas. This should be a formal legal requirement.

Entrance areas, boarding and loading areas, the full length of the barriers, parking areas and work areas should all be sufficiently lit to prevent interference in the boarding or loading of the ship and to avoid anyone entering it surreptitiously. It is important to note that many of these measures have been adapted from or complemented with several IMO documents noted at the foot of the page.

As regards the Captain, some captains are often heard to say that they are not policemen, that they are there to sail the ship, that they do not carry a gun, etc. With the greatest respect for these professionals, here is an outline of the figure of the captain.

Traditionally, according to documentary evidence of the duties of a captain, there is a general consensus classifying them as public, technical and commercial. Although it was more true in the past, the captain does, to a certain extent, have a degree of legal authority, he controls the sailing of the ship and, although to a lesser extent these days, he represents the ship owner in the business part of the voyage.

Regarding his public duties, the fact that ship represents a part of the sovereignty, sailing on seas and oceans away from the government controls of the country whose flag it flies thereby greatly weakening the control by government authorities, justifies the captain being given the authority to carry out such duties.

A captain's public duties are those that support his competence and legal authority to carry out certain acts which allow discipline to be maintained aboard and to punish, if necessary, any misdemeanours committed by the crew (art. 610.2 and 3[18]) or the passengers (art. 700).

Referring to the passengers, article 700 of the Code of Commerce states that "In all areas related to keeping the peace and the presence of police on board, the passengers will unconditionally comply with the regulations laid down by the captain". We understand that the public duties of a captain more than justify the new security demands that are being imposed; although, it would be a good idea for this ancient law to contain the new requirements as the Code of Commerce dates from 1885. The situation is obviously different today and that the Captain needs to have the help and support of other persons responsible for security.

The measures that a captain should take must be aimed towards preventing the ship being taken over, and its illegal use, as well as avoiding personal risk, and risk to third persons, the cargo, the ship, the crew or the passengers, if need be. What is more, these are obligatory measures.

We are fully aware of the difficulties that these responsibilities imply, but we believe that the figure of the Captain is, and must continue to be, at the very top of the security ladder aboard ship.

---

[18] See Código de Comercio (Code of Commerce)

B. Controlling access to the ship

The ship's hull constitutes a clear and easily defined boundary. The protection of this boundary creates a physical and psychological deterrent for individuals trying to enter without authorisation or cause material damage or personal injury. The measures taken to protect it make intrusion difficult and help the crew and security guards detect and, if necessary, capture the intruders or prevent the attacks.

All the doors, gangplanks and other means of access to the hold or storerooms which are not being used while the ship is in the port should be kept locked and supervised by the shift personnel.

During the night the deck and the full length of the hull should be well illuminated.

The areas of the ship which face out to sea should be equipped with adequate security measures to prevent small boats from pulling alongside or even get within 50 metres of it. It would be useful to install floating barriers on the side of the ship open to the sea.

On the ship itself double armoured doors should be fitted so that there is a sealed space between them both at the entrance to the bridge where the command post is, and at the entrance to the engine room. This way the possibility of keeping the control and operation of the ship safe from terrorist attack would increase. However, this measure, in extreme situations, puts the Captain in a real dilemma, as the people who have taken control of the ship will be controlling the rest of the crew and passengers and will put serious pressure on him to give in to their demands.

The strict measures which affect the immediate security of the ship itself will be the responsibility of its security staff, especially:

- Access control
- Close control of the perimeter of the part of the ship above water[19]
- Passenger control
- Crew control
- Marking sensitive areas and restricting passengers' use of them
- Lighting close to the sides of the ship
- Lighting on deck
- CCTV
- Specific identity cards for crew and passengers. This helps with security on board and, above all, when passengers and crew are checked when they re-enter the ship after one of the various stopovers.[20]
- Reporting security requirements to the port and harbour authorities, to the Dirección General de Marina Mercante (Merchant Navy General Management) and, more specifically, to the security forces.
- Communication links with the people responsible for port and maritime security and public safety.

---

[19] It may be discussed whether the inspection of the submerged part of the ship, as a preventive measure, should be done at the expense of the ship owner who can contract a private company to do it, or if the service should be carried out by members of the security forces. These decisions are to be made by the governing authorities.

[20] These measures are being implemented by the big cruise lines. The card will have many uses on board, including access to their cabins and a debit card for paying for services on board.

The ship can also be accessed from below the water line (the keel). Systematic inspections of the submerged part of the hull should be carried out on certain ships when they arrive at the port to deter potential attackers and check there are no explosives stuck to them. These tasks fall to the underwater activity groups of the Guardía Civil (Spanish Civil Guard), as previously mentioned.

The cost of the security measures, at least on board the ship, which have to be covered by the shipping companies is, obviously, a disadvantage. However, we cannot forget that what would be really worrying would be costs resulting from a lack of security, especially now that threats are becoming a real problem.

5.9 Structural layout of the ship

Due to its design, the layout of the interior and exterior spaces and structures of the ship make the people on board highly vulnerable in terms of security. The crew are less vulnerable because of their knowledge of the construction of their working environment, but the passengers are highly vulnerable as they are in strange surroundings: a ship which makes all kind of movements due to external factors (state of the sea and the strength of the wind).

In normal conditions, in buildings on dry land, the evacuation of a large number of people can be chaotic, unorganised, and subject to psychosocial pressures in an emergency. They are, however, moving on stable surfaces, with gentle slopes leading to a single exit point and familiar surroundings (little difference in the interior layout of buildings). On board it is another matter. The sideways movements and lurches forward throw bodies off balance and cause steps to be taken unevenly on deck. People need to hang on to solid fixtures and the incline of the stairs varies in accordance with the degree to which the ship is listing or moving, making the space available on the steps different at each moment.

Security equipment for the different types of emergency that can occur on a ship are found on levels different to those that passengers are used to in buildings on land. For example, the lifeboats are on the upper decks, not at the flotation line which would be the equivalent of street level in a building.

The behaviour of the passengers at the beginning of an untimely alarm situation will be governed by the typical responses we see in everyday life. This can lead to the possible creation of a crisis situation in crowd control, with loss of efficiency, added risk, increase in time taken to evacuate to other areas or to abandon ship.

In order to establish an environment which aims to avoid unwanted circumstances of shock and panic among passengers, the design of the evacuation passages inside the ship are governed by the classic regulations applicable to any building on land. This, understandably, does not take into account the special conditions to be found on a ship which is moving to a greater or lesser extent out at sea. For this reason they should be considered within a theoretical framework that must later be proved in reality via simulations, and drills carried out to emulate the different situations the ship may find itself in. On the other hand, the passageways designed for evacuation to the boarding decks have specifications established in a maritime regulation[21].

---

[21] Resolution A.757 (18) dated 4th November, 1993. Regualtions for calculating the width of staircases constituting evacuation passageways in passenger ships.

The prevention system has put a lot of emphasis on the subject of evacuation in recent years, and not only with reference to the equipment available, because, even if there is a considerable amount, it is not always used to its full effect if the people do not reach the muster points in the right condition.

There are several procedures in existence to measure the design parameters of access and evacuation passageways, corridors, doors, stairs, etc. which diverse groups of people (who may be neither experts nor mentally stable at the time of the emergency) may pass through on their way to their meeting points or safe areas.

The problems associated with the evacuation passageways should not be treated as a need to create space, but, rather, from the opposite point of view. In other words, consideration should be given to the real use that is conditioned by the needs of the ship, by the number of persons that may be on board and by the special inclusion of the human factor as a final measure which will positively or negatively affect all other aspects.

For transit areas, the surfaces in question need to be considered, for example, whether they are for horizontal or vertical traffic flow. The first of these is more usual, with a fewer number of vertical type being desirable. Ideally, the latter should be replaced by slight slopes, although this is not always possible. When dealing with the idea of traffic flow, the following are important: the size of the doors, doorways, entrances, the way a door opens, the types of lock, lighting, distribution and location of lights as well as of emergency muster points, signage, the nature of the deck and its surface coating, absence of obstructions, available communication point, corridors designed with fewer bends and dead spaces, etc.

When looking at stairways, the following must be considered: their incline, the width and height of the steps, the size of the landings, the way they face, and physical components such as light, how much of a grip there is on the floor, etc., as they will lead to a conclusion regarding the coefficient of crowd build-up and speed of traffic flow. It is accepted that the horizontal speed component on a stairway is equal to the cotangent of its vertical component. The most significant parameters in the case of a stairway will be its length, width and degree of inclination (Fig. 5.1).

FLOW AT THE FOOT OF A STAIRWAY

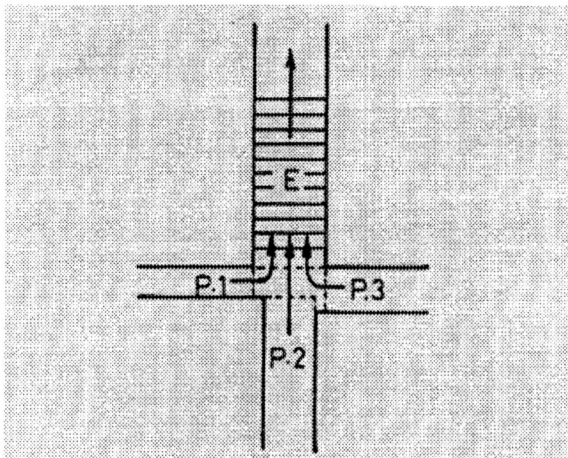

Fig 5.1

The points where more than one flow of traffic meet, or the point where two of them cross over gives rise to new complications in the calculation of the traffic flow. In such cases it is signage and instructions that help improve the situation, as well as the calculation of new width measurements after the point of convergence, which must be designed with the expected flow in mind (Fig. 5.2).

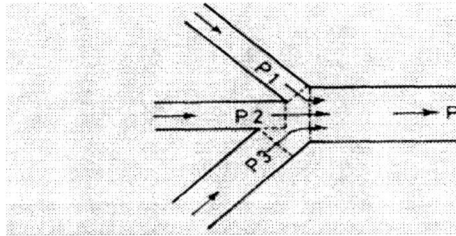

Fig.5.2

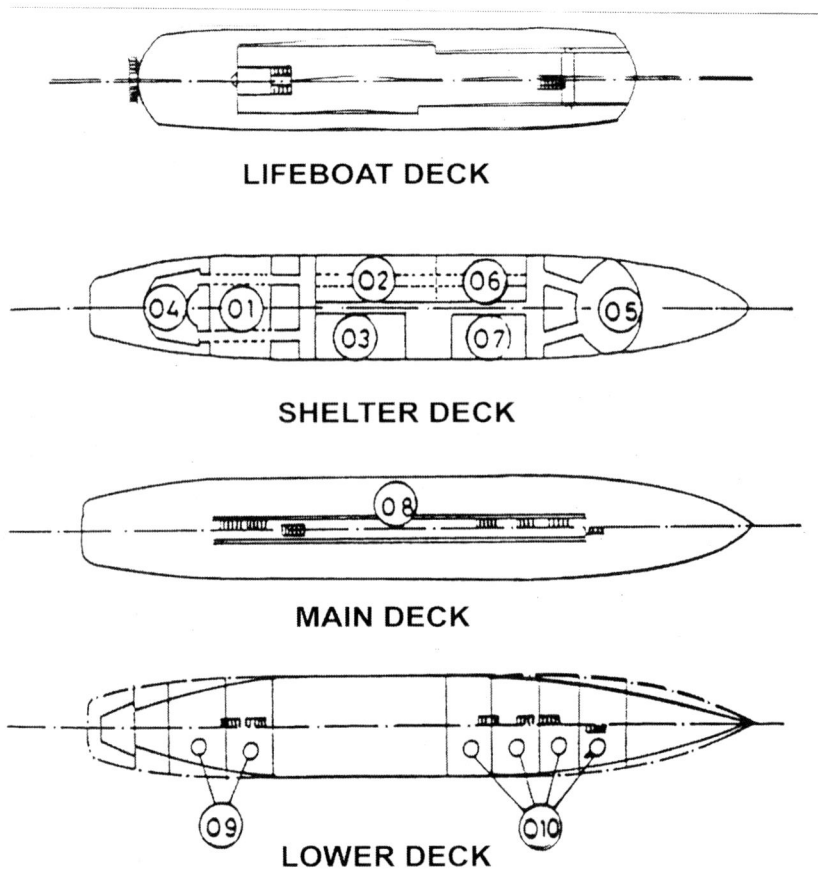

LIFEBOAT DECK

SHELTER DECK

MAIN DECK

LOWER DECK

Fig. 5.3

The density of the flow (i.e. the number of persons per unit of time) will be mainly determined by the number of persons on board (passengers and crew), and the size of the entrances and evacuation passageways leading from the cabins and areas of high concentration (chambers, cafeterias, etc.).

Taking the occupancy per deck as a starting point (Fig. 5.3), and considering three possibilities of distribution according to the time of day or the circumstances in a given moment (Table 4.1), the evacuation time needed for each area of the ship can be determined.

The physical characteristics of the people who will be using the passageways also influence the possibilities greatly, taking into account whether they are only crew, in the case of a ship without passengers, or not. It is important to consider the possible ways of dealing with places used by the public according to their age ranges, whether there are any passengers with physical disabilities or impediments, etc. as when added together these factors can negatively affect the evacuation times, making them longer by causing obstructions in the evacuation passageways. The parameters used are flow density and evacuation speed in metres per second (Fig 5.4).

Characteristics of flow in corridors   Characteristics of flow on stairways

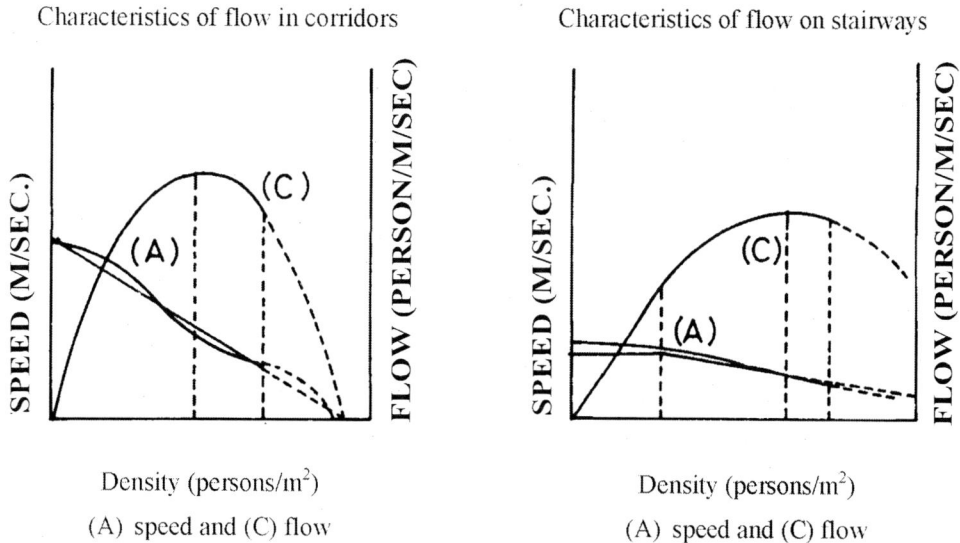

Density (persons/m²)   Density (persons/m²)

(A) speed and (C) flow   (A) speed and (C) flow

Fig. 5.4

Several experimental studies have made it possible to calculate the speed of evacuation and the maximum flow capacity for the following equations:

$$V_e = 1,65 - 0,30\delta, \text{ when } \delta = \text{flow density (p/m)}$$

$$Q_{max} = 2,27V_e . \Delta t, \text{ with } \Delta t \text{ being in seconds.}$$

The final destination of any evacuation should be a large area sufficient to hold or accommodate the number of persons allocated to the life saving equipment, as the following step after meeting at the muster point.

POSSIBLE DISTRIBUTION Nº PASSENGERS			
ORIGIN	Nº 1	Nº 2	Nº 3
0.1	205	165	125
0.2	55	105	75
0.3	105	75	55
0.4	105	75	65
0.5	125	95	65
0.6	105	90	55
0.7	65	60	25
0.8	105	315	505
0.9	55	55	55
0.10	55	45	55

TOTAL 1-800 PEOPLE

Fig. 5.4

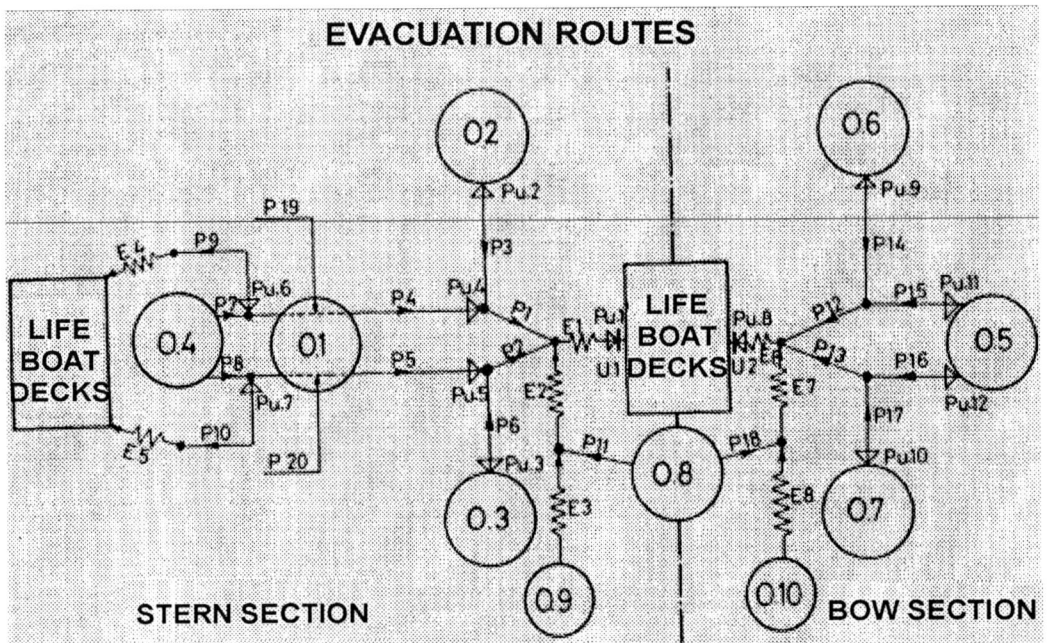

Fig. 5.5

With the dimensional parameters of the passageways and the characteristics of the people who will travel through the evacuation passageways, a plan of the real situation in a given ship can be drawn up (Fig. 5.5).

5.10 Preventive measures on board

The objective is to establish some permanent or routine procedures which will lessen the likelihood of a critical event taking place.

Prevention constitutes the wide base of a pyramid. This is then followed by evacuation, when it is the best solution for saving the lives of the passengers and crew. At the apex, is intervention, which is always a doubtful and predictable final outcome.

The plans of action to be taken will be based on prior knowledge of the ship itself and the sea port environment, as well as on the type of passengers according to transit areas and population. To do this, it is necessary to obtain information by doing the following:

- Creating a map of areas most at risk. Firstly those on the ship itself, and later those in the port, depending on the characteristics which pose the greatest risk.

- Identifying and making a list of the operations on board which are considered routine. With this list it is then very easy to pick out any that are strange, unusual, problematic and which are generally going to require a response from the crew.

- Ensuring every member of crew wears an identity tag stating his/her name, job and place on board the ship. Coupled with the uniform, it creates an image of order, professionalism, leadership (when necessary), and authority bestowed or transferred by the command. However, a photograph is not required as persons cannot then be swapped if need be.

- Ensuring passengers are also identified with their names and surname(s) on their boarding passes. These should coincide with their official identification (ID cards, passport, etc.), the list of which should be provided by the staff on land who have carried out the first requirement of verification.

- Establishing access control screening and ensuring it is always carried out. The suitability of the means of protection in the immediate area and farther away (control room) should be analysed to guarantee total control at all times and in all situations. The entrances and exits should be well signposted as well as displaying clear instructions for their use.

- Checking the efficiency, the message, the placement, the picture, the colour and the suitability of the signage used on the ship. Special attention should be paid to those that indicate direction, bearing in mind that, as they are permanent fixtures, they will always be pointing in the same direction when, in reality and in certain circumstances, it may be necessary to go in the opposite direction to that indicated by the sign.

- Physically marking the boundaries of public, private and restricted areas with the correct procedures. Confusion caused by people in places they are not authorised to enter, or passengers in crew-only areas or control centres (bridge and engine room) without the accompaniment of a member of the crew must not be allowed.

- Using signs at determined points which pose a risk within the facilities if special care is not taken. Such points include inflammable liquids and gases[22], electrical channels[23] and switchboards, etc.

In as far as these courses of action can be seen and evaluated, they will provide a more objective view of the level of vulnerability of the ship, as well as the strong and weak points of the system and, resulting from that, of the areas where supplementary measures need to be taken to reinforce security.

5.11 Conclusions

In terms of vulnerability, a ship is an element which can be considered as an area closed off from its surroundings (independent) and totally isolated during its voyage. Regarding security, this is something which criminals do not like as they do not have total freedom to escape after they have committed their crime. On the one hand, another positive aspect (preventive and dissuasive) is that the ship's human resources are rigidly structured in a hierarchy. The personnel are very professional and specialised, not leaving the criminals many opportunities to act. Plus, the structure and design of the ship can be compartmentalised, a useful tool allowing attacks to be isolated. On the other hand, a negative aspect is the fact that maritime activity can rely on many (land-based) authorities which have a responsibility towards the ship, and this can make it difficult to identify a spokesperson in case of negotiations with the criminals. Finally, there is a particular factor which affects the vulnerability of the ship: the diversity among passengers (origins, customs, beliefs, responses) when it comes to conflicts (crises) on the ship. This increases the variability of situations and possible ways of dealing with them to regain control and get back to normality.

---

[22] UNE regulations 1063 and 48103
[23] UNE regulations 21086 and 21089

6 Protecting the ship

6.1 General

Given the wide variety of types of ship and the characteristics specific to each one (merchant ships, passenger ships, leisure craft, etc.), it is not possible to establish any solid regulations to cover the surveillance and custody in each specific case.

The correct procedure is for each shipping company, via its technical department, to establish these regulations itself (or outsource the work to companies specialising in this field), to carry out an analysis and to determine what measures regarding organisation and procedures will be required to come in line with the comprehensive security plan.

Fundamentally, the analyses and studies considered refer to:

- The vulnerability of the people and the ship, or ships, which are to be protected
- The threats affecting the people and ships being protected
- Risks that can interfere in protection
- Level of security required
- Security measures to be adopted
- Cost to establish and maintain the security measures in the short, medium and long term

The general recommendations for carrying out a security study on a ship are also included and are analysed in the following sections.

6.2 The information plan

This plan should provide information on everything related to the object to be protected, right down to the very last detail, as it is very difficult to protect something you do not know absolutely thoroughly. This means an exhaustive inspection must be carried out to get to know the ship and analyse it perfectly:

- The ship which is to be taken custody of, including everything related to the ship itself and its access areas and location.
- Which are the areas that can be freely accessed, are under surveillance, are controlled, are restricted or are where access is prohibited.
- How many people need protecting, who are they and what level of protection do they need.

The information plan is divided into two parts: the interior and exterior of the ship.

A. The interior of the ship,

The following elements have to be observed, learnt and analysed:

a) *Accesses*
- Inner and outer doors and hatches (number and robustness)
- Doors (number, position and alarm systems for protection already installed)
- Characteristics of corridors and stairways (length, irregularity, steepness)
- Lifts and goods lifts
- Access to areas at risk, such as the engine room, bridge, control rooms and communications rooms
- Trap doors, air ducts, or other holes which, due to their size, could allow a person to enter

b) *Conductor networks*
- Lighting: electrical switchboards, general switches, fuse boxes, emergency equipment, etc.
- Heating and air-conditioning systems, if applicable
- Water: location of the water tanks, stopcocks, auxiliary pumps, etc.
- Fuel and gas circuits: valves, identification (labelling)
- Alarms: system, ways of connecting and disconnecting, reach and efficiency, etc.

c) *Decks outside*
- Layout
- Lighting
- Air vents
- Entrances to the ship

d) *Service levels*
- Layout of interior communications
- Engine room
- CO_2 room
- Room where archives, plans and confidential documents are stored
- Extinguishers
- All crew on board the ship

B. The exterior of the ship

The following elements have to be observed, learnt and analysed:

a) *Accesses to the ship*, all the different kinds of entrances to the ship and accesses from land.

b) *Surroundings*, especially:
- Distance to the nearest ships or dock (normal mooring depending on port)
- Sea traffic in the area (small boats, fishing boats, etc.)
- If nautical events are normally held, such as regattas, etc
- The vulnerability if docked (roads, isolation)
- Buildings, maritime stations and the nature of nearby ships

    c) *Auxiliary surveillance measures*
- Ship's own lighting facilities
- Other facilities (check they are working): port patrols, access controls at the entrances to the terminal or station, closed circuit television in the port

6.3 Protection

Once the information plan has been put together and analysed, the vulnerability can then be seen; in other words, which places are more or less left unprotected, which are the places where a just a general control is needed, and which are those that need special attention.

As a result of the conclusions drawn from this, the action needed to protect the ship will be decided, as well as what personnel and tools will be needed to achieve this objective.

When studying the action to be taken for protection, it is important to take into account tense or serious situations. This means that to guarantee the security and control of the ship in any situation, two protection plans are needed, one for normal circumstances and another to be used in more difficult situations.

Protection will comprise the following two concepts: fixed protection and mobile protection.

a) *Fixed protection*

This presumes the existence of a closed in area equipped with a wide range of mechanisms and devices (optical, acoustic, infrared, photoelectric cells, closed circuit television cameras, etc.).

In an emergency situation, protection will be reinforced with specially trained personnel located at high points around the ship so they can communicate with each other and the person in charge of the surveillance operation either verbally or by radio.

b) *Mobile protection*

Regarding the protection based on surveillance patrols, these should be carried out by one or two security guards who, if possible, ought to be accompanied by dogs specially trained for the purpose.

Rounds will constantly be made throughout the area, although with no regularity in the timing and following different routes. These guards must be equipped with a good communication system which will allow them to communicate with all members of the protection group.

Taking into account the difficulties associated with transmitting and communicating indoors and inside metal structures (Faraday effect), they should carry a map (or have prior knowledge) of the areas where the signal is weak or non-existent, and have alternative technical procedures available to them for solving the problem of a break in communication.

6.4 Exterior protection

This protective circle combines the use of personnel and systems, as this gives the best results when it comes to preventing or controlling access to prohibited areas.

The circle is made up of the following elements:

People:

- Guards posted in areas which allow them to watch the outside of the ship
- Patrols in small boats, or motor vehicles if the layout of the port where the ship is moored allows for it.

Systems:

- Television cameras trained on the side of the ship
- Photoelectric cells

6.4.1 Access control

With people already on board, the basic objective of access control is to identify individuals who want to enter certain areas, preventing, monitoring or allowing entry according to pre-established criteria.

Means of compartmentation

The most usual classification of the physical means for compartmentation is established by taking into account the type of risk "causal agent" which is applied. Depending on the need for the interior of a passenger ship to be divided into sections, there are three main groups using passive methods:

1. Protection against unauthorised access: screens, doors, security chambers, locks and locking mechanisms
2. Protection against coercion and aggression: counters, cabins, reinforced/bullet proof/armour-plated doors/glass…
3. Protection against the handling of property: cupboards, glass cabinets, safes

Passes

To be able to monitor the internal traffic of the ship, one of the most common and easiest systems to use is one of *passes.*

Because there are different internal services operating on board, and because the personnel providing these services may be on a rota, by wearing a pass the following security terms are met with:

1. Physical identification

    In private areas defined just with signs, the pass will be the only means for habitual users to identify those who have authorisation for entry.

2. Prevention

    If confronted with one or more persons who are not carrying the required pass, habitual users of a restricted area are within their right, and in fact are obliged, to take the preventive measures they consider appropriate according to the circumstances.

3. Dissuasion

    The simple presence of a pass creates the image of internal organisation and control, and this may well dissuade a person from entering an area without the appropriate authorisation pass.

Electronic identification

The pass can be used as a basis for electronic identification devices, in accordance with IMO proposals regarding the personal identity card (IC).

To guarantee the correct functioning of the pass, it has to meet certain quality and design requirements. The minimum characteristics considered necessary are the following:

1. Physical characteristics

    - Approximate size of a credit card
    - Secure transparent laminate which does not allow the pass itself to be removed or the details on it to be changed
    - Electronic identity chip

2. Basic information: company logo, background colour indicating level of authorisation.

3. Personal details

    - Name, position, photograph

    Thanks to recent developments in technology and the widespread use of computer systems, the passes needed can quickly and effectively be produced using the following equipment:

    - The physical materials and the basic information needed
    - Computer with digital card
    - *Software* for making passes
    - TV camera
    - Printer

6. 4.2 The structure of a control system

The basic structure of the system is made up of the following elements:

a. *Data collection unit*

This refers to equipment used to take down or read information, the most common of which are:

    - Keyboards.
    - Card readers (these can use any of a number of different technologies: magnetic strips, wiegand, proximity or chip).

b. *Control unit.*

This is the piece of equipment designed to analyse the information received, to compare it with the pre-established data base and to decide on the course of action to be taken in each situation. The basic characteristics of this equipment are:

    - Capacity for information
    - Programming process
    - The length of time it will continue to run if there is a power cut.

c. *Response unit.*

Electro-mechanical devices which physically block entry; these will open automatically when the control unit sends the correct signal. The most commonly used devices are:

    - Electric doors and locks
    - Turnstiles.

The basic set up described here is used to control an entrance, in one or both directions. The programming of the pre-established data is done on site and directly into the control unit. This is called the *autonomous access control system* (Fig. 6. 1).

It is possible to connect several different control units to a "central management" control system, which will programme, update and personalise the data bases for each of the units. Communication is maintained via a data network installed for this purpose. This configuration is known as a *centralised access control system* (Fig. 6.2).

The *centralised access control system* allows for greater flexibility in the process of entering and deleting data, as well as the storing of all action or incident reports in once place. That means that, although it will be more expensive to install a communications network, the operational features gained will be numerous.

AUTONOMOUS DOUBLE DIRECTION SYSTEM

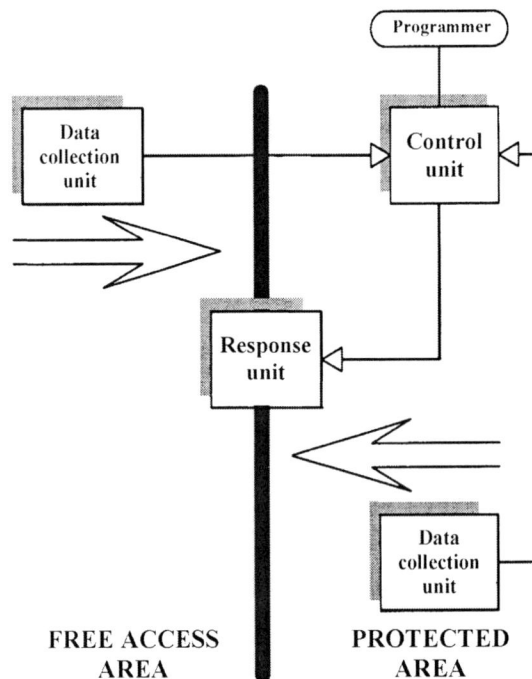

Fig. 6.1

This collection of means used could be physical or passive, technological or active, or specialised security personnel.

Some of the technological means which can be used to check and monitor people, mail and vehicles are the following:

- Metal detectors, archways for persons to pass through
- Manual metal detectors, to check people over
- X-ray machines, to check handbags and parcels
- Metal detectors, to check mail
- Machines to detect explosives by picking up gases

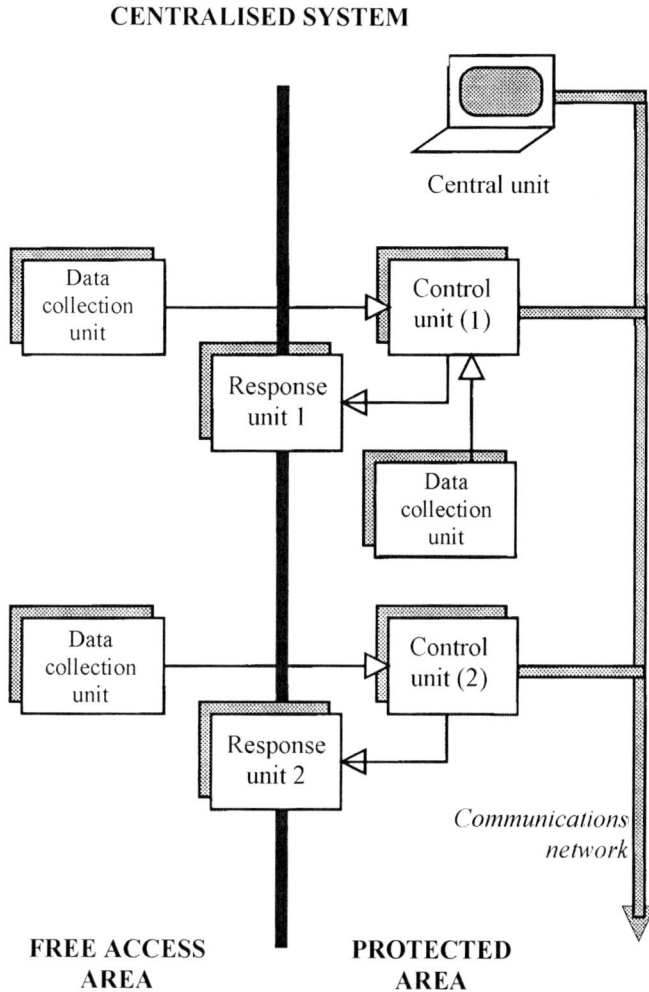

CENTRALISED SYSTEM

Central unit

Data collection unit

Control unit (1)

Response unit 1

Data collection unit

Data collection unit

Control unit (2)

Response unit 2

Communications network

FREE ACCESS AREA

PROTECTED AREA

Fig. 6.2

The security personnel which man these control points will carry out all the operations necessary to verify whether a person has been authorised entry and that they enter in accordance with regulations. They must prevent non-authorised persons from entering the ship, and to be able to do so they will have to identify everyone who wants to do so.

In summary, we can say that access control is carried out in a particular place where an individual or object is identified and authorised to enter the ship which is to be protected. Therefore, the best location for this is on land, before the boarding (waiting) lounges and the immediate entrance to the ship are reached.

6.5 Procedure

It is important to take into account the fact that several types of people have access to a specific target, such as:

- Personnel who live and work permanently on board ship

- Persons or personnel who appear on ship temporarily (visitors, passengers, consignees, pilots, the authorities, etc.)

According to the operating criteria of the ship, depending on the case, the personnel may belong to:

- The staff employed by the company or body which owns the ship

- Another contracted company providing some kind of service (cleaning, maintenance, etc.)

To carry out the control, an individual's identity will be checked with a security authorisation document, or other type of document.

Regarding regular staff, for each crew member the following should be taken into account:

- The level of authorised access (quite easily done on board)

- The time access is authorised for (not so easily done on board)

With these parameters well defined, everyone can be granted access to the area which corresponds to them in accordance with their position and duties.

6.6 Centralisation concept

6.6.1 Definition

Centralisation is defined as the unifying link between the equipment and/or systems that make up the security structure, creating an optimal relationship between themselves, the environment and the system operators or users.

The unifying function of a centralisation system, fundamentally, has the following objectives:

a) To provide accurate information on the security measures available.

b) To immediately provide the maximum information regarding any event which it will be necessary to control.

c) To present the information in an easy and comprehensible way for the user.

d) To be able to activate the prepared action plans.

e) To ensure all routine and planned action does not require the intervention of an operator to activate it.

f) To be able to modify, under full protection, the basic details of the control process.

g) To automatically record all data and events.

6.6.2 Operating criteria

The basic concept of centralisation is to enable the system operator to become more of a supervisor in the processes, rather than the "executor" of all the action taken

The basic hypotheses of automatic action, which are normally considered in the integration of systems, are:

- Authorised opening
- Non-authorised opening
- Alarm warning

INITIATING SIGN	AUTOMATIC ACTION	
Access control	Authorised opening	Blocking of alarm signal in alarm system
	Non-authorised opening	Activation of alarm signal in alarm system and corresponding routines
Alarm system	Alarm warning	Selection on TV monitor of image corresponding to area in question. Recording of selected image. Activation of area warnings. Electrical control of doors and lighting.

6.6.3 Structure

The actual structure recommended for the location of the centralisation equipment is one which allows the different functions to be independent of each other. These are basically the following:

a) *Monitoring area*

A location where the operator has a general vision of the different systems and has all the management tools necessary to allow him/her to check or modify the cover.

b) *Alarm area*

The area which allows an incident to be coordinated, whatever its type. For this it must have the maximum priority communication systems and the specific information from the "place of the incident".

c) *Case study area*

This is where certain situations experienced (both actual incidents and not) are reproduced and analysed, along with the corresponding action taken.

d) *Technical area*

The area which allows technical teams access to carry out preventive or corrective maintenance service, without disturbing operations.

Depending on the type or complexity of the activities to be carried out, the aforementioned areas can be manned by one or more people. What is important is that, depending on the activity to be carried out, the personnel should always have the *task in hand* clearly identified, and there should be no *interference* between the various activities.

7 Means of protection

7.1 Introduction

The objective is to always rapidly detect incidents and help the human team restore the situation to its previous (routine) state.

The security package constitutes three factors which must be combined as integral parts of a whole. These factors are:

- The human factor: Comprising the ship's own security personnel or other contractors (security guards).

The role of the personnel depends on the duties assigned to them as part of the ship's organisation. This is generally specified in the emergency procedure plans or in the responsibilities assigned to certain members of the crew.

- Technical factors: a) Passive: physical and mechanical, b) Active: electronic.

- Organisational factors: Security, emergency and intervention plans reinforced with internal regulations and strategies.

Of all the external agents which can cause damage or loss (natural, nuclear, chemical, antisocial, etc.) the ones that come under the term *security* are those which intentionally target goods and property.

7.2 Criteria for choice

Regarding safety, any expense must be justified according to the probability of the threat being carried out, and of any consequences it may have. The technical department in charge of preventive safety follows a Total Loss Control procedure in which the sum total of all the expenses incurred by the emergency in question is calculated. This includes people as well as equipment and materials, whether they are damaged in the incident or added to prevent it. If the expected loss is only small and the cost of the prevention is high, then the action is not considered beneficial from a financial point of view, although it may be, to a certain extent, on a human level. This safety sector deals with human responses where the personnel are exposed to known risks from the activity or machines. The solutions found can be closely bound to objectivity. The area of security deals with humans confronted with other humans with an extremely high number of different situations, conditions and circumstances. In all cases justification depends on the nature and possible frequency of the type of threat, given that the resources, having been created by a person, will eventually be overcome by another person.

For this reason, when making choices regarding security, certain criteria should be followed. These include:

- The cost/efficiency ratio which will show the possibility of implementing the measures without them being so expensive that they are not viable.

- Special attention should be paid to the quality of the equipment chosen, taking into account recognised standards which have been tried and tested.

- Careful installation carried out by specialised companies to aim, in terms of security, for less vulnerability to sabotage, whether due to the technology or the actual installation and start-up procedures. It is often a good idea not to hide the security equipment from sight as it can act as a deterrent for passengers. In other situations, however, it can train a hidden eye on unwary criminals.

- One of the biggest problems with any security equipment is maintenance. It is best to choose equipment which is low maintenance, but of an equally high standard and with all the same functions.

- The job of almost all security equipment ends with the information it provides human beings with. Sometimes these humans then have to use controls on the equipment to retrieve the information they require. This process can lead to mistakes and be a waste of time. All equipment must be easy to use.

- The best way of personalising the system for the end user should be found. This requires ergonomics be applied to the characteristics of the person in areas of communication, master keys (number, type, technical specifications), location and presentation of specific maps, creation of procedure codes adapted to the security personnel, etc.

7.3 Passive technical measures

The aim of the passive technical measures is to impede or delay the appearance of a risk or threat. Together, these passive measures are known as physical security.

Physical security is made up of:

- Static and permanent elements which can create an enclosure for the facility to be protected, and which make up the first obstacle for intruders, thus forming what we will call *perimeter protection*.

- Other static and permanent elements which prevent access to the main ship itself or to the security nucleus, thus forming what we will call *periphery protection*.

- Means for protecting property, comprising locked areas or rooms (display cases, safes, vaults, etc.).

7.4 Capacity

This is determined by the following parameters and characteristics:

> • Reactive security. On their own, the components in this type of system provide time and space for reaction, especially reactions that mean the shutting down of the perimeter of the facility, as they are located at a distance from it.

> • Percentage of false alarms. The alarms from these elements reach us via active components within the passive elements, but not via the passive elements themselves.

> • Vulnerability to sabotage. This may well be high as this is the protection which is farthest away from the control centre. Sabotage can be reduced by the amount of active elements in place as well as by established guard posts.

7.5 Active technical measures: electronic security

The function of the active measures is to sound the alert locally or farther away when there has been an attempt to damage or sabotage the established physical security measures. Together these active measures make up what is known as electronic security.

Its main functions are:

> - Detecting intruders both inside and out

> - Access control and monitoring human traffic, packages and mail

> - Visual surveillance via photographs or closed circuit television

> - Communication over the public address system

> - Protection of communiqués

The electronic security system comprises the following elements:

> - The system is activated by an electrical current, therefore it must always have a source of electricity available to make it self-sufficient in case of a general power cut or of the power supply being intentionally cut off. This is generally achieved with energy accumulators or batteries.

> - The security equipment constitutes the brains of the whole system. It receives impulses from the detectors and, after analysing them, it converts them into signals which it sends to the local and/or remote warning signs or devices.

Detectors are devices placed inside and outside targets at risk of intrusion. They are used to relay information to the central control room of any atmospheric changes in the area they are protecting and which would indicate, therefore, intruders had entered.

The warning signs or devices form an important part of the system as if the intrusion is successful, information will be needed about what is happening and where, to allow for an efficient response.

7.6 Alarm systems. Security equipment

The basic elements of an alarm system, which a chip may have, are the following:

A.   *Intrusion detectors*

These sensors work by detecting a physical bulk. Any variation in its normal dormant state, trigger the alarm. The basic elements used are:

-   Specific (mechanical or magnetic) detectors to be used to monitor a door or an element of the security system.

-   Lineal detectors using infrared beams to create an imaginary line of protection between a transmitter and a receiver.

B.   *Manual activators*

This refers to an individual reacting to a warning when confronted with a situation of risk. The basic elements used here are:

- An alarm button (a mechanical element that is adequately identified).

- An alarm code (an access keypad can activate the alarm when a predetermined number is entered rather than the access code).

- Alarm by omission (a mechanical element that sounds the alarm when it is not attended to in a routine operation).

An alarm system may be *autonomous*, which means it only sounds in the immediate area, or *centralised*, which means it sounds in the immediate area and/or discretely in the control room.

As previously mentioned, the security system is the brains behind the supervision, monitoring and indicating all the signals produced within the security facility.

Although there is a wide range of security systems available on the market, all of them basically consist of:

Power supply modules. These transform the 220 V alternating current of the industrial power network into the 12 volts of continuous current needed for the electronic circuits of the security system to work.

In addition to this it keeps a battery charged to ensure the security system keeps working if there is a power cut.

The time the system can run only off the battery depends on the charge capacity of the battery and how much electricity the equipment consumes.

Loop supervision module. This element continually checks the detectors are in a dormant state. When the state of any of these detectors is altered, it passes the information to the control module.

Control module. This module processes the signals it receives, activating the corresponding output according to the type of alarm.

Signalling module. This module signals the alarms received either in the immediate area (sirens, lights) or elsewhere (telephone keypads). This element is normally started up with either a keypad or a key.

C. Detectors

These are the basic components of an electronic security system. They are alarm indicators and are used to keep a watch on a specific area to then send a signal to the security equipment when an alarm situation is detected.

The choice of the type of detector to be used depends on the characteristics of the area to be monitored and the possible causal agents of intrusion. The detector needs to be chosen in line with these parameters.

The possible causes for the triggering of an intrusion detector are: movement of intruders, moving the detector itself, pressure on the detector and breakage of the object under protection.

Generically, detectors are divided according to their use: for indoor or outdoor use.

1.   Detectors for indoor use

As the name implies, these detectors are located on the inside of the ship, cabin or other place to be protected.

Depending on their location and the cause which will trigger the alarm, they can be subdivided into groups of *penetration* and *volumetric* detectors.

Penetration detectors note any intruders entering via existing openings for access into the area being monitored.

'Openings' can refer to gaps for doors or windows, etc. as well as surface areas that are slightly less resistant than those normally used in construction.

They will, therefore, detect the opening of devices designed to be used in that way as well as the breaking of any elements of construction which are normally joined to the structure, before any intruder actually enters.

The volumetric detectors are designed to capture the movement of an intruder by the atmospheric disturbance caused by the movement in the protected area. In other words, the intruder is detected once inside.

The most common indoor detectors are:

Penetration detectors: glass breakage detectors, piezoelectric detectors, vibration sensors, inertial sensors, foil tape and magnetic contacts.

Volumetric detectors: sonic, ultrasonic, microwave and passive infrared.

Proximity detectors: capacitance or precision sensors.

2. Outdoor or perimeter detectors

Outside the ship, the function of electronic security is to detect risk as it approaches and at the moment of first contact.

The farther away the perimeter from the nucleus of the target, the more time available to make decisions aimed at neutralising the risk and to help external auxiliary services find a definitive solution.

Some of the most commonly used external detectors are the following:

*   Fixed to the hull: electric cable sensors, inertial sensors, woven wire sensors, electrical fields.
*   At intervals around the perimeter: laser barriers, active infrared detectors, microwave detectors, electrical fields.

- Differential pressure detectors: seismic detectors, magnetic detectors, seismic-magnetic detectors, precision detectors, electromagnetic detectors.

All these systems can be used on their own or by combining any two of them to achieve a double line of electronic perimeter defence. This provides a better level of security and allows for a second element of detection which can confirm the activation of the perimeter and thereby eliminate false alarms.

3. The basics of detectors

Detectors can be classified according to the following functional systems:

- *Vibration*

  - Microphone. Device made up of a microphone and an evaluation circuit which is activated when an acoustic vibration of a certain level is detected.
  - Microphone cable. Comprising a coaxial cable, it is able to capture low-frequency vibrations in the surface onto which it is attached. It is activated when the vibrations have certain characteristics.
  - Geophone. A device made up of a microphone transducer able to capture vibrations produced in the area around where it has been placed. It is activated when the vibrations have certain characteristics.
  - Inertial detector. Comprises a balancing inert mass. It is activated when the vibrations in the surface it is attached to (and is monitoring) throw it off balance.

- *Displacement*

  - Magnetic. A device comprising an electrical connection and a permanent magnet. The movement of the magnet in relation to the connection will cause the device to be activated.
  - Mechanical (taut wires). A device comprising a collection of cables subject to a certain degree of traction. It is activated when the tension varies as they are moved.
  - Electro-mechanical. A device comprising an electrical connection and a moveable part attached to the connection. The device is activated when this part moves.

- *Pressure*

  - Electromagnetic. A long or flat device comprising an electrical connection which is activated when it receives the pressure of a certain weight.
  - Capacitive (differential). A device sensitive to the differences in pressure on its capacitive elements. It is activated when it receives the pressure of a certain force.
  - Hydraulic. The same as the previous device, but with a hydraulic circuit.
  - Pneumatic. The same as the previous device, but with a pneumatic circuit.

- *Movement*

  - Microwave barriers. Device comprising transmitter-receiver equipment placed in opposition, at a distance of up to 200 or 300 metres depending on the model.
  As it totally or partially passes through a body, the stream of microwaves generated by the transmitter produces a fade in the signal which is captured by the receptor and conveniently evaluated by the system, thus triggering the alarm.
  - Infrared barriers. A device similar to that of a microwave barrier, only that the waves generated are infrared. They have a range of between 80 and 100 m. The stream of waves transmitted is much less than that of a microwave barrier.

- Laser barrier. A device which produces the transmission and reception of a coherent beam of light. It is activated when the beam is sufficiently interrupted by the movement of an intruder as s/he passes through it.
- Passive infrareds. A device which picks up the infrared radiation generated by the elements in place in the area being monitored. It is activated when it has assessed the difference between the atmospheric radiation and that generated by the movement of the intruder.
- Ultrasonic. A device comprising an ultrasonic sound wave transmitter. These sound waves reflect off the different objects in the room and are picked up by a receiver. Any movement by an intruder changes the characteristics of the reflected signal and activates the alarm.
- Doppler radar. A device comprising a microwave transmitter-receptor which is activated when certain variations in frequency as the signal is reflected off a moving body (Doppler effect).
- Coupling of conductors. A device comprising one conductor that transmits electromagnetic signals, and one or more other receiving conductors placed in parallel with the transmitter and which they are coupled with via air or earth. It is activated when it detects a variation in the coupling field caused by the movement of a body within the monitored area.
- Electrical field (capacitive). A device consisting of the installation of conductor wires around the perimeter of the target which generate an electrostatic field. The cable is used as a sensor and the intruder need only approach it for the alarm to be activated.

- *Breakage*

  - Electric. A device made up of a band of conductive material (foil tape) or of an electrical conductor (conductor network) stuck to the surface to be monitored. They are activated when broken.
  - Alarm glass. These are sheets of tempered glass which have an electrical circuit incorporated into them during fabrication. When the glass is broken it causes an interruption in the continuity of the electrical circuit and the alarm is activated.

4. Signals and warnings

Depending on their location and the way they work, these can be classified in the following way:

a) *Local:* acoustic, electronic sirens, mechanical sirens, optical, sudden light, flashing lights, bash.

b) *Distance:* telephone calls and telecommunications by wire or radio.

c) *Special:* photographic machines, closed circuit television, film cameras and others.

It is advisable to install two or more warning devices to increase the level of security and share the work between them.

The requirements for an acoustic warning system should be that: it is impossible to tamper with the connection cables, it has its own power supply (battery), it has a low energy consumption, that the power is correct in accordance with the current regulations, and that it is guaranteed to work in adverse weather conditions.

Reliability

The reliability of a protection system is defined by the following parameters:

- response guarantee
- percentage of false alarms
- vulnerability to sabotage

The response guarantee is related to the correct functioning of the elements comprising the system.

The areas boasting a high level of guaranteed response are those with constantly monitored special circuits, with lines established to warn of sabotage that monitor all elements in the area 24 hours a day, especially the local alarms.

Any attempt to put any of these elements out of order will cause an alarm to sound either in the control room or outside the ship, even if equipment is not in use at that moment.

Given the high number of components in an electronic security system, a high percentage of false alarms may be given.

7.7 Closed circuit television

As a measure to complement the physical and electronic systems, the idea of installing closed circuit television (CCTV) should be considered.

Closed circuit television has the following functions:

- monitoring the whole area and the exterior points of access
- checking the alarms which are produced by the perimeter systems installed
- recording the images corresponding to an incident.
- possibility of linking the closed circuit to specific risk detection systems.

Essentially, closed circuit television comprises:

- television cameras which can be either fixed or equipped with a positioning system, and can film continually or for a specific amount of time, as considered necessary.
- monitors located in the console of the alarm control centre which will show what the cameras are filming.

When installing CCTV, it should be planned in such a way that all areas to be monitored are covered and that each of the different areas is associated with a specific camera so that the correct camera can be quickly activated if an alarm sounds.

When drawing up this plan, it is important to consider whether fixed cameras or cameras with a positioner will be the best choice for combining the necessary views and for the correct amount of attention being paid to the screens.

Usually referred to as *closed circuit television*, this system is a tool designed to provide security staff with information. It captures images of an occupied or empty area to help in the evaluation of the resources needed for any preventive or emergency action needed.

The basic elements of a television surveillance system on board ship are normally:

Camera

This is the component which captures the image. The basic characteristics to be considered when choosing a camera are:

- the technology. Currently the most recommended system is a CCD sensor
- the kind of image. Black and white or colour

- the optical features: focus distance, iris diaphragm mechanisms
- sensitivity or minimum amount of light needed to make out the picture
- resolution or number of vertical lines

Additional elements needed for the installation of the camera are the casing, the bracket and the positioner.

Monitor

This is the where the image is actually seen. The basic characteristics to be considered when choosing

a monitor are:

- the type of image: black and white or colour
- the resolution or number of vertical lines
- the size

The basic uses are:

- to provide information to the control centre
- to be dissuasive in access areas

Recording systems

This is a regular feature in consumer electronics which security professionals have benefitted from:

- magnetic tape recorders
- magnetic storage media for computers
- video recorders

Management systems

These are the different types of equipment which work with or analyse the images:

- Sequencers, which allow different images to be seen or recorded in sequence.

- Multi-flexors, which allow different images to be seen or recorded simultaneously.

- Video matrices, which allow images to be sent out to different places in a fixed, sequential or programmable form.

7.8 Communication systems

These systems are used to transmit the information from the monitor or the security control system for processing so the necessary measures can be taken.

The main forms of communication are: the human voice, the telephone, telegraph, radio, bells, lights, sirens, computer network.

The information transmitted by these communication systems generally refer to: the condition and working order of the security system, the condition and working order of the sensors, normal situations, and situations or incidents which require a response or reaction to an alarm.

7.9 Alarm centre. Control and alarm centre

As previously mentioned in section 5.5, when discussing the general aspects of the system, this is the nerve centre controlling all the alarms produced by the variety security equipment connected to it.

This centre receives the signals, processes them and acts according to the operation required for each alarm. It must have the components, equipment and systems needed to receive and check the alarm signals and to transmit them to the control posts.

To be able to connect apparatus, devices or security systems to alarm centres, it is important that the equipment has been installed by an approved security company.

Before creating the connection, the alarm centre operating companies are required to instruct the user on how the service works. They should explain the technical and functional characteristics of the system and the responsibilities that the come with the installation of the system.

To function correctly, the alarm centres rely on all their integral parts. Each one of these parts has a certain degree of importance, and they can be grouped in the following way: human resources, technical means and organisational means.

Human resources

The role of humans can be considered essential for the development of the correct running of the centre, although the technical and IT support is, of course, also needed for it to work.

These personnel must make the right decision at the right time whether under normal working circumstances or in real emergency situations. No margin for error can be allowed as the safety and security of people and belongings will often be in their hands. For this reason, it is essential that they are chosen and trained well.

The alarm centre must be attended at all times by the operators needed to provide the services required. There must never be fewer than two people manning the post who will be in charge of making sure the receivers work and transmitting the alarms received.

The alarm centres may use security guards as an alarm response service. Keys should be coded using a code which is not known by the security guard carrying them and which is changed periodically, in accordance with the ship's general security plan.

7.10 Other control systems

As well as the main security service systems, there are many other systems which provide a wide range of additional services, such as: controlling the connection and disconnection of the security systems, opening and closing of vaults and rental safes, controlling technical parameters, interrupting power and water supplies, etc., looking after keys, monitoring the traffic of personnel in restricted areas, coordinating with the technical services if urgent intervention is required, monitoring entry times and monitoring the rounds.

7.11 Alarm reaction procedure

The first step which should be taken in the control centre when an alarm sounds should be to check it.

The alarm received will, therefore, be checked using the means available in the control centre. Any false alarms will be filtered out once they have been proven to be so and the due course of action will be taken when any real alarms have been verified.

If an alarm is verified, the action taken if the ship is at sea will be to report the alarm to the officials as expressed in the ship's comprehensive security plan. If the alarm sounds whilst in port, the following will apply:

- The same as at sea, but it will also be reported to the harbour master or the permanent control centres in the port, as long as this is detailed in the ship's comprehensive security plan.

- The alarm should be reported to the security forces when necessary due to the possible implications on a grand scale.

- The response service should be mobilised. This includes the following of the ship's comprehensive security plan, both from the control centre itself and from the mobile service created for such circumstances, depending on how the service is organised.

The reporting of alarms which have not been thoroughly checked out should be avoided to ensure the security forces are not deployed in vain.

8 Security Management

Security management requires a general and complete overview so that prevention, protection and reaction policies can be established. As will be shown at the end of the chapter, certain synergies exist. The prevention plan is constantly kept up-to-date by risk evaluation and, as a result, by the emergency plan.

From an operational perspective, for the development of prevention and surveillance procedures, and to be able to structure and plan a response for a crisis situation, it is first essential to establish, define or classify situations that are linked and then establish the possible chain of events.

8.1 Definitions

> ➢ Event: Anything new or unexpected which arises during work and is given consideration by the security service.
> ➢ Incident: Materialisation of a risk during an event causing little or no personal injury or damage to property which could, in turn, lead to an accident.
> ➢ Critical incident: An incident which affects a critical element of organisation, or an incident which has surpassed boundaries and become a serious incident, whether intentionally or not, and which requires crisis management.
> ➢ Emergency: A situation occurring during an accident.
> ➢ Crisis. In the official dictionary of Spanish language there are three definitions for this concept: a) a turning point for better or for worse, b) a situation where its continuity is in doubt, c) an extremely difficult or complicated situation.

8.2 The general process

Any situation, anywhere, can lead to an incident (whether intentionally provoked or occurring by chance) which can quickly turn into an accident. In some technological systems this is known as a contingency.

An accident can be of any type. It can cause casualties or not, involve a specific technological system or cause related systems to fail in succession, create situations of panic or go either fully or partially undetected by the passengers (and even the crew).

There are currently three basic courses of action which are fundamental for the outcome of events and can determine the success or failure of any intervention:

• Detecting the incident (technology - IT - human), thereby ensuring it is quickly reported to the body responsible for decision making (whatever their position within the organisational structure), and the response is activated.

• Being able to analyse the severity of the accident or passing it urgently on to whoever can do so.

• Activating the reaction procedure.

Depending on the reaction, the accident can be controlled (though not necessarily totally resolved) or stay uncontrolled and worsen.

The response procedure should be included in the emergency plan. It should, therefore, be the result of a technical or technological reaction using the available resources, and dealt with in a certain way, normally according to specific guidelines.

A ship has many emergency plans and procedures in place, and the people responsible for acting on them and those in charge of them are only too familiar with them. Such procedures include: fire, man overboard, abandon ship, collision, leakage, etc. An emergency plan, then, is a technical tool used by well-informed and trained personnel to guide their actions. This will ensure a response designed to minimise, stop or at least prevent an unfavourable development of the risk that has materialised.

However, if it is not possible to control the situation once the risk has materialised, and it develops unfavourably, escalating in terms of severity, then the situation becomes a critical incident.

Apart from a technical response, the situation then requires a response from top management, because the incident has stopped being simply technical and has entered the social and political field. In this case the concept of the 'political' field does not only refer to the possibility of it interfering in government politics, but it is also applicable to company policies. A situation like this could affect a company's strategy, and even cause concern regarding its place in the market or its continuation.

In this situation the *direction of the crisis* is determined. Chronologically it consists of a beginning with an incident, an aggravation as an accident, a response within an emergency plan and a final exceeding of the limits resulting in a crisis situation.

The crisis requires the participation of the person with the most authority within the company. It is dealt with in a generic fashion and there are few guidelines to follow. The process must go through all the intermediate stages, except the different situations can cut down on the amount of time spent at each stage. The times can vary greatly and can almost produce a situation where there is no loss of continuity between the incident and the crisis.

All incidents and accidents should be considered possible causes of the crisis. The correct response to the process consists of a series of organised and complementary general activities which deal with the problem as a whole. These include "preventive activity" (covering action taken as a precaution, preventive action and action taken to establish the emergency plan), "emergency intervention" (carrying out the emergency plan as intervention), and "crisis action" (covering the intervention and also the later rehabilitation).

8.3 The comprehensive security system

Once the risk and vulnerability analyses have been done, the level of security required is determined and the security system can be decided upon. This will be a response to the level of security needed in each case, according to the risks and vulnerabilities that exist.

In other words, the security of the object under protection generally depends on three types of resources:

- Human resources (technicians and security and surveillance specialists)
- Technical resources (the necessary material elements)
- Organisational resources (plans, regulations, strategies)

These resources are interrelated and interdependent in such a way that a security system does not depend on the quality of each of its components (resources), but rather on the coordination and adjusting of them via operational procedures and orders received. In other words, it comes down to the preparation and training given to security personnel.

An efficient security system should be both defensive and offensive at the same time.

The defensive aim of the system is:

- To detect any attempt at attack, intrusion or any real danger.
- To stop or impede damage being inflicted by the source of the danger.
- To identify and localise the danger to be able to act on it.

The offensive aim of the system is:
- To provide a guarantee and a reaction time when faced with danger.
- To provide immediate investigation.
- To quickly neutralise any attempt at attack, intrusion or any real danger.

8.3.1 Components of a security system

A security system is made up of two kinds of elements:

- Physical or tangible elements
- Non-physical or intangible elements

8.3.1.1 Physical or tangible elements

These are the elements which help provide physical protection for the system and which have a tangible physical presence. These elements are:

- Barriers. These are used to channel access to protected areas and can be either natural or artificial.
- Doors. These are barriers which are used to channel and control access to protected areas.
- Monitors or control resources. These are the control resources designed to maintain surveillance on doors and other areas under protection. They may also be: human (security guards, patrols, etc.), animals (dogs, etc.) or electronic (closed circuit television, radio, etc.)

- Communications. These are the channels through which information provided by the monitors (or information from any other source) is relayed.

This information will lead to the corresponding security measures being taken.

Communicated reports, which can take various forms (human voice, telephone, telegraph, radio frequency, etc.) normally refer to the state and working order of the security system.

- Response force. In the case of an emergency situation, the system tackles it with a response force. This will be discussed in the section on human resources.

- Visibility. This is the system's capacity to see, via the monitors and the response force, the security conditions in protected areas and perimeters and their surroundings. Visibility is achieved with the use of lighting, night vision equipment, radar and different types of sensors, etc.

- Distance, space and time. Distance and space are both elements which, along with other passive protection measures, serve to channel and delay access to protected areas, creating time to initiate a correct response from the security system.

8.3.1.2 Non-physical or intangible elements

These elements are essential for the smooth-running of the security system although their physical presence is not as evident or noticeable as elements in a physical system. These intangible elements are:

- Information. This is everything communicated to the security system, either internally via the system itself (sensors, etc.), or externally or not within the system itself (knowledge of attack rates in the area, activity or type of ship, etc.). This information is used to add to, modify or change the system.

- Security policies. These are the main, general courses of action taken by the security system, as well as the procedures used to achieve them.

- Security plan. This is the detailed planning of an action programme to respond to specific security needs and with the aim of being able to implement a security policy.

- Security programme. This is the set of courses of action designed to reach an object within a specific time. The programme is based on a policy and is created in accordance with the plans.

- Security procedures. These are a specific set of courses of action to be taken to reach a specific goal. They are the means used to carry out part of a plan, of a programme or of a policy.

- Position orders. These are written documents which tell the specialist personnel what to do, who should do it, when and how to do it, what resources should be used to do it and in which situations it should be done.

- Security organisation. This is a group of people forming a functional unit which has been trained to meet specific security objectives.

8.4 Security theory

Perfect security should cover all the space in a sphere around the object to be protected (person, sector, or object); in other words, if we take this object to be the central point, then the secure area should be all the space above, below and to the side of it, at such a depth as to cover all the required security needs in each case.

Security cannot only be considered on one level, it must aim to cover three dimensions against possible attacks (vertical and horizontal sectors), while recognising the importance of the horizontal plane as it is the most accessible.

8.4.1 Comprehensive security

It is generally understood that comprehensive security refers to security measures as a whole and which become more restrictive the nearer to the object under protection they are. It is as if, around the person, object, materials or processes within a facility, we were to draw a series of concentric circles and we were to reinforce each of them with these security measures.

These circles are known as *security areas* and can include the following:

A) Area of influence: a concentric space outside the exclusion area. It is quite possible for attacks to be carried out on the protected area from here. It is not normally property of the operator (port facilities, other ships, etc.).

B) Exclusion area: a concentric space outside the protected area which, being clearly indicated, is for restricted use and access is limited. It has to be property of the operator (sectors, decks, etc.).

C) Protected area: a space enclosed with physical barriers and with access control points. There is also a certain control of movement within the area and of the length of time spent there.

D) Critical or vital area: this is the space enclosed by barriers within the protected area. Access and length of stay in the area are closely controlled. Movement within the area is also strictly controlled (officials on the bridge and in the engine room).

E) Controlled area. This can be considered the space covered by both the protected and critical or vital areas together.

F) Restricted area. This is generally considered to be any space with specific restricted access or which is monitored for security reasons or to ensure the safety of persons and/or property.

8.4.2 Security plan or scheme

All security plans should fulfil four basic functions:

1. *Deterrence.* This function uses defence tactics in the form of physical security measures (enclosures, obstacles, etc.) to:

   - Stop any attack or intrusion
   - Delay the attack or intrusion thereby allowing for intervention
   - Restricting or controlling the intrusion to the degree or level permitted by its own security
   - Channel or direct the intrusion as desired

The simple presence of any security measure, human resources included, will help deter attack or intrusion.

2. *Detection*. This second function is a necessary complement to the physical or containment measures used and involves the organisation of technical and human resources to:

- Maintain surveillance of the specific or general area to be monitored.
- Raise the alarm by sending out a signal.
- Recognise the alarm by studying, comparing or interpreting the signal received.
- Send out the agreed signal once it has been confirmed.

3. *Reaction*. This completes the defence cycle (containment-detection-reaction) and it includes the following stages:

- Alarm. This means the arrival of the agreed signal, mentioned in the previous stage
- Checking of the signal received
- Evaluation of the level of risk
- Decision. To be made regarding the level of security risk and whether intervention is required or not

4. *Intervention*. This final function is a matter for human resources. A course of action will be taken or a response made depending on the threat they are faced with.

8.4.3 Efficiency of the system

A system's efficiency depends on the concepts related to efficiency itself. These are:

- Delay time: This is the time between an alarm being given and an intruder reaching their objective within the controlled area.

- Response time: This is the space of time it takes for the security forces to act. It is counted from the moment the sensors are activated by an intruder to the moment they are caught.

8.4.4 Styles of systems

A security system can generally be any of the following styles:

a) Disguised

It is important here that many of the security measures are kept hidden, either to guarantee impenetrableness, to avoid portraying the wrong kind of image, or to simply avoid giving an idea of the value of the property being protected.

This style is only dissuasive to professionals because they know measures for protection will be in place, but as they cannot gain enough information on these security measures, they will choose to abort their mission or look for more reliable information.

b) Open or visible

This style of system is designed, above all, as a deterrent. It is based on the fact that the value of the property being protected is not known. Not only does it not project a worse image, but it actually enhances the image portrayed.

Uniformed security personnel with communications equipment not only provides real efficiency, but also ensure quick coordination in the reaction to a situation.

However, one of the characteristics which makes this style more vulnerable is the fact it is easier to get information on the extent of the deployment and also the possible and inevitable security routines.

A "mixed" style is generally favoured, as it brings together elements of both styles, ensuring all the security measures are not discovered whilst keeping up an acceptable level of deterrence.

The choice of one style or another does not just depend on one, single factor, but on several. These include the location of the object under protection, its physical characteristics, the possibilities for using the available resources and the quantity, quality and characteristics of these resources.

8.4.5 Criteria for coverage

Basic procedure

Any study made with the aim of controlling or reducing a risk should be carried out realistically and following a systematic process which, taking the existing general or total risk as a starting point, takes into account all the different situations that can arise as well as the possible criteria and resources needed to cover it.

The process involves the following:

a)   The methods of protection to be adopted must always be individually tailored for the case in point; using general security measures normally causes problems in the carrying out of basic activities; in this case, in receiving, accommodating and transporting passengers.

b)   For a passenger ship to be run correctly, in both terms of general organisation and security, it is very important to adequately divide up areas and keep the different activities been carried out in each one separate.

c)   To achieve a good division of areas and activities, one of the basic objectives of the security plan is to control access to the different areas of the passenger ship by providing users with the corresponding authorisation.

d)   Access control involves identifying users prior to their entering and checking their corresponding authorisation.

Subdivision

Depending on the severity of the risk evaluated in each of the areas, or corresponding to each of the activities, they will be subdivided and the corresponding controls considered necessary for each case will be applied.

The possible options are:

-   Open. When there is a free circulation of traffic through all areas.

-   Signposted. There is no particular risk, but access is restricted for organisational reasons. This means elements for enclosing spaces, normally doors, are not blocked and signs considered necessary are on display.

- Blocked. Access to areas at risk is blocked. As there is a low level of circulation of internal traffic, we can choose to block the way. This means using the corresponding elements for enclosing and locking spaces; normally doors and locks.

- Controlled. Access to areas at risk is controlled. As the level of circulation of internal services is high, it is not possible to block the way. This means using security personnel or elements for enclosing spaces with electronic control systems on them.

Identification

Except in the case of free access, all cases require users to be identified prior to entry if they are to be correctly implemented.

By the term 'identification' we mean a decision being made as to whether a person belongs to a pre-established group and is, therefore, authorised access.

Possible means of identification are: something that is known: access codes, something that is owned: keys, radio transmitter, infrared transmitters, identity card, card with a magnetic strip, wiegand card, proximity card, intelligent card (chip); something that is: the retina of the eye, the shape of the hand, fingerprints, the voice.

8.5 Guide to creating a security plan

a) A staff motivation and awareness policy. Regulations for the restriction of internal movement. Personnel to control reaction areas. Subdivision of areas with different levels of risk and different activities.

b) Provide physical measures of resistance that can make it more difficult to enter the critical areas.

c) Provide means of observation in areas that need to be kept under surveillance.

d) Install alarm systems which complement or substitute surveillance.

e) Train enough security personnel to be able to deter or limit the actions of individuals.

f) Create a security presence which leads others to presume the existence of further security measures apart from those that are visible.

9 Public safety

In articles 104 and 149, the Spanish Constitution grants the State exclusive authority over public safety, indicating that the state security forces and bodies, under Government authority, are assigned the duty to protect citizens' rights, liberties and to guarantee public safety.

This objective led to the establishing of Organic Law 1/92 regarding public safety. Said law is designed to ensure the keeping of the peace, the eradication of violence and the correct use of rights of way and public spaces, as well as the prevention of crimes and misdemeanours.

Public safety is the responsibility of the security forces under different government authorities. These consist of:

> - The state security forces and bodies under the state government: The National Police Force and the Civil Guard. Organic Law 2/86, of the 13th March, regarding security forces and bodies puts the Civil Guard in charge of the protection of the coast, ports and airports.
>
> - The police forces under regional government: regional police.
>
> - The police forces under local council authority: local police.

All of these should act in accordance with the principle of mutual cooperation which is coordinated by the Security Policy Board and the Local Security Boards.

The following persons and bodies are also especially obliged to collaborate in ensuring public safety: Those persons or bodies whose duties imply the surveillance, security or custody of people or property or provide services of public or private ownership, helping the security forces when needed.

Public safety will be upheld by the State security forces and bodies assigned the following functions:

> - To ensure laws and legal resolutions are complied with by carrying out the orders received from the authorities within their field of expertise.
>
> - To help and protect the general public and ensure the safety of any property in danger for any reason.
>
> - To watch over and protect the ships and public facilities as required.
>
> - To provide protection and security for VIPs.
>
> - To maintain and re-establish, if necessary, public order and safety.

- To prevent crimes being committed.

- To investigate crimes in order to find and arrest the suspects, to secure the instruments used in the crime as well as personal effects and evidence, to be available to the court or tribunal and to prepare the technical and expert reports needed.

- To obtain, receive and analyse data of interest regarding public safety, and study, plan and carry out crime prevention procedures and techniques.

- To collaborate with the Civil Protection services in cases of high risk, catastrophe or disaster affecting the public according to the terms of Civil Protection legislation.

All these functions will be carried out in accordance with the following land-based jurisdictions:

- The National Police Force covers capitals of provinces and other boroughs or towns specified by the government.
- The Civil Guard covers the rest of the national territory and territorial waters.

However, when needed, both forces may carry out investigations and collect data throughout the national territory, whilst always keeping the other abreast of their actions.

Independently of ships' interior security protocols and plans, and of the measures ship owners, port authorities and the merchant navy have to take, the security forces must play a fundamental role in the prevention of terrorism and in the investigation of terrorist elements and groups, as well as being aware of the current methods and procedures used by such groups. They have to be able to coordinate all parties involved in security and, in particular, monitor a data collection system which, whilst maintaining communication between the different shipping companies, is able to sort data, signs and traces that can be used to ensure adequate prevention and planning.

9.1 State security forces and bodies

9.1.1 The Civil Guard in ports

Organic Law 2/86, dated 13th March, regarding the security forces and bodies, assigns the Civil Guard the responsibility of watching over the coast, ports and airports among its other duties. It is perhaps time to consider replacing the current duties of the Civil Guard, (which are closely linked to fiscal assignments and, therefore, somewhat reduced these days due to the elimination of borders within the EU), and moving towards strengthening and taking on port security assignments as the law requires it to and as it has done in airports.

For this to be done the objectives of the port police should be taken into account. The port police must work with the Civil Guard as an auxiliary force in procedures which they themselves draw up, albeit very generally, in their capacity as a judicial police force. They must make all the information they have available to the Civil Guard and hand over anyone they arrest and any property they confiscate, whenever they are acting according to their public functions or with the necessary legal cover.

There is no distinction made between the custody assignments assigned to the Civil Guard in ports and airports. The word custody implies constant surveillance. Perhaps it is the sheer volume of passenger traffic energising our tourist industry that has ensured the heads of the Civil Guard always give preferential treatment to airports in the deployment of the limited personnel available. This is logical, especially in current times when port activity is developing slowly.

Ports are not only the destination of the majority of cargo entering a country, but also of cruise liners and their passenger traffic. Plus, in this age of pleasure-seekers they will become a significant reference point. This is a traffic which requires police presence for the custody of the facilities, and the security of ships, people and cargo which could become targets for terrorist attack, not forgetting the fight against illegal immigration, drug trafficking and, to a lesser extent, contraband, all of which enter by sea. In practice, in many ports the duties pertaining to public order, public safety and even those belonging to the judicial police are carried out by the National Police Force. This is due to the wide availability of officers who are deployed throughout large cities and are able to reach the scene quickly. Justification for this is found in article 11.6 of the organic law regarding security forces and bodies. With the aim of achieving optimum use of available resources, and a rational distribution of forces, the Home Office can order any of the security forces to take on all or some of the functions exclusive to another force in particular areas or nuclei.

As regards terrorism on a national and an international scale, extremely specialised units should be deployed which have monitoring resources and sophisticated investigation methods. These units will be able to access the relevant information and coordinate with other international bodies.

Regarding our subject area and in support of the arguments hitherto portrayed, the aforementioned Organic Law 2/86 states:

- "The State is exclusively responsible for public safety. The maintaining of it falls to the Government of the Nation (1º.1)"

  The Constitutional Court has made several declarations regarding this. It accepts regional and local police forces as the only exception to the rule when the respective statutes of autonomous regions so include them.

- "Members of the Security Forces will act in accordance with the principle of reciprocal cooperation, and will be coordinated by the bodies created to this effect as established in this Law (3)".

- "Everybody must provide the Security Forces with the help required in the investigation and persecution of crime and criminals...(4º.1)".

- "Persons and bodies which carry out surveillance, security or custody duties involving public or private people, property or services are obliged to help and collaborate, at all times, with the Security Forces (4º.2)".

The port authorities, especially via the port police, carry out security, surveillance and custody duties involving public property or services including general ports and, specifically, any cargo and facilities to be found in them. Now, more than ever, private security guards are also present in ports. As collaborators, and members of security firms, all security guards must be regulated by the security forces, and all are obliged to collaborate in this.

9.1.2 Jurisdictions

The jurisdictions for the state security forces are distributed territorially in the following way (Art. 11.2):

a) The National Police Force (from hereon NPF) in the capital cities of the provinces and in any boroughs and urban nuclei at Government request.

b) The Civil Guard will cover the rest of the national territory and territorial waters.

The assigning of the first spatial jurisdiction is being considered. This will not include crime investigation and data collection which any of the forces may carry out throughout the national territory.

There is no doubt that the surveillance of maritime areas comes under the jurisdiction of the Civil Guard, and this is carried out with naval and air units. The concept of territorial waters should be interpreted in a wide sense as outside these waters, both in the adjoining area and in the area of the continental platform and the exclusive economic zone, there are other rights of jurisdiction and police responsibilities to take into consideration, without interfering in our Navy's military jurisdiction.

To ensure an optimal use of resources, the Home Office will be able to assign one force's assignments to any other force. In the majority of cases these decisions will be made by Government officials and sub-officials.

For spatial distribution, a physical distribution of jurisdictions is established (Art. 12):

a.   Covered by the NPF:

   -   Control of Spanish nationals and foreigners entering and leaving the national territory.
   -   The provisions in the legislation on foreign nationals, refuge and asylum, extradition, expulsion, emigration and immigration.

b.   Among other duties, the Civil Guard will cover:

   The monitoring of roads, coastlines, borders, ports, airports, as well as centres and facilities that so require it.

Perhaps the security forces should have their responsibilities more clearly defined and outlined for them in reference to ports, as well as developing procedures and police units which are efficient in giving reasonable responses to the policing problem in these areas.

The Civil Guard is slowly taking on board its security responsibilities for surveillance and custody in ports which, for diverse reasons and at a rate which is possible or suitable for them, it has to develop in the future with the deployment of its Maritime Service and the merging of the coastguard services and the old fiscal services posted in the ports to create one Unit. In the near future the decision-making bodies will be concerned with organising and coordinating these services and supplying them with aerial surveillance resources better suited to the marine environment.

9.1.3 The Civil Guard Maritime Service

The RD 246/91, dated 22nd February, regulates the Civil Guard Maritime Service and assigns it the functions, in Spanish waters, of being a judicial police force and a governing body, maintaining public order, carrying out fiscal and administrative duties, as well as continuing with its military functions. To achieve this it must be provided with material and human resources to be able to carry out the duties it has been assigned, principally:

1.   Ensuring the Law is abided by.
2.   Helping and protecting people and ensuring the conservation and protection of any property found to be in danger.
3.   Watching over and protecting public buildings and facilities which so require it.
4.   Preventing crime, etc.

In summary, it is to carry out the duties of a judicial police force, administrative, fiscal, governmental and public order duties, etc. as well as its own military duties. These are all duties which the Royal

Decree from the creation of the Civil Guard states will be carried out "up to the outer edges of the territorial waters determined by current legislation and, on occasion, outside the territorial waters in accordance with current International Treaties." In this way, the policing of the marine environment was assigned to the Civil Guard and the first patrols received their baptism in the events in Barcelona and Seville. However, it is one thing to assign jurisdictions, and quite another to create a maritime police force overnight.

Today the Civil Guard has 15 PMS (Provincial Maritime Services) and 26 patrol boats stationed along the 8,000 km of Spanish coastline. The human and material resources are scarce in comparison with other European countries around us and inadequate for the duties to be carried out. However, the fact that the deployment of the Civil Guard Maritime Service began barely 6 years ago and is still continuing must be taken into account, as must the fact that the aim is to create at least one PMS in each province with coastline, and to later take the further step of using other naval resources (deep sea patrol boats) which will allow greater range and a more effective presence, not only in territorial waters, but in other areas where Spain has sovereign rights, such as the adjacent area or the exclusive economic zone. All this depends on the budget to be approved in the coming years as well as the acceptance of the priorities described, such as the previously announced intention for the Civil Guard to exercise greater control in the Gibraltar Straits.

This service, as it continues to be equipped with material and human resources and concludes the deployment along the peninsular and insular coastline which it is committed to doing, and as it becomes able to organise itself as a force uniting the remaining Civil Guard units with surveillance responsibilities in the ports and along the coastline (the objective of the recently created Fiscal and Border Headquarters) and the units of the national police force responsible for foreign nationals, immigration and the fight against drug-trafficking, and its Department annexed to Customs & Excise, each of which have their own jurisdictions, but collaborate in those they share, will be required to carry out comprehensive maritime police duties in the future. It must be able to give an operational response (as soon as it has the information and air surveillance support) to the problems and challenges posed by organised crime at sea. This includes terrorist threats which have reached significant levels of importance and which Spain is not immune to.

In the same way, terrestrial units will lend any support needed in the ports, particularly in the control of different fleets, and in close collaboration with authorities of the Spanish Navy, the Merchant Navy, state ports and other police forces. The Law on ports includes other security duties such as those detailed in article 15.4. This article refers to the service area within ports under state jurisdiction and requires reports to be issued by the Home Office regarding public safety and the monitoring of the arrival and departure of persons in national territory, before any plans for the use of port space, or for the significant modification of them, can be approved.

Article 26, section e), states that, in order to fulfil the general objectives, State Ports must define the technical and economic criteria for the use of the forces for security and that any security action taken must be in collaboration with the Home Office.

The Project on General Regulations for Staff and Police in Public State-run Ports is currently in the process of being drawn up[1]. A study of the draft provided in October 2000, shows an opportunity has been missed to broach the subject of what the responsibilities of port authorities should be in terms of port security, and how those responsibilities should be organised, what channels should be used and

---

[1] This complies with the mandate established in article 106 of Law 27/92, dated 24th November, regarding Ports Belonging to the State and to the Merchant Navy in the draft provided by Law 62/97, dated 26th December.

how the necessary cooperation, coordination and collaboration should be overseen. This is a serious omission, especially when we take into account the fact that ports have been opened for other uses and other facilities. Today a port is no longer a perfectly marked out area, little by little our ports have begun to merge with cities, opening themselves up to them, and this should have provoked a redefinition and reassigning of the different police jurisdictions and activities in public ports, starting with the legal statute and the responsibilities of the port police.

The Civil Guard Maritime Service needs to promptly unite the jurisdictions currently dispersed among the Harbour Masters, environmental authorities, port authorities, national and regional fishing authorities, different police forces, etc. The current situation means that, for the moment, coordination is weak, that personal impulses are followed rather than a comprehensive model designed for maritime control and, from a coordination point of view, the carrying out of responsibilities at sea, in all the different areas, requires a great deal of good will on behalf of everyone involved for the solving of any problems at sea.

It is clear that a policy needs to be developed for analysing risks and threats and that, as a result, channels for response will have to be established.

9.2 Public safety. Public order

The largest ports are, for the most part, located within the cities that surround them. For this reason it is the National Police Force that, for practical reasons, normally sees to public safety in port areas, even if there is nothing from a legal point of view impeding the Civil Guard form carrying out such duties. The Civil Guard would probably have fewer officers concerned with public safety in these areas. However, if the jurisdictions are large or are not clearly defined, it is often necessary to stick to a criteria of efficiency because, as far as civilians and facilities are concerned, the most important point is that problems are solved.

The distribution of police jurisdictions and responsibilities in ports is a matter still pending, and that is not including the possible jurisdictions claimed local police and which are not fully defined given that ports are like balconies jutting out from large cities and forming an integral part of these boroughs.

In some ports the port police forces have been developed and enhanced to such a level that they have, in fact, been compared to state security forces. In others, on the other hand, police duties have been absent in recent years and the agents of authority (as almost all obsolete port regulations and the Projects for future regulations recognise them to be) with their title of security guards,[2] have only been carrying out administrative work, monitoring unloading and dock workers, controlling entry to the service areas, etc. All these are duties which could be carried out by other professionals, given their private nature.

These port police forces which the Law on State Ports unbelievably makes no reference to, form part of the special police forces referred to in Organic Law 1/92 regarding public safety. We hope that the law reform currently underway will include the figure of the port police officer in the end. Regarding the duties of the port police, the debate today centres on the limits of their public duties and on the

---

[2] In a collective agreement they have renounced the right to carry firearms, meaning they are no longer sworn in by the governing authority.

private assignments they carry out. They are sincerely in need of a redefinition which will reaffirm their status as agents of authority able to take on security duties along with the custody duties that, in ports, come under the jurisdiction of the Civil Guard.

9.3 Responsibilities, duties and limitations of the State Security Forces

Among the responsibilities of these forces, the following stand out:

- Preventing all types of criminal activity via the systematic investigation of the terrorist groups operating both within their territory and internationally.
- Investigating naval resources to which they may have access for committing crimes.
- Establishing channels to collect the right information from all state and private port operators.
- Creating groups specialising in maritime and port surveillance.
- Guarding the waters of the sovereignty or waters under Spanish jurisdiction and port areas.
- Providing a point in each public port where shipping operators can give any information of interest or have their suspicions looked into.
- Coordinating other groups in both the public and private security sectors which may carry out duties in the ports.
- Maximising surveillance measures on the arrival of sensitive ships, considered so because they are likely to present a greater risk, as well as keeping in contact to ensure a greater and better cooperation between themselves and other persons responsible for security inside the ship, in the port itself or from the shipping company.
- Taking charge of any person handed over to them by the Captain or persons responsible for security on board, and starting the proper procedures if the premises of international criminal jurisdiction are met. Organic Law no. 6/85, regarding judicial authority, states in article 23:

"1. According to criminal law, criminal acts and misdemeanours will be judged under Spanish jurisdiction when they are committed on Spanish territory or aboard Spanish ships or aircraft[3], without affecting the international treaties that Spain forms a part of.

2. Spanish jurisdiction will also cover judgement of acts described in Spanish criminal law as crimes, even if they have not been committed on Spanish territory, when the persons responsible for the crime are Spanish or foreigners who have acquired Spanish nationality after the crime and where the following requirements are met:

a) That the act is a punishable offence in the place where it was committed.
b) That the affected party or the Department of Public Prosecutions reports the crime to the Spanish courts or files a complaint with them.
c) That the criminal has not been absolved, pardoned or punished abroad, or, in the latter case, that s/he has not served the sentence. In the case of a sentence having been partly served, this will be taken into consideration and the new sentence reduced accordingly.

4. Spain will also be responsible for judging crimes committed by Spaniards or foreigners outside the national territory when they are classed, according to Spanish criminal law, as one of the following crimes:

---

[3] This is known as the flag principle

a) Terrorism[4]

b) Piracy[5] and the illegal seizure of aircraft

5. Action will be taken regarding ships flying foreign flags, if the premises of Article 27 of the 3rd United Nations Conference on the Law of the Sea[6] which lays out the terms of criminal jurisdiction on board a foreign ship in the following way are met:

1. The criminal jurisdiction of a coastal nation should not be exercised on board a foreign ship sailing in territorial waters, with the arrest of an individual or the investigation of a crime committed on board ship during its passage not being permitted, except in the following cases:

a) When the crime has repercussions in the coastal nation;

b) When the crime is of such a nature that it could disturb the peace of the country or order in territorial waters;

c) When the Captain of the ship, or a diplomatic agent or civil representative from the consulate of the country whose flag the ship is flying, requests the assistance of the local authorities...

2. The regulations above do not affect the right of the coastal nation to take any measures necessary, authorised by its laws, to arrest persons and investigate aboard a foreign ship sailing through territorial waters that has come from internal waters.

3. In the cases previously mentioned in paragraphs 1 and 2, the coastal nation, at the request of the Captain and before any measures are taken, will notify a diplomatic agent or civil representative from the country whose flag the ship is flying and will enable contact between this agent and the crew of the ship. In case of emergency, notification may be given as measures are being taken.

4. Local authorities must take into account the purpose of the voyage when deciding whether to proceed with any arrests and how they should be carried out.

5. Apart from in cases stipulated in Part 12[7], or in a case of the laws and regulations established in Part 5[8] being broken, the coastal nation may not take any measures on board a foreign ship passing through its territorial waters to arrest anyone or to carry out any proceedings regarding a crime committed before the ship entered the territorial waters, if that ship comes from a foreign port and is only passing through the territorial waters without entering internal waters."

- When taking action it is important to remember that the stipulations of the criminal procedure act[9] must be taken into account, as this act considers domestic merchant ships to be

---

[4] Spanish criminal law is used to pronounce judgement in cases of terrorism, in accordance with the principles which allow the Spanish regulations to be applied outside national territory. This case refers to a principle known as the Principle of Universal Justice.

[5] The same as terrorism, except it is important to point out that the Spanish legislator, when writing the 1995 Penal Code, forgot to include this crime, not taking into account international regulations nor its inclusion in the Organic Law of the Federal Judiciary. In Spain maybe the figure of the pirate has lost its place.

[6] 3rd United Nations Conference on the Law of the Sea, dated 10.12.1982, ratified by the Document BOE 14-2-1997 dated 20.2.96

[7] On the protection and preservation of the marine environment.

[8] Regarding the specific regulations for the Exclusive Economic Zone. Article 55 and following.

[9] Especially article 554.

dwellings. Neither may anyone enter and search foreign merchant ships without the authorisation of the Captain or, if the Captain were to refuse, without the authorisation of the nation's Consulate.

Regarding foreign warships, if the commanding officer refuses to grant authorisation, his authorisation can be replaced by that of the ambassador or minister of the nation in question.

9.3.1 Duties

According to Article 104 of the Spanish Constitution: "The security Forces and Bodies, under Government control, will be entrusted with the mission of protecting the free exercise of rights and liberties and of guaranteeing public safety."

Organic Law 2/1986, dated 13th March, regarding security forces and bodies, lays out the basic lines of procedure and organisation of the police forces and their duties, both in territorial deployment and the physical jurisdictions to which we have already, partially, referred.

9.3.2 Limitations

Many of the limitations are the logical consequence of the complexity of Public International Law, as ships do sail, on occasion, under flags that hide their actual nationality, at least as far as capital and responsibility are concerned.

The high seas are still an extraterritorial area and the application of the flag principle, of the universal justice principle or of the personality principle is not always understood in the same way among all nations. It is difficult to exercise sufficient control over this zone although attempts to do so have systematically been made in the many Agreements drawn up to try and find efficient solutions.

We could say that we are living in a period of history which will mark a turning point in the concept of security. Terrorism is now showing itself to be real threat which demonstrates an exceptional cruelty. The leaders of our current societies need to be concerned with ensuring the responses are both correct and proportionate, with the procedures agreed on internationally, not forgetting the diffusing of bitter conflicts, avoiding unjustified inequality and reducing the amount of hatred in the world. All this will help take the edge off nationalist, social, ideological, religious and ethnic extremists.

9.4 Private security

Private security was born out of a government initiative aimed, initially, at protecting banks. However, in reality, this has led to the evolution of the concept and to a number of companies in business and industry requesting the services of private companies, in accordance with several factors such as:

- The increase in criminal activity and damage to persons and property.
- The crisis regarding personal and family values which has meant an increase in maladjusted individuals and social outcasts.
- The crisis in and development of economic and social systems, with the appearance of deprived areas which are breeding grounds for all kinds of crime.

- The progressive and startling increase in drug use, especially among young people who are beginning to take drugs at younger and younger ages. This has greatly contributed to the increase in crime rates.
- The development of criteria stating to what extent the State believes individuals should be responsible for the protection of their own property and, to a lesser extent, of people, notwithstanding their general responsibilities in this area.
- The slow increase of security.structures within companies themselves, which has led to the creation of comprehensive protections plans and the contracting of security services and equipment.

Private security has a variety of characteristics which differentiate it from public security. Among them are the following:

- The exclusive nature of risk prevention, avoiding all direct action in response, except that which helps avoid personal injury or the injury of a third person.
- The local nature of private security which focuses on a specific objective and cannot carry out general security services.
- The nature of its activity being controlled by the government in several ways, including, the registering of the company, the authorisation for specific services, inspections and other control procedures.
- The private nature itself, given that the work is carried out by businesses with the aim of achieving the same results as all other companies.

As a result of these characteristics, and of the developments made within the field of private security, it was necessary to pass Law 23/92, dated 30th July, which regulates surveillance and security services for the protection of persons and property rendered by private legal persons or natural persons who will provide complementary and subsidiary services to the public security sector.

In accordance with this law and the regulations that led to its development, security firms may only offer the following services and carry out the following activities:

- The surveillance and protection of property, premises, shows, competitions and conventions.
- The protection of specific persons, once the corresponding authorisation has been granted.
- The deposit, custody, counting and classification of coins and notes, bonds and other objects which, due to their economic value or the expectations they produce, or due to their dangerous nature, may require special protection in addition to the security measures already taken by the financial entities themselves.
- The transport and distribution of the objects described in the previous section via different means.
- The installation and maintenance of security equipment, devices and systems.
- The use of control centres to receive, check and transmit alarm signals and their relaying to the security forces, as well as supplying response services which are not the domain of the security forces.
- The planning and assessment of the aforementioned security activities.

We can see, therefore, that private security firms are subject to quite strict government control, as it is considered they are doing security work delegated to them by the State and, because of the nature of this delegation, the State has the right to check the delegated work is being carried out in accordance with the corresponding legal regulations.

Both types of security are of a complementary nature, as much in the logical sense of collaboration between similar entities as in the strength of the regulations which, as we have already seen, impose the category of auxiliary units on private security personnel in relation to the security forces.

Finally, it is important to note that private security firms should seek the help of the public security forces when carrying out their duties, as there is no room for isolated operations or a lack of coordination in such an important matter.

9.5 The work of the International Maritime Organisation

The first time the IMO was made aware of acts of piracy was in 1983 when Sweden asked the senior technical body of the organisation, the Maritime Safety Committee (MSC), to investigate a situation which they described as "alarming".

Having discussed the matter, the MSC prepared a written document that was later presented in the thirteenth session of the IMO assembly (the governing body of the organisation), held in November 1983. It was approved and was adopted as assembly resolution A. 545 (13).

Although the number of acts of piracy and armed robberies have decreased in some areas, in others the problem has become more acute. For this reason, in November 1991 the IMO Assembly adopted a second resolution regarding this matter, resolution A. 683 (17). This resolution notes "with great concern the still increasing number of incidents involving piracy and armed robbery against ships and the increasing violence against personnel on board such ships"

The reports provided by the various experts were presented to the IMO secretary's office towards the end of March 1993, and a definitive report was then prepared for the secretary general. He, in turn, passed it to the MSC, the IMO's senior technical body, which then examined it in its 62nd session (MSC/circs. 622 and 623), with the assembly adopting resolution A. 738 (18) dated 4th November, 1993 (See Appendix 4).

The response of the Maritime Security Committee came in the form of a document entitled *Measures to prevent unlawful acts which threaten the safety of ships and the security of their passengers and crews*. To everyone's surprise, the resolution was approved immediately and unanimously, by all 136 member countries, in the fourteenth assembly (governing body of the International Maritime Organisation), and recorded as resolution A. 584 (14), adopted on the 20th November, 1985.

All this happened very quickly, but was truly transcendental. From the moment the resolution was adopted and onwards, it has become evident there is an approved and internationally recognised formula which establishes, clearly and fully, what ports and ships should do to provide adequate protection against terrorist attacks. Since the 26th September 1986, we have had a document which can be used by politicians, lawyers, journalists and the general public to determine whether a certain port or ship has taken what are considered "reasonable measures" to protect its passengers and crew: the MSC 53/24, Appendix 14 *"Measures approved by the Maritime Safety Committee of the International Maritime Organisation to prevent unlawful acts against passengers and crews on board ships"*.

And finally, after the hijacking of the transporter "Avrasya" by Chechen rebels in the Black Sea in 1996, a set of wide-ranging measures were proposed for the fight against terrorism and other threats to passenger ships, and these were dealt with by the Maritime Safety Committee in its sixtieth session.

The principle measures suggested were the following:

- searching of passengers, luggage and vehicles
- prevention of unauthorised access to the ship
- action taken to avoid weapons and explosives being transported
- establishing restricted areas in ports and on board ships

The most debated clause was the one referring to what exactly the searching and viewing on screen of everything taken on board would mean in terms of cost and delays. It was finally subtly changed so that the inspections undergone by passengers' luggage and vehicles would be adjusted according to "the risk of unlawful acts", "a high level of threat will mean an increase in security searches/screenings, and sufficient trained personnel, equipment and systems must be available."

In spite of the IMO directives being highly influential, they are only directives, and several countries have decided to reinforce them by making them laws.

9.6 United States Maritime and Port Security Act (1986)

Throughout the eighties, in the United States, there was increasing concern that the protection offered sea travellers was falling behind with regards to that provided to air travellers. During this time some meetings were held prior to the Congress Delegation meeting chaired by Mr. Mario Biaggi. In October 1985 the Delegation published a report emphasising that, in spite of the fact that many cruise line companies were voluntarily adopting their own safety measures, other were providing none, and as the Coast Guard did not have the required authority to insist on a minimum level of preventive measures being taken, it was necessary to create legislation to that effect. As a result of this report, the 1986 Maritime and Port Security Act and the 1990 Aviation Security Improvement Act were established.

The aforementioned 1986 Act established the following objectives:

1. The projection onto a screen of the cargo and luggage that go through a port in the same way that this is done in an airport.

2. Security measures restricting access to the cargo, ships and port facilities to authorised personnel only.

3. Additional security on board the ships.

4. Appropriate basic security levels when granting authorisation or passes.

5. Other appropriate measures to prevent unlawful acts committed against passengers and crew on board the ships.

The 1986 act also granted the president the power to withdraw the right of entry into the United States, or to operate from its ports, from any passenger ship coming from a country which uses its territory as a base for terrorist operations, or which is known to have used ships as political instruments. Finally, the act promotes the provision of pertinent, relevant and full warnings to travellers.

9.7 Warnings to travellers

The United States Department of State Travel Advisory service was designed to inform Americans travelling abroad of any circumstances which may affect them adversely.

In official words:

"These warnings are not based on isolated cases of international terrorism, but describe the potential danger of violence and physical harm that exist in certain places. These are tendencies and models that appear likely to last some time, a period of time during which the United States Department of State considers the local government will be reluctant or unable to provide adequate protection."

In this way, in 1991, during the Gulf War and in anticipation of possible terrorist attacks, the United States Department of State published a Warning to Travellers in which 23 countries were blacklisted. As a result, without any violent acts being committed against Americans, within a matter of days nine of the major cruise line companies had cancelled their voyages in the Far East.

All countries can issue warnings to travellers and, when they do so, they are fulfilling a legitimate function. The public expects the government of its country to keep an eye on the world situation and to publish warnings to ensure nobody travels to a conflictive area without being aware of the situation. However, there can be a negative side to this if government departments take commercial factors into account when they decide which countries to include in their black list.

The ship's administrator and the Captain face the dilemma of whether to ignore the warning to travellers and continue with their itinerary, or to opt for an available alternative port and, if possible, one which is equally as attractive. The decision is not an easy one to make because if they ignore the Warning and an incident occurs once within the blacklisted port then this can increase the possibility of large compensation claims.

9.8 Aviation Security Improvement Act (1991)

On the 16th November, 1990, President Bush signed and established in law the Aviation Security Improvement Act, thereby creating the position of director of intelligence and security within the Transport Secretary's Office.

The tasks assigned the new office included advising the Transport secretary on national and international security issues and developing programmes related to the security of travellers.

The office was created with the intention of ensuring high security standards, not only on aircraft, but also aboard ships, including ships flying foreign flags but transporting American citizens and ships which dock in US ports.

Both the Department of Transport and the United States Coast Guard have publically expressed their intention to make the IMO directives obligatory. The members of the new office are currently evaluating the basic regulations that need to be established in ports and on passenger ships with the aim of deciding when they should be implemented.

9.9 The Coast Guard

The members of the US Coast Guard, who are totally independent from the Intelligence and Security Office, also have the objective of ensuring passenger ships satisfactorily comply with security standards before they enter ports in the United States. To avoid problems when an official inspector boards the ship, it is essential that it has a well-designed security plan that shows its efficiency and complies with IMO directives and United States legislation. If the ship does not have an appropriate security plan it could cause problems and lead to delays.

It is logical to presume that, thanks to the effort of the Coast Guard and the interest shown by shipping companies, security inspections by Coast Guard officials will become as routine as safety inspections in the near future.

9.10 The United Kingdom Aviation and Maritime Security Act (1990)

In 1988, the situation at the time led to UK government concern over the attractiveness of car and passenger ferries as terrorist objectives. As a result, a series of discussions with the navigation industry began to try and establish a set of basic, voluntary guidelines which could be put into practice by the industry. The aim of the government was to "educate the industry in the acceptance of the fact that decisions on protective security must become permanent characteristics of their policy."

After the tragic terrorist bomb attack on flight Pan-Am 103, the government decided to increase its authority in the matter and to create an act regarding air safety. The Department of Transport made the most of the initiative and had the law expanded to include the maritime sector. The result is known as the 1990 Aviation and Maritime Security Act.

The most important functions of the Act are:

- To assign a person to be responsible for all security related matters.

- To form port security committees.

- To design and put in to practice extensive contingency plans, training and retraining the required personnel.

- To design restricted areas.

- To establish entry systems.

- To locate physical protection systems.

- To establish strict controls at access and exit points, ensuring these are equipped for carrying out inspections.

The law also highlights the responsibility of the ships' administrators and the captains to use the IMO directives as a model.

These standards are now legal requirements applied in all UK ports and to all passenger ships which enter these ports. The Inspectors began their job in 1991 and since then a vast amount of reports have been presented. There is currently a strong emphasis on making the industry understand the need for these new regulations and work is now underway to perfect them, as the appointment of the first Chief Inspector of Transport Security, Mr. H. Ditmas, who has prepared a set of "Instructions" to explain the requirements.

9.11 The maritime police model

Since the promulgation of Organic Law 2/86, dated 13th March, regarding the security forces and bodies, (which was a development of Article 104 of the Spanish Constitution that assigns the security forces and bodies the task of protecting the free exercise of rights and liberties and guaranteeing public safety,) and since it set out in article 11.2.b, that the Civil Guard had full jurisdiction of the territorial sea, and in article 12.1 assigned the Civil Guard the responsibility for the custody of roads, the coast, borders, ports, airports and any centres or facilities which may so require it, the ministerial departments, bodies and institutions related to the sea have been debating not only the methods and resources required to carry out these duties, but also to what extent and in which areas these jurisdictions should be exercised and what model the maritime police should introduce.

With time further changes came about and what are today Harbour Master's Offices (previously known as marine commands) fell under the jurisdiction of the Ministry of Defence as just one more responsibility of the Spanish Navy. The idea was first to free the Navy of responsibilities which were not strictly military. Since then many things have changed regarding jurisdictions and the organisations related to the sea, mainly with the introduction of the 1992 Port and Merchant Navy Law, which coincided with two historic events that year: the Barcelona Olympics and the Universal Exposition of Seville.

9.11.1 Towards a comprehensive model of maritime policing

Spain has opted for a complex model of very small and disperse jurisdictions. Since 1992, the year the Civil Guard Maritime Service was started, this body has only carried out police duties, albeit in a comprehensive way:

- Judicial Police

- Administrative Police

- Public Order Police

It shares responsibilities with regards to fishing:

- Inspection by Ministry of Agriculture, Fisheries and Food. Outer waters

- Inspection by the Autonomous Communities. Internal Waters

- Fiscal Police:

- Shares jurisdictions with the Customs Surveillance Service

The Civil Guard itself should act as arbiter in a model coordinating the following aspects:

- Surveillance and security in ports assigned to them in article 12 of Organic Law 2/86, dated 13th March, regarding the Security Forces and Bodies.

- The maritime service.

- The fiscal service. The judicial police service with technical resources adapted to marine conditions.

- An air service with aeroplanes and helicopters with enough range to be effective. This may carry out SAR (Search and Rescue) missions only.

Perhaps the solution lies in a headquarters, within the Civil Guard, capable of coordinating the different aspects mentioned, if integration is definitely not a choice that is going to be made.

However, it is one thing for the law to assign responsibilities, and quite another to have the human and material resources available to be able to carry out the duties effectively and efficiently. The Civil Guard Maritime Service, which is beginning to get going, must be strengthened in the next few years with airborne resources, qualified personnel and deep sea patrol boats, to achieve just a minimum of efficiency in carrying out its duties in the marine environment.

9.11.2 Division of responsibilities

1. The Ministry of Defence

The Ministry of Defence has military responsibilities and responsibilities for the defence of the national territory as well as those stated in Law 60/62 regarding aid, salvage, discoveries and retrievals at sea. The latter are surplus responsibilities which are pending further development so they can be transferred to the Ministry of Development.

Our Navy also has collaboration agreements with the Ministry of Agriculture, Fisheries and Food for the control of the local and deep sea fishing fleets. To carry out this task it uses two ships provided by the ministry itself. The ministry is in charge of the maintenance of the ships, whilst the Navy provides the crews.

2. Ministry of Development

    Merchant Navy Command:

    - Harbour Master's Offices
    - Inspection of ships

3. State Society of Sea Rescue and Safety

4. Communications Bureau

5. Public Body of State Ports in Domestic Ports

    -Port authorities and port police

A. Home Office

Civil Guard Management Bureau: Several sea-related specialities which are beginning to be coordinated.

Pollution: The Maritime Service for pollution from ships and the Environmental Protection Service for pollution originating on land.

Judicial, Administrative and Public Order Police, etc. for territorial waters and, occasionally in other areas: the Maritime Service and Judicial Police Command Teams.

Surveillance from the air: Helicopter units. These basically consist of unsuitable helicopters which have insufficient range for sea crossings and surveillance.

Fiscal and anti-drug investigation: Fiscal units and groups.

National Police Force: Both drug-trafficking and immigration fall under the jurisdiction of the National Police Force, but it does not have jurisdiction in territorial waters. To carry out operations at sea, with regards to drug-trafficking, it uses the air and sea resources of the Customs Surveillance Service. Together they have carried out major operations. This is, perhaps, due to the Civil Guard not having any deep-sea patrol boats as yet.

B. The Treasury

Customs Surveillance Service: Until the Government decided to establish a maritime police force and assigned it to the Civil Guard, the only public service, apart from the Navy, which has maritime resources was the Customs Surveillance Service. This service, which has significant maritime resources that are currently far superior to those of the Civil Guard Maritime Service, also has some helicopters and aeroplanes. Its naval resources include a deep-sea patrol boat with sufficient range to be able to carry out trans-ocean crossings.

Its responsibilities are basically related to contraband and it has jurisdiction both on land and at sea. The philosophy is to wait patiently and act on specific occasions when provided with information regarding a particular operation. Its boats carry out very few preventive missions.

Recently, this service, which has been questioned in several forums and tribunals, seems to have become embroiled in a crisis with regards to its future. It is, perhaps, time for it to take a good look at itself and outline its philosophy as well as its duties. Opinions have especially been expressed with regards to it acting as a judicial police force, a role which many dispute.

C. Ministry of Agriculture, Fisheries and Food (MAPA)

This ministry carries out inspections of fishing boats outside internal waters and, if they are Spanish boats, anywhere in international waters. State jurisdiction regarding fishing begins outside the baselines or straight baselines.

To carry out these duties, the Spanish Navy has two ships armed and managed by itself in the Exclusive Economic Zone. A third is being constructed and will be armed and piloted by the Civil Guard. This is all based on collaboration agreements.

The ministry has its own team of inspectors to fulfil these responsibilities in collaboration with the Navy and the Civil Guard. The responsibilities are also met by the Civil Guard via the Maritime Service.

D. Autonomous Communities

Spain's autonomous communities have exclusive responsibility for fishing in internal waters, the gathering of shellfish and for fish farming in all areas.

Development legislation for the organisation of the fishing sector.

The autonomous communities have their own inspectors with the responsibilities of the administrative police in this area.

Their jurisdiction covers marinas as well as fishing and commercial ports which are not domestic ports. They have also recently been granted responsibility for the management of domestic ports, including environmental responsibilities and the deployment of their own port police.

9.12 Crew control department

It can be said that the control of immigration, as well as small scale contraband and drug trafficking, via the monitoring of crews reaching the Spanish ports, coastline or anchorage, as well as the monitoring of certain ships which are forced to enter specific areas, is not even remotely organised.

The responsibilities are so disparate and are distributed in such a heterogeneous way that the lists of crew members may, or may not, be presented to the harbour master; the consignees may, or may not, give the lists to the National Police Force responsible for immigration; nobody normally checks the lists of crew members on their arrival in Spain, and certainly not on their departure, regardless of the country of origin of the ship; and it is not strange for some crew members to "disappear" from the lists. There are cases in point, and they are not few and far between.

Other countries with a similar problem of mass illegal immigration have established serious control measures to monitor crew members on their arrival in the ports and, depending on their nationality and origin, they forbid some, or all, of the crew members to disembark. Sometimes the ship and its crew are checked again, only moments before they leave the port.

It is now fairly common for crew members to abandon their ships in our ports. There is now an organised illegal immigration which uses the cover of appearing on a list of crew members. This selective immigration, which we believe to be ongoing, like a drip feed, is usually organised in conjunction with an official on board the ship and happens frequently.

It would not go amiss to record all foreign crew members when they disembark as well as when they embark to leave. This would, of course apply to certain crews according to the risk factors such as:

- the origins of the crew members
- the type of trade
- the ship's country of origin

Or, for the lack of authorisation of the:

- ships
- crews
- freight.

A personalised and authorised written document should always be required for anyone leaving the ship, and those ships which have a prior record of similar events, apart from being heavily fined, should not be issued with authorisation permits until a certain time has passed. This will act as a deterrent and oblige ship owners and charterers to strictly monitor their crews.

9.13 Port Authorities

Security, whether public or private has been questioned within ports because of the deregulation of traffic and the creation of Free Ports with relaxed jurisdiction and favourable customs regulations. The sales dynamic currently far outweighs the subject of security and it is clear all interests must be combined, including the port authorities in security matters, as they need to be able to manage a security system which is profitable but without damaging the trade itself. To sum it up, the security system has to be a commercial operation but not get in the way of commercial trade as far as is reasonably possible. Current technical resources should be boldly used to achieve this.

The security of private cargo should be left to private firms, but with all the guarantees in place to ensure the law is complied with. These private security firms need to comply with certain terms and conditions to ensure an efficient collaboration with the security forces. Private security firms should move from simply defending private property to ensuring legality and that the legal requirements and regulations that they are in charge of are complied with.

All this, of course, will be controlled by the security forces.

The security forces need to organise the private security forces belonging to the different firms that are stationed in surrounding ports to monitor the amount of cargo. This has not yet been done in a conscientious manner, but they must insist on the security of traffic on other levels.

9.14 Merchant Navy Command and the Spanish Marine Safety and Pollution Agency

As has already been mentioned, in Spain two of the main pillars supporting maritime security are the Merchant Navy Command (known as the DGMM), a subsidiary of the Transport and Energy Ministry, and the Spanish Marine Safety and Pollution Agency (known as SASEMAR).

The possible collaboration procedures for DGMM and the police forces, the Civil Guard, customs and any others, should undergo a period of testing and feedback to ensure they are put to the best use and they are as efficient as possible. We do not believe that this is where links, relationships and agreements to be united on a government or institutional scale should be made, but whatever the path chosen, it is bound to be an important step towards the fight against crime at sea and the criminal organisations that commit them today.

SASEMAR, among other duties, is responsible for the control of maritime traffic via a large network of control towers in ports and at strategic points where there is an intense flow of sea traffic. Equipped with the latest ship positioning and monitoring technology (Radar, ARPA, a communications network, radiogoniometer, etc.) this should, in our understanding, be part of a possible network of remote stations which could monitor any vessel approaching the coast. Many of them would not need to cover great distances, just short distances to monitor the ships before any illegal persons disembarked, or any drugs or contraband was unloaded, thereby being able to alert the security forces in the area.

It is clear that the two aforementioned functions of the DGMM and SASEMAR would cover both the land and sea-based aspects where a ship or vessel was the common denominator, an element little understood by land-based authorities, much in the same way the maritime authorities know little about jurisdictions on land. We believe that a country in today's world cannot afford to do without support, especially support that is already available, if it wants to achieve its crime prevention objectives in its fight against all types of crime. Responsibilities and jurisdictions should not be cause for discrepancy between both areas, especially when the maritime side is complying with its responsibility for inspections and monitoring of ships (SASEMAR for those in passage and DGMM for those in ports, whether moored or anchored) in compliance with the regulations established by international organisations, among them the IMO, which basically consist of collaborating in warning the corresponding police authorities about any irregularities.

The recent IMO resolution A.872 (20) dated 28.11.97 details regulations for the prevention and suppression of the illegal traffic of drugs, psychotropic substances and chemical products in ships dedicated to international maritime transport. Although the resolution is essentially international, it has been agreed that it could also be applied to other types of navigation, including that between peninsular ports and the Balearic Islands, the Canary Islands, Ceuta and Melilla.

The LPEMM,[10] article 66.1, regarding the concept of port services, states that port services are those services designed to meet the objectives assigned the port authorities by the Port Law and which are

---

[10] Ley de Puertos del Estado y Marina Mercante (Law on State Ports and the Merchant Navy)

carried out on its territory. The following, among others, are obliged to be considered as such: surveillance and security services and port police, as well as those services provided by the Home Office or other government organisations.

Section 2 of the additional 4th regulation, deals with inter-ministry collaboration, explicitly stating that the Public Works and Transport Ministry[11] can request the collaboration of the Home Office Maritime Services[12] when required for the general needs of shipping, the safety and security of people and property, or for maritime transport.

---

[11] Today the Ministry of Development.

[12] Today the Home Office Maritime Service is the Civil Guard Maritime Service

10 The human factor as the cause of a crisis

This chapter deals with aspects and peculiarities of human behaviour, as it is human behaviour which conditions the way people relate to each other and the experiences they have, as well as acting as a trigger to a crisis, or resolving it efficiently and effectively.

In a confrontation between parties (i.e. between passengers themselves, or between passengers and crew), either one can be the first to cause disruption, with an initial intervention being made or not by the crew members responsible for control. These crew members must, however, intervene at some point and ensure the incident is peacefully resolved. During this phase or period, the analytical capacity for identifying the situation and possible behaviour of the persons involved (in order to provide the correct response and control the incident) can come from the inherent ability of the people in charge themselves, (although it is impossible to be able to deal with all the possible incidents that come under the term *security*), or from the use of techniques and procedures whose efficiency has been more than proven and which are used by experts in the field.

10.1 Personality

A common way of speaking about personality is to associate it with someone having a certain social attractiveness. People say that someone has *personality* or *has a big personality*, meaning that they have a certain social attractiveness, possess outstanding qualities which make them shine above all others, or that they have characteristics such as self-confidence, kindness, being good with people, etc. It is quite normal, therefore, that we all aspire to *have personality*. Although it is not far from the psychological concept of personality, this is a colloquial, not a scientific definition. We are going to look at how personality is really related to a person's qualities and how it affects what others think of us.

An person is made up of several dimensions (somatic, neurological, affective, temperamental, motivational, and experience and education) and shows itself in a person's way of thinking, feeling and expressing him or herself and in their attitudes, habits and behaviour.

Personality and character are terms that are frequently used interchangeably, but they are not the same. Whilst personality is the outer self that others see, character defines the beliefs of the inner self which determines behaviour and makes decisions.

Below are three recognised definitions of personality:

1. It is the collection of structural properties and dynamics of a person which organises human experience and shapes a person's actions and reactions to their surroundings. [Pervin].

2. It is the collection of relatively stable and permanent aspects of a person which distinguishes them from all others and, at the same time, forms the basis of our predictions in relation to future conduct. [Wright].

3. It is the dynamic organisation, within a person, of all the psychological systems that determine their behaviour and characteristic think. [Allport][1].

10.1.1 Three aspects of personality

A) Personality is a collection of elements which make up the person and act as their own individual stamp. This is what we could call, in keeping with some of the authors writing on the subject, *temperament* or personal style. It is what shines through us and is observed and perceived by others.

B) Personality is also the way a person responds to stimuli and circumstances in life, in other words, to their surroundings. It is formed, above all, by the people they live with and interact with in all kinds of relationships, but also by things such as the place where they live, their work, etc.

C) Personality is the collection of mental functions which all people have and which result in certain behaviour or conduct: reactions to stimuli.

10.1.2 The structure and function of personality

Personality has a structure and that is how it is understood and explained in the different schools of psychology. Each one of them does, however, give a different explanation:

a) The somatic dimension:

- Morphological: size, weight, skeletal and muscular structure, etc.
- Physiological: pulse, breathing, hormonal aspects, etc.

b) Neurological dimensions

This refers to the central nervous system (CNS) and how it works. This system is a fundamental part of each person and absolutely decisive in their mental life. It is the centre of certain important aspects such as thought, memory and reception. The whole of a person's mental life is, in general, ruled by the supercomputer that is the brain.

c) The cognitive dimension.

---

[1] His contributions are the first humanist theories that influenced many others, including Nelly, Maslow and Rogers (Montezuma, Indiana in 1897, Cambridge, Massachussets in 1967).

This includes everything that has to do with thought, perception, memory and attention. They are social, cognitive (from cognition/knowledge) processes, and distinguish human beings from other animals. Linked to this is everything that has to do with any form of human learning such as, for example, learning to drive a car or what readers are doing as they read this: learning a subject.

d) The affective dimension

This is to do with feelings and emotions in general. All feelings and emotions are expressed in types of behaviour, actions and reactions; they are life experiences that a person has which, on the one hand, depend (in their expression) on what a person is like and, on the other hand, help to make a person how they are. A person becomes emotional or feels depending on the kind of person they are, but the collection of emotions as a whole also makes a person what they are, for example, calm to a greater or lesser extent, more or less in control in a crisis situation, etc.

e) The temperament dimension

This refers to certain dispositions, linked to our physical make-up (biotype), which lead a person to act in a specific way (psychotype). Since the times of ancient Greece (Plato and others) the diversity of human temperaments has been discussed. People were categorised into groups according to their different types of behaviour. Everybody has heard of someone being described as having a nervous disposition, or having a phlegmatic, choleric or sanguine temperament. Many other writers on the subject have established different classifications of temperament, although it cannot be denied that each person has certain predispositions or tendencies to act in one way or another. In any case, it is a variable which needs to be taken into account when discussing personality as a whole, based on a biopsychic unit, the symbiosis of soma (body) and psyche (mind) which makes up every human being.

f) The motivational dimension

This includes the driving forces behind human behaviour. Different types of behaviour are always motivated by something, there are reasons for the behaviour. Among these motivators, the following stand out:

• *Needs*: organic, social, etc. Needs must be acted on or an imbalance is created. For example, thirst and hunger, or, among the social needs, the need for human relationships.

• *Interests*: these are focal points for our attention and our behaviour. We guide ourselves, and we tend to do the things we are interested in. This explains pastimes, hobbies, cultural pursuits, etc.

• *Attitudes*: These are the positions we take, when confronted by important aspects of life, which affect and explain our behaviour. They are related to behavioural habits. Political, social and religious attitudes can be said to explain our position and behaviour in these areas.

g) The experience and learning dimension

This is made up of a collection of learning processes (in any area) and of experiences (of all kinds) that a person has accumulated over time. Together they make up a person's knowledge and form an integral part of themselves. This includes education (family and school), influences from different people, experiences with people, things and situations, problems or crises which have been resolved or not, etc. These include the learning processes a person has been through and which have constituted their education, in the widest sense of the word. It is hardly surprising it is said that each person is a story in themselves. A human being is a being in evolution, and the different stages and learning processes have gone through, as well as the experiences they have had, all form part of their personality.

10.1.3 Personality theories

Human behaviour is complex and not determined by one factor alone, but by a complex network of factors. This explains why there are so many widely different concepts surrounding the human personality. Psychologists have established several behaviour observation systems, with different instruments of measurement and different scientific starting points, and these have given rise to the various theories about personality. Regarding our subject, the most relevant and useful are:

A) *Personality type theories*

> The main representative in this field is Sheldon [Sheldon]. His theory is based on the hypothesis that there is a link between the somatotype and the psychotype of a person. The somatotype represents physical structure and this author gives three basic types: the endomorph (plump), the mesomorph (muscular) and the ectomorph (slight). Each person tends towards one of these somatic types, although there are no pure types; a person has a greater proportion of one or another.

To correspond to the three somatypes, three psychotypes, or psychological types, were established.

He therefore established the viscerotonic type (the endomorph), people characterised by their love of physical pleasures and comfort, their enjoyment of other people and by their even character; the somatotonic type, related to bodily movement, a love of action and adventure, and self-confidence; and the cerebrotoninc type (ectomorph), characterised by social inhibition, a heightened state of self-awareness and chronic fatigue.

B) *Personality trait theory*

> A person's personality traits belong to them only and are permanent characteristics, underlying a person's behaviour. It is behaviour that leads us to discover a person's traits, as the behaviour depends on them. These traits, as well as human behaviour, are structured hierarchically.

The main representative of this theory is Eysenck [Eysenck][2] The theory fundamentally establishes two main dimensions of personality: extroversion-introversion and neuroticism-stability.

Extroverts are sociable, prefer to be kept busy and are impulsive. Carefree and altruistic, extroverts likes change, have mood swings and do not control their feelings well. Introverts are calm, introspective people and are more distant when it comes to personal relationships. They plan things in advance and do not like excitement. They take life seriously and control their feelings well. They are reliable, rather pessimistic and ethical criteria are of great importance to them. It is rare to find a person that is an extreme case of either of these two opposing types, it is more normal for a person to be found somewhere between the two. Most people are neither totally introvert nor totally extrovert, although they do tend towards one or the other.

---

[2] H.J. Eysenck (Berlin, 4.3.16 / London 4.9.97)

The trait of neuroticism is similar to emotional instability. Persons at this end of the scale are prone to anxiety, are easily perturbed, often have headaches and have problems sleeping or with food. At the opposite end of the scale is emotional stability.

Personality factors are not directly inherited, but each person does inherit a nervous system which makes them more or less likely to develop one way or the other. This predisposition and the interaction of a person with their environment throughout their life determine the final configuration of their personality.

10.1.4 A sound, mature and fulfilled personality

A. A sound personality is really an ideal. It may never be fully achieved, but it can be striven for through constant effort, learning and self-criticism. A person with a model, sound personality would have the following characteristics, recognisable in their actions and behaviour:

    a) These people know themselves well. They know their abilities and limitations and know how to live with them.

    b) Their needs and satisfactions or achievements are well-balanced, meaning they do not experience permanent inner conflict. They are at peace with themselves and this produces a feeling of inner happiness.

    c) They are productive and know how to channel their worries through the correct channels of activity and rest, managing them well.

    d) They have satisfactory relationships with others in their family, workplace and in general social environments.

At the opposite end of the scale to this model image there are many types of personality which are not sound for many different reasons, and this leads to difference or instability. It is important to remember that there is no correlation between this and a person's level of intellect. A person can be very intelligent, and even successful (in the artistic, political, social field, etc.), and still be unbalanced personality-wise, lacking a sound personality.

On the other hand, there are also people with a lot less talent or less education who are totally balanced, self-confident and who feel happy, and all of this is shown in their behaviour.

B. The term maturity or maturing is applied to personality in the same way as it is applied to cheese and biological processes. It is important to remember that not all people mature in the same way, at the same rate or at the same age. When we detect an inadequate correlation between the chronological age of a subject and what is considered to be psychologically "normal" for someone that age, then we talk about an immature personality. The traits or criteria for maturity are the following, according to the most representative authors in the field (Allport, Maslow[3]):

    e) The extension of the self. This means having independent interests of one's own, with the ability to be strict with oneself and to put effort into every task or activity that is of value. It involves having goals in life and setting oneself objectives to be reached. It means being able to love, to be intimate with another person and to respect the dignity of everyone else.

---

[3] Abraham Maslow (Brooklyn 1.4.1908, California 8.6.1970)

f)   Self-objectification. This is the same as realism when understanding oneself and others, when setting oneself goals and when making judgements or evaluations. It includes sense of humour and is an adult way of being realistic and objective about things.

g)   Philosophy of life. This refers to a way of understanding and channelling one's own existence, thereby creating emotional stability. Having such a philosophy means a person tolerates well the inevitable frustrations that life throws us all and can freely express their beliefs and feelings. They have the characteristic of spontaneity, which is synonymous to simplicity, naturalness, unaffectedness and a lack of falseness in behaviour.

h)   Independence, both on physical and social level. This ensures a person can keep calm, in control and relatively happy in circumstances which would make other people vulnerable or bring them down.

i)   Close interpersonal relationships and a greater capacity to identify with others.

j)   A love of life in the widest and most profound sense.

An immature personality, on the other hand, tends to have several or all of the following traits:

a)   Superficial or incorrect understanding of self
b)   Incoherent reasoning
c)   Poorly defined or non-existent goals in life
d)   Little emotional stability
e)   Intolerance of frustration
f)   Difficulties in giving and receiving love
g)   Lack of emotional control
h)   Inconsistency from lacking a true philosophy of life
i)   Frequent intolerant and inflexible behaviour
j)   Highly influenced by the opinions of others
k)   The present is almost all that matters
l)   A tendency to act on impulse (I do what I want)
m) Lack of responsibility and will-power
n)   Difficulty in accepting who they are, accepting others and accepting the realities of life in general
o)   Tendency to escape from the real world via the imagination, through a fantasy world
p)   Lack of autonomy and independence

C.   We say a person is fulfilled when they have achieved stability in different areas, managing to (or at least establishing solid groundwork to) satisfy their needs and carry out the majority of their projects. This brings with it the advantages of freedom, independence, control of situations, being well-balanced and finding harmony with the world.

However, fulfilment is quite a subjective concept, as individuals create different goals for themselves and what is an achievement for one may not be enough for another. Personal fulfilment is linked to the concept of vocation, itself synonymous with dedication to a task which gives meaning to life and fulfils it sufficiently.

A fulfilled person is not simply one who has reached a high social or professional status, etc., but one who feels happy with what they are doing, who has positive ambitions that drive them to do better each time, but without comparative anxiety about their destiny. They do not feel responsible for what they consider due to bad luck, unavoidable circumstances, etc.; that is something that is simply *out of their hands*. When we are unable to control behaviour, it is beyond us, out of our reach, we can, and generally do, experience frustration, blamelessness, depression, etc. if, on the other hand, we see an event as depending on us, on how we are, on our behaviour, we internalise the control and then feel responsible for the event.

All this is related to the so-called *attribution theory*. Whatever happens to us we attribute it to something. And this attribution is sometimes wrong. It is wrong, for example, to attribute a failure to personal reasons (individuals tend to be quick to blame themselves) when the mistake was made by another or is due to inevitable circumstances. It is also wrong to for a student, for example, to blame the strictness of the teacher, or bad luck, for failure when it is actually down to their not having studied enough. It is often the case that a person involved in an accident will consider circumstances, rather than their own negligence or imprudence, to have been the cause. At the same time, if that person blames the accident on another person, they will attribute it to mistakes made by the other driver rather than to circumstances.

A person who has good self-control is one who is able to attribute causes or motives correctly to facts, and these causes may sometimes be found within ourselves, sometimes outside of ourselves and, sometimes, in both places. A person with good self-control knows how to distinguish, in each case, where their behaviour originated. That person is also one who will particularly try to control what affects them from the inside, from their inner self.

10.1.5 The theory of self

The main representative for this theory is C. Rogers [Rogers]. The theory is based on a belief in man whom it considers deep down is always moving in the direction of progress and maturity. A normal person (as opposed to a neurotic one who acts on irrational and aggressive impulses) is free to live and fulfil their basic nature which makes them a social being, worthy of trust and constructive.

The key concept is the *self*. Man tends to work towards self-fulfilment driven by a basic impulse. People tend to move from dependence to independence, from inflexibility to change, from fixed ideas to free expression and creativity. Self-awareness is also important as is congruence between the self and experience, a characteristic which defines a psychologically healthy person. This consists of knowing oneself well and being consistent as regards what one is and what one does.

Rogers view is clearly optimistic and is based on a person getting used to and accepting themselves, blindly trusting their possibilities. This can clearly be applied to education and therapy.

A) Psychoanalytical theories

The various theories derived from those of S. Freud are based on childhood experiences and, particularly, on an individual's relationship with their mother. They define the personality of a person as positive (adequate development) or negative (illnesses, psychological problems). A person's actions are spurred by conscious and unconscious motives with the following psychological layers or strata being distinguishable in every person: Id, Ego and Superego.

The success of a mature and balanced personality involves the triumph of the Ego over the impulsive requirements of the Id and the censorship of the Superego. It consists of gaining areas of consciousness and in overcoming the many conflicts and vicissitudes that the libido (erotic force or instinct) experiences throughout the different stages of the development of the personality.

B) The developmental theory of Erikson [Erikson]

A person's personality is never finished, it is always being developed. This development happens over a series of ever-increasing consecutive phases. Each phase represents a critical moment which the person deals with more, or less, satisfactorily. If dealt with favourably, it makes access to the next phase easier, whilst if dealt with in a negative manner, it compromises the person's ability to confront later phases and, therefore, makes general development more difficult.

According to this author there are two basic suppositions underlying the development phases:

> - Personality is developed in accordance with the increasing capacity of the person to interact with their surroundings.
> - Society invites everybody to make this interaction.

A healthy personality is one where a person is in control of their surroundings, has integrated all the elements of it well and is realistic in terms of the self and the world.

10.2 Medical profiles for human response

A. *The neurotic*. With neurosis, a person has a large *superego*. They are very repressed, they are not generally criminals, and they have a very high regard for morals and ethics. This person is paralysed by rules and regulations and this creates anxiety and depression.

B. *The psychopath*. The absolute opposite of the above. In a psychopath the *id* is predominate, causing them to act impulsively, without thinking. They do not even take morals into consideration; they feel no guilt and do not differentiate between right and wrong. They mix socially with both women and men, they spend a lot of money, they do not think before acting and they are unpredictable. It is important not to confuse the psychopath with the psychotic. This is an antisocial personality disorder, but a sense of reality is maintained.

C. *The psychotic*. The psychotic loses the sense of reality. With the *ego* distorted, this person is mentally insane. They are incoherent and a delirious or have hallucinations.

10.2.1 Anxiety neurosis

Anxiety is an emotional state with many aspects and which manifests itself in many different ways. It is one of the most common emotional disorders.

Only man is capable of planning for the distant future, thanks to the mental capacity of anticipation. For this reason only man can experience anxiety. Anxiety accompanies intellectual activity and curiosity as the shadow accompanies the body.

The inherent nature of life today is a source of anxiety. Man is constantly striving to find himself. His future is limited by the undeniable fact of his imminent death. For this reason we constantly move from our future to the past, from anticipation and plans to memories, longing and regrets, and all this is tainted with anxiety. Only man can make decisions, and each decision involves a risk. We are constantly surrounded by uncertainty and are overwhelmed by it. Therefore, anxiety is essentially the fearful anticipation of danger.

Anxiety normally resides in our unconscious and does not enter our consciousness until we know what we are afraid of and are experiencing fear itself. For example, an unexpected danger causes a normal state of anxiety. If the danger is real, and we cannot act efficiently, we feel fear. This tension then becomes a normal anxiety. Anxiety can also be produced by a feeling of absolute isolation, of separation and of exclusion from the normal run of things. Anxiety can also reflect a fear of being destroyed, with no possible way on defending oneself. This is a neurotic attitude in that it lacks a definite something to adhere to. It is the fear of the unknown and the incognisable, of the unusual, the undefined, the mysterious. This disagreeable state creates a feeling of impotence, as there is no specific way to react to an unknown danger.

Anxiety is the universal phenomenon of our era. Hand in hand with anxiety go feelings of insecurity and uncertainty with regard to the future. Normal anxiety keeps us vigilant and aware of the problems we have to face. However, this becomes a worrying and damaging phenomenon when it keeps coming back time and time again at inopportune moments.

Anxiety frequently causes unpleasant and painful physical sensations. The most common are: difficulty breathing, pain around the heart, palpitations, dizziness, increased perspiration, general weakness and tiredness, stomach pains and cramps, and migraines.

An anxious person will complain of the fear of an indescribable danger, the fear of an imminent illness, irritability, insomnia, restlessness, loss of appetite, unclear thought, a feeling of confusion.

The most common signs presented are: cold and clammy hands and feet, dry mouth and lips, a change in pulse rate, a change in blood pressure, tension, immobility and tension in the stomach muscles, irritable bowel and exaggerated reflexes.

10.2.2 Phobias

A phobia is the fear of something which does not really constitute a source of danger, but when the person is faced with it they react with real fear, even though they understand their reaction is inappropriate. A phobia is a persistent fear without foundation, the origin of which has been forgotten,

There are two theories regarding the origin of phobias: the conditioning theory and the dynamic interpretation theory.

    A. According to conditioning theory, phobias are due to a traumatic emotional incident, feelings of guilt, and repression of memories of the experience. Later on disorders surface every time the person finds themselves exposed to the same circumstances as in the original emotional trauma.

    B. The dynamic theory generally maintains that the phobia is a defence mechanism used by the person to relieve themselves of the anxiety produced by an impulse. An unconscious impulse creates an emotional state: the impulse is repressed, but the emotional state continues.

The person tries to give an explanation for their profound emotional stress, and attributes the cause to a particular object, situation or idea. A real situation can be avoided, whereas an impulse is unconscious and cannot be tackled.

Therefore, a person with a phobia gets rid of the anxiety by avoiding certain objects or situations. Anxiety attacks can happen in many situations, and each one of these can help explain the attack. With time, if the attacks continue, the person becomes a prisoner of their own phobia.

In summary, a phobia is a morbid fear provoked by a specific previous experience. It is a defence mechanism to combat severe and permanent anxiety. For example, a man is afraid to use lifts, or to be in closed spaces, etc. In other words, he has claustrophobia, and with the right therapy it may be discovered that the root of the problem lies in his childhood because his father used to punish him by locking him in a dark room. It is quite possible for claustrophobia to appear at the age of 20 or 25 without the subject ever having felt this fear beforehand.

10.2.3 Hysteria

The word hysteria comes from the Greek word votépa, which means uterus. The Greeks believed that this ailment was exclusive to women and was an illness of the womb. The theory lost all credibility during the First World War when many soldiers displayed the typical symptoms of hysteria.

The current understanding of hysteria is that it is a spontaneous, non-premeditated attempt to adapt to problems which are so great that they overwhelm an individual, by fleeing towards incapability.

This loss of function may be physical or psychological. However, it should not be considered as a conscious attempt made to deliberately avoid a situation, or to fake illness, as a person fitting this medical profile is not aware of the true motives which are driving them. The physical symptoms often include paralysis, tics, shakes and spasms. There is also "glove anaesthesia" and "stocking anaesthesia". In these two cases the person loses all feeling either in the hand up to the wrist, or the feet up to the ankle.

With conversion hysteria a person may also experience problems with vision. These problems can range from lesser symptoms such as "tunnel vision", where the patient can only see in a straight line, to total blindness. In some cases, the desire to flee from a situation can provoke memory loss.

One thing worthy of note, and which comes under the umbrella of neurosis, is hypochondria. This is far more prevalent in current society than it is generally believed and can reach a point where it affects activity on board if a passenger suffers from it.

10.2.4 Hypochondria

Today hypochondria is not considered an illness, it is an attitude taken towards illness. A hypochondriac is constantly introspective, worrying over every detail of their bodily functions (digestion, constipation, etc.) and over possible symptoms of illness.

By focussing all their attention on a specific function and emotionally charging it, a hypochondriac can provoke physical changes and create real, functional and organic symptoms due to the psychological impact.

The main symptom of hypochondria is worrying about health. A hypochondriac is constantly thinking about their symptoms, even taking into account signs that we are normally unaware of; the intensity of their heartbeat, pulse, digestive functions, the fact that mineral water helps digestion, the exact temperature which is best for them, etc. they develop a subtle ability to detect their inner bodily functions (cenesthesia).

They will describe their case in detail, describing their symptoms to the doctor and others many times as it is their favourite subject of conversation.

The most typical symptom in cases of hypochondria is self-suggestion. Sufferers experience this along with a negative change in their state of mind, making them phobic towards their pains which they think are always the beginning of serious illnesses. The hypochondriac will end up giving up everything to stay at home with their "illness".

A hypochondriac passenger can cause trouble by constantly asking for things they think they need, even though they will normally have everything already. They will ask for seasick tablets, water, say they do not feel well, etc. On voyages without a doctor on board, this can cause a crisis if they ask for one and find out that the service is not available.

They will demand all our attention, preventing us from carrying out other tasks or tending to other passengers who may need our help, especially in the case of an accident on board.

10.2.5 The psychopath

In reference to the "nature versus nurture" debate, the psychopath is born as such, not made. Jurists do not know how to act when faced with such individuals as there is no treatment for them, the only solution is to deprive them of their freedom because they pose a danger and they are fully aware of what they are doing. They are fully conscious of their actions, and these are premeditated. They never feel remorse. They are very intelligent, they cheat and they seduce their victims. They let themselves be led by what they see, what they feel and what they fancy, for what seems best to them at any given time.

Their main traits are:

- They never commit suicide, they love themselves too much to lose their lives
- They are inconsistent, they do not follow any norms
- They are liars. They fell no guilt or shame
- They do not adapt socially, they are out of place everywhere
- They do not learn from experience, they are insensitive to punishment
- They are egocentric, they only love themselves. They are unable to love, everyone around them is considered trivial. They are promiscuous.
- They do not think about the consequences of their actions, they do not care
- They are always searching for emotions
- They have a tendency to become drug addicts
- They have a lack of respect for authority, they do not pay attention to anybody, only to their instincts
- They are aggressive

More and more we are seeing that the American line is being taken. This makes no distinction between neurotics and psychopaths, referring to them both as personality disorders.

10.2.6 Paranoid personality disorder

A person with a paranoid personality disorder is distrustful, very proud and has great self-esteem. For this reason they are easily humiliated and believe that everybody wants to bring them down. This person should not be confused with a true paranoiac. For example, in a case of jealousy where a man starts following his wife for unfounded reasons, the man with the paranoid personality disorder can be made to see that his suspicions are unjustified; a man with delusional (paranoid) disorder, never. The latter will always believe his own reality. One of the dangers facing a person with a paranoid personality disorder lies in the use of drugs which will only serve to intensify their false beliefs.

10.2.7 Schizoid personality disorder

A person with a schizoid personality disorder is not psychotic, as they do not have hallucinations or delusions. They are emotionally cold, not very expressive and are introverted. They have no social contact, and do not tend to commit crimes because they shut themselves off from the world and do not bother anybody. Here the danger also lies in the use of drugs, as they can cause brief periods of psychosis (toxic psychosis). In other words they can become psychotic (irrational) and can get persecution complexes which can lead them to attack someone out of fear during their psychotic period.

10.2.8 Schitzotypal personality disorder

People with schizotypal personality disorders have a disorder with traits similar to that of the schizophrenic. They are known for their odd ideas, strange feelings and unusual experiences (they believe in aliens, spirits, etc.). They are not usually conflictive and some may experience a schizophrenic episode around the age of 16 or 17. Others do not experience schizophrenia, but they are very strange.

10.2.9 Borderline personality disorder

People with this disorder have a very negative image of themselves. They are unstable, impulsive and always bored. They overcome the feeling of emptiness by eating a lot, with bulimia, alcoholism, etc. When they gamble, they push themselves to the limit. They cannot control their impulses.

10.2.10 Histrionic personality disorder

People with histrionic personality disorders like to be the centre of attention. They are seductive, superficial and use their physical appearance to attract attention. They are theatrical and exaggerated. They often "attempt" suicide to attract attention, as opposed to the depressed person who really does commit suicide.

10.2.11 Narcissistic personality disorder

The narcissist is characterised by feelings of success and by their arrogance. They lie to prove how great they are, they tell tall stories and even believe their own lies. They are pathological liars and believe they are special and unique. For them there the line between fantasy and reality is very unclear. They need to be admired, and they dress in a flamboyant way.

10.2.12 Avoidant personality disorder

People with avoidant personality disorders are pathologically shy. They hide away and are afraid of social contact. They feel other people are not going to like them and are afraid of being criticised. They are hypersensitive. Normally, these are people with issues stemming from a childhood where their parents or tutors valued them very little.

10.2.13 Dependent personality disorder

These people are unable to make their own decisions, preferring others to make the decisions for them, or needing someone to approve the decisions they have made. This is all due to a childhood scarred by an authoritarian mother or father.

10.2.14 Obsessive-compulsive disorder

This is one of the most common disorders and is among the most severe kinds of neurosis. The most obvious characteristic is the search for security. Obsession: a specific idea which can not be put to one side or forgotten about (e.g.: tidiness, cleanliness). Compulsion: behaviour (e.g.: spending).

According to Maslow, "persons with obsessive-compulsive disorder desperately try to order and stabilise their world to avoid the reappearance of uncontrollable, unexpected and undefined dangers. They establish a whole range of rituals, rules and formulas to anticipate any possible incident recurring and to avoid new ones."

In general terms, obsessive-compulsive behaviour is repetitive compulsion. In fact, this characteristic is typical of all neuroses and reflects the inability of the neurotic person to change their behaviour. In a specific sense, the obsessive-compulsive behaviour refers to ritualised activities.

The obsessive-compulsive neurosis includes hand-washing and other senseless ritual behaviour; an obsessive fear of dirt, of germs or of accidentally hurting another person.

These obsessions are generally accompanied by ritualised precautions; hands must be washed a specific number of times a day, objects must be laid out a certain way, etc.

These obsessions and compulsions are attempts at rejecting feelings of guilt provoked by unconscious sexual or aggressive desires, or at correcting or repairing them.

The main aim of the obsessive-compulsive activity is to prevent the appearance of more serious symptoms. Therefore, it can be said that the compulsive neurosis is a secondary line of defence against the activation of repressed material. In other words, the hand-washing ritual is observed or useless things are bought impulsively to avoid the tension which the imbalance produces, to avoid it getting worse. As the imbalance becomes more acute, symptoms characteristic of hysteria, schizophrenia and paranoia, etc. can develop.

The characteristics of obsessive-compulsive neuroses are: compulsive rituals (e.g.: hand-washing ritual), the obsessive fear of dirt and germs (accompanied by cleaning and tidying rituals), the obsessive fear of wounding someone (accompanied by precautionary rituals), the compulsive need to count or repeat certain phrases, the act of deliberating on trivial matters or matters which have nothing to do with the problem in hand, the compulsive need to work or keep busy with a specific activity, compulsive attention to detail, often to the detriment of other more general and more important aspects of the task, the compulsive adherence to demanding rules of work, high morals, or regulations, compulsive pseudo-attempts at suicide, the compulsive tendency to avoid feared situations (crowds for example) or the compulsive fear of certain situations, compulsive habits and mannerisms (tics for example), obsessive hypochondria, the compulsive tendency to avoid people, or obsessive fear of people, the obsessive fear of being poisoned, cheated or attacked, obsessive doubt, vacillation and worry, compulsive sexual behaviour (masturbation for example), compulsive aggressive or emotional outbreaks (anger or quarrelling for example).

10.2.15 The affective disorders

These are alterations in the state of mind of a person, of their mood or other emotions. These include depression, which all human beings can suffer from at some point in their life.

A distinction is made between exogeneous depression and endogenous depression, depending on whether it is caused by something external in relation to the subject, i.e. a death in the family, a bad time in their life, etc., or whether it is not caused by any traumatic event in the subject's life, but rather it is fundamentally due to biochemical alterations in the brain (the first neurotransmitter affected is serotonin).

In certain situations mood changes constitute illnesses as the tonality of mood is pathologically altered, for example, if sadness is persistent it is defined as *dysthymia*; on other occasions the mood swings are frequent, easily passing from euphoria to depression, and this is *cyclothymia*.

Deep depression alternating with bouts of manic exaltation is known as manic-depressive psychosis.

10.2.16 Manic-depressive psychosis

Given that happiness and pain are clear and important aspects in human life, it is hardly surprising that their opposing pathologies, mania and melancholy, were among the first mental symptoms discovered by medical scholars.

There is no doubt that both the manic and depressive conditions can co-exist within the same person, although that does not mean that one is always followed by the other. In some cases of depression the tendency to enter a manic phase is not observed, and in others the manic condition is the only symptom and is not complicated by a depressive condition.

Depressive or manic disorders can be suffered singly, whether manic or depressive episodes, or mixed (bipolar), bouts of depression alternating with other bouts of mania.

This is an illness which appears cyclically. Each phase lasts several months and when the depressive or manic episode ends, the patient returns to normal without any kind of mental deterioration.

It tends to appear a little later than schizophrenia, around the ages of 25-30 years. The illness affects 1% of the population. There is a hereditary factor which influences its appearance; if one of a child's parents suffers from it then the child has a 23 % chance of inheriting it.

There are also biochemical reasons for the illness. Alterations in the neurotransmitters in the brain have been discovered where levels of serotonin are very low. In such cases, anti-depressants which increase levels of serotonin in the brain improve the symptoms. A general decrease in hormone levels is also observed in the thyroid, gonadal and suprarenal glands.

10.2.17 Mania

During the manic phase of manic-depressive psychosis, the patient experiences the overwhelming urge to keep moving (hyperactivity). They cannot relax or stay still, not even for a moment. They have racing thoughts (taquipsidia: quickness of thought), which are immediately acted on.

If the person has not been not hospitalised, it is probable that they are running several businesses at the same time, are involved in two or three romantic affairs and, in general, that they are whipped up in a whirlwind of hyperactivity.

They spend a lot of money, which sometimes they do not even have; some even spend all their family's wealth.

Exaltation in every sense of the word: sexual impulses and needs are very high; they want to go out, to drink, to gamble, etc. They self-esteem is very high and they have feelings of grandeur.

Due to their profusion of ideas, there is an uninhibited verbal flow. If asked a question, the patient will be able to reply correctly, but the fleeting thoughts and reactions to external situations will soon make them go off on a tangent from the original answer until they find themselves tied up in a confusion of their own ideas. They will commit sexual indiscretions or make indiscreet or outrageous proposals.

They have insomnia and do not feel tired. They can stay awake for days and be fully functional and active throughout.

They hardly ever finish their sentences and the mere sound of words can cause them to recite and create rhymes in the form of one word repeated tirelessly. In many ways manic patients are similar to a person who is drunk. They can be happy and in a good mood one minute and angry and hostile the next. Perception is generally lacking or faulty.

10.2.18 Major depression

In the depressive phase the opposite condition to mania is observed, this includes hypoactivity, lack of initiative and energy, and a general depressed attitude are common symptoms of this aspect of the psychosis.

They feel sad and cry easily. They experience a loss of hope and are not interested in anything. Apathy. They lose their self-esteem. Sexual inhibition. Thoughts of catastrophe.

Many patients complain about their inability to think and concentrate. They lose the power to express themselves and the ability to conceive ideas. When they are asked a question they answer correctly, but very slowly, carefully and deliberately.

Whilst they are in this depressive state, many patients consider suicide is the only way out. They do not expect anything from life, they are useless beings, or they have sinned, or they are somehow responsible for the suffering they see in the world.

Many people with major (chronic) depression end up committing suicide. This is endogenous depression which, as previously explained, is caused by very low levels or a lack of serotonin.

Patients are normally prescribed drugs which contain lithium (discovered by the Romans who ate oysters to combat despondency and sadness because of their high lithium content), which raises these serotonin levels.

Anti-depressant drugs, Prozac, etc.

There is another form of suicide, known as *extended suicide or suicide through compassion*, which statistically occurs every so often throughout the world and in very different places. It refers to seriously depressed individuals who see things negatively not only for themselves, but they also see a negative future for their spouse and children. For this reason, and to avoid future suffering, they kill their closest family members and then commit suicide themselves.

10.3 Occupational stress

This is basically the effect of a lack of the balance needed between perceived requirements and the perceived capacity of an individual. It also refers to an imbalance between external requirements and the capacity of the person to deal with them.

The greatest level of *stress* that can be reached is caused by an external situation which implies a threat to person's life (or that of those close to them) and produces physiological, psychological, behavioural and social changes.

THE CHANGES
VARY FROM
PERSON TO
PERSON,
DEPENDING ON ...

THE SUBJECTIVE PERCEPTION OF THE
SERIOUSNESS OF THE THREAT

HOW CLOSE THE
DANGER IS

EXPERIENCE

KNOWLEDGE AND AWARENESS
OF ABILITIES

However, the *stress* accumulated on a daily basis, such as that produced by demands at work, can be devastating. For this reason it is very important that it is dealt with properly. If we want the crew to have a good relationship with the passengers and also be able to establish a clear leadership to control the public in an emergency situation, then their levels of activity must be kept far from dangerous levels.

Crew members are not machines. For them to be effective in a crisis situation, they must first deal with their own fears and control their emotional stress levels. If these levels are already routinely high, then it will be much more difficult for them to control them in an emergency situation.

10.3.1 Concepts related to occupational stress

These concepts have to do with a person's work itself, i.e. conflicting roles, the ambiguity of their role, work overload, underload (a low level of activity) and psychological changes.

They are related to an individual's function, threats to their person, physical working conditions, and personal characteristics.

They can be external factors: stigma/stereotypes, the press, legal aspects, conflicts, family or work.

They can be internal factors relating to the company: bad training, interpersonal relationships, competition, lack of integration, salary, bureaucracy, cutbacks.

Crew members cannot always leave their problems outside the ship, they take them on board, they live with them and they are conditioned by their consequences in many areas of their personality. For example, below is a list of events which produce certain amounts of stress according to several surveys.

Event	Stress level
Death of spouse	100
Divorce	73
Death of a close relative	63
Serious illness or physical injury	53
Marriage	50
Dismissal or stopping work	47
Illness or change in health status	44
Pregnancy	40
Sexual problems	39
Change of workplace	39
Change in economic status / level of income	38
Change of field of work	36
Change in habits / arguments between spouses	35
Change in responsibilities at work	29
Personal success	28
Starting or ending a job (spouse)	26
Starting or ending studies	26
Change in standard of living	25
Change in personal habits	24
Problems with the boss	23
Change in working conditions or hours	20
Moving house	20
Change in holiday habits	19
Change in sleeping habits	16
Change in frequency of family visits	15
Change in eating habits	15
Getting ready for a holiday	13
Christmas	12
"Minor" law offences	11

As can be seen, the majority of the causes to come out of this large survey are synonymous to changes in a person's life. Even changes which are considered happy events are thought of as stressful.

A stressful situation suffered by the crew can be faced successfully, or ignored, and in both cases there are generally no symptoms. However, when one fails, the following appear:

1. *Physical symptoms*: tachycardia, palpitations, high blood pressure, difficulty breathing, headaches, gastritis, diarrhoea, constipation, muscular pain.

2. *Psychological symptoms*: aggressiveness, irritability, anxiety, fear, depression, difficulty concentrating, fatigue.

3. *Changes in behaviour*: changes in sleep patterns, changes in sexual behaviour, changes in appetite (anorexia, bulimia), drug use.

10.4 Handling and prevention

When faced with the appearance of one of these disorders, the crew member (if possible with the aid of a medical or psychology professional) should evaluate all the generating factors to try and discover which of these is producing the imbalance. The isolated situation of the ship during a long voyage should also be taken into consideration. Resistance needs to be improved via relaxation techniques and training on problem solving, which are currently the most commonly used methods.

10.4.1 Critical situations

35% of male and 25% of female crew members on passenger ships have found themselves in a situation where their lives were in danger. Anxiety was obviously higher in people who have experienced such situations. This data refers to crew members with more than 10 years experience and thousands of sailing hours.

10.4.2 Comments

The fact that fear and anxiety exist on board is a reality that we must all regard as something normal, something physiological, especially when there is cause for it or an incident has taken place, a rough sea, for example. The problem becomes serious when there is anxiety but no reason for it, when it is disproportionate or when it is in anticipation of something (the mere thought of boarding the next day made him anxious).

The crew members, and passengers, should be given more information about how the ship works and, especially, about its structure and how resistant it is to stormy weather or adverse weather conditions. Better training, including group emergency training and training in communications techniques, to increase the feeling of trust between the bridge, the engine room crew and the crew most in contact with the passengers. This will help create good relationships between all the groups on board. There should be improved prevention measures applied, including a better selection process, better diagnoses and a better rehabilitation process (obviously the work of a psychologists if possible). Any crew members showing signs of anxiety in relation to the ship should be trained in relaxation techniques and should undergo the correct treatment.

10.5 Intoxication from alcohol or drugs

The effects of excessive doses of different substances given the generic name of 'drugs' (including ethylic alcohol) on the central nervous system and other organs of the body are very complex and to a great extent unknown. It is quite normal for any (intentional) intoxication on board to be produced by a variety of substances with different effects, and this complicates diagnosis and treatment enormously.

10.5.1 Alcohol

The term alcohol is used a synonym for ethanol or ethylic alcohol, which is a substance found in alcoholic drinks. The consumption of a greater quantity than the body is able to eliminate (30 ml per hour) produces clearly recognisable signs: slurred speech, difficulty with movements, double vision, changes in behaviour with acts of aggression and, often, with social inhibitions, dizziness, etc. sleepiness is gradually added to these symptoms and, if consumption is continued or the alcohol continues to be absorbed through the stomach, this can easily lead to a coma.

The methods for handling an individual with ethylic intoxication essentially depend on the seriousness of the patient's condition, i.e. their level of consciousness.

If the patient has not lost consciousness, it is advisable to induce vomiting with the normal procedures, to avoid more ethanol being absorbed. The patient should then be kept warm and made to rest as time is the best healer in these cases. A patient should never be put in a cold or luke-warm bath, nor should they be given analgesics, vitamins or tranquilisers, etc.

When the patient is in a coma they should be sent to hospital, making sure all the while that their tongue does not block their airway and that they do not choke on their own vomit.

Alcohol withdrawal symptoms may start early on and be not too serious, or start later and be more serious: *delirium tremens*. These generally include signs of agitation, with sweating, tachycardia, nausea, vomiting, irritability, nervousness, anxiety and insomnia. Sedatives can be used to handle the patient until they can be handed over to a doctor or hospital.

Intoxication by alcohol should never be considered just a police matter: it is a health problem which can be very serious. Intoxication by alcohol is very frequent, but is by no means the only drug responsible for all afflictions of consciousness.

10.5.2 Opiates

With intoxication produced by the most widely used drug in drug abuse, heroin or "horse", the most normal symptom is a profound sleepiness and stupor; if it is impossible to wake someone up then we must consider them to be in a coma. On opening the eyes of the patient, the small size of the pupils (myosis) is obvious. This also tends to be accompanied by bradypnea which can, occasionally, be intense (4 – 5 cycles / minute).

These three symptoms (coma or sleepiness, myosis and bradypnea) are almost exclusive to a heroin overdose and require urgent medical intervention.

In addition to these symptoms, the following can also be observed: cyanosis of the hands, lips, ears and feet, hypothermia and major muscle relaxation.

On many occasions the patient dies suddenly, especially when the dose administered was particularly high. The cause of death in this case is usually respiratory failure, and the consequent lack of oxygen in tissue.

Patients must be moved urgently to hospital with oxygen therapy and life support measures, especially respiratory support.

In cases of abstinence, the first symptoms may appear six hours after the last dose of heroin. These symptoms include anxiety, insomnia, rhinorrhea, watery eyes, sweating, shivers, goose pimples. In these cases sedatives may be used to control patients until they reach the hospital, but always under strict medical control.

10.5.3 Amphetamines

These drugs are very popular as memory stimulants and appetite suppressants, but they can very harmful in cases of overdose, although it is normal that this only happens towards the beginning of the addiction.

Intoxicated patients are sweaty in appearance, agitated, they have the shakes (generally a fine tremor), they are irritable, and they say they can see, hear and touch objects, animals or people which do not exist.

They are normally confused and are frequently dizzy and complain of pain, especially chest pain, and palpitations. When the patient is examined, they very often have high blood pressure and an irregular heartbeat. In serious cases they may have a fever and experience convulsions.

These symptoms will require the patient to be transferred to a specialised centre where they can be sedated, normally with tranquilisers, and have their heart rate monitored, as the arrhythmia can have serious consequences.

The patient should not be moved forcefully, unless it is by experienced personnel, as the patient may suffer a crisis comprising agitated movement and severe aggressiveness, which could compromise the physical well-being of the patient and the persons attempting to move them.

10.5.4 Cocaine

This central nervous system stimulant is, perhaps, the drug which has most increased in use in recent years, probably due to the popular belief that chronic use of the drug causes few problems.

Several cases have been reported of the deaths, on board ship, of people carrying bags of cocaine inside their bodies (body packers). In these cases the bags have suddenly broken, causing a fatal intoxication by cocaine. Today, apart from the serious damage that the drug can cause having been absolutely proven, it is perfectly well-known that an overdose via inhalation (sniffing) or the intravenous use of the drug can have serious consequences. In fact, many deaths attributed to an overdose of heroin are actually due to an overdose of cocaine.

Acute intoxication produces symptoms similar to those described in the case of amphetamines, with the most notable being agitation, euphoria, strange sensations of touch including intense itchiness, and the feeling they have bugs on their skin, a sensation which leads the patient to constantly touch, pinch or scratch different parts of their body. An irregular heartbeat and convulsions are very frequent symptoms.

The treatment process in these cases is similar to that described in the case of the amphetamines. It is important to move the patient to a centre where they will receive the correct treatment, avoiding the use of force where possible.

10.5.5 Barbiturates and anxiolytics

As with an overdose of opiates, an overdose produced by barbiturates has an equally serious prognosis. When the intoxication is only slight, the symptoms may be indistinguishable from that of ethylic intoxication, except for the absence of previous alcohol consumption and the typical smell on the breath.

In more serious cases, the most obvious symptom is a loss of level of consciousness, with tiredness and confusion that can alternate with phases of irritation, especially when the patient is stimulated. In these phases the pupils may be small.

If the drug continues to penetrate the intoxicated person's blood, the level of consciousness is reduced even more coupled with the appearance of bradypnea and the resulting cyanosis of the hands, feet and face, and a drop in blood pressure and body temperature.

The treatment for this type of overdose should always be carried out in a hospital but, in the meantime, the usual life support measures should be taken.

10.5.6 Cannabis

This term includes all preparations of the product (marihuana, ganja, hashish, hash oil, etc.). An acute intoxication produces symptoms of a stimulated nervous system, hallucinations and delusions, with feelings of fear or panic, confusion, disorientation in space and time, and agitation. A certain increase in heartbeat may also be observed, with redness of the eyes being another typical symptom. These symptoms do not normally require immediate treatment; it will be sufficient to ensure that the patient rests with the least number of stimuli present possible.

10.5.7 LSD (Lysergic acid diethylamide)

This substance is one of the most used hallucinogens. An acute intoxication produces a large variety of symptoms, including visual hallucinations, temporal disorientation, dilation of the pupils, profuse sweating, increased blood pressure and heartbeat, as well as an increase in the number and depth of breaths taken, hair standing on end, nausea, vomiting and a very dry mouth.

Without any previously known predisposition, it is possible that the overdose leads to fear, terror or a panic attack and aggressive reactions, especially aggression aimed at the self, resulting in self-harming and suicide attempts.

The treatment here needs to psychotherapeutic, based on calming the patient down and placing them (without using any force whatsoever) in a place where there are as few stimuli as possible and which is accepted by the patient.

Generally, drugs overdoses require the attention of a doctor who should determine the severity and decide on whether the patient should be admitted to hospital. Of all the different types of intoxication, only those produced by heroin, barbiturates and cocaine, if they are severe, require the urgent removal of the patient to hospital and the use of aggressive cardiorespiratory resuscitation measures.

In the rest of cases, just trying to keep the patient calm and avoiding them hurting themselves or others is sufficient. In these phases recriminations obviously have very little therapeutic value and can even be harmful.

10.6 Panic and its effects. Fear and anxiety

At this point it is advisable for us to distinguish between two concepts which are related to each other, but which are not exactly the same and which show themselves in different psychological ways:

a)   Anxiety: This is an unpleasant emotional reaction to an imminent, although not necessarily specific, danger. The anxiety is noticed above all in changes or signs of a physiological nature. For example, sweating, change in heartbeat, tightness in the stomach or chest, "a knot in the throat", etc. A kind of paralysis is produced in the person who becomes afraid.

Anxiety is noticed most of all in the area or field of psychology. It comprises a collection of sensations, vague to a greater or lesser extent, of something unpleasant, of defencelessness, of tension, of a threat to the subject, even with the possibility they will die. Fright and worry are predominant here rather than paralysis, so the person will tend not to be able to stay still and to show general agitation, etc.

When the anxiety attack increases progressively with nothing to stop it, a panic situation is reached. Before it reaches this extreme there tends to be an increase in symptoms and subjective situations which could be summarised in the following way: violent heartbeats which beat the chest and have repercussions in the neck and head until the first panic is experienced. The subject believes this is a heart attack and thinks about death. This fear increases and new feelings and symptoms appear such as dizziness, a feeling of suffocation, and loss of balance. They endure truly horrific moments and do not know whether to run, flee or shout. If they are medically examined, for example in accident and emergency, they normally leave feeling relieved to find there is nothing *physically* wrong with them, and just merely telling them *there is nothing wrong* calms them down. However, they obviously do have *something*, and that *something* is this psychological problem, with certain causes (of which the subject is aware or not) producing it.

b)   *Distress*: A reaction of fear when confronted with an indeterminate or unknown danger. The term distress is also used as a synonym of extreme anxiety. If it increases in frequency and intensity until it becomes chronic then we are talking about a distress neurosis or anxiety neurosis.

c)   *Fear*: This is an emotional reaction when faced with a real and specific danger, and is consciously recognised as such.

d)   *Panic*: This is the acute stage of an anxious state.

10.7 Aggression

A) Interpersonal relationships can occasionally take on the form of aggressive behaviour. The word aggressive has its etymological roots in the verb meaning to approach, to start an argument, and is normally used to mean the propensity of a person to attack, destroy, injure someone or do damage to something, although it can also be used as a synonym for creative assertiveness, initiative, entrepreneurial spirit, for example, when we talk about an "aggressive salesman" or an "aggressive sales policy".

It is, however, important to recognise aggression as a human dimension or component, as something necessary for life or to survive and as an equivalent to '*to face or stand up to*'. In this sense it is necessary because without it a person would be unable to resolve many of the problems they come across. Destructiveness, on the other hand, is negative aggression, an aggression which annihilates things, which destroys people, including the person themselves when they attack themselves (physically or mentally) through self-destructive behaviour.

It is interesting for us, however, when dealing with public order security, to look at the destructive side of aggression, how far it is related to instinct and in its capacity as a force not adequately controlled by the person in question.

B) The main theories which attempt to explain aggression are the following:

- *Innatist theory*: This theory presumes that aggression is an innate temperamental disposition, associated to a specific biotype and psychotype. However, it has been proven that aggression is more a social than a biological problem and its roots and causes are, therefore, social. It has also been demonstrated that there are hardly any grounds to link aggression to genetic aspects (and even less so as linked to a specific chromosome as defined by Lombroso[4] [Lombroso] when discussing the *"born criminal"*.

- *Psychoanalytic theory*: Aggression is a psychic energy of a destructive nature, a *death instinct*, as opposed to a *life instinct* or *libido*. When attacking, the person is reacting against all frustration and conflicts.

- *The frustration-aggression theory*: This is a variation or continuation of the previous theory. Wherever there is aggression it has to be believed that some previous frustration exists. One of the most recent versions is that of Berkowitz [Berkowitz], whose main proposals are the following: "There are emotional states which make people predisposed to aggression. There is no aggression in which extreme factors or certain triggers do not play a part. Aggression is learnt and can become behaviour or habits which are reinforced through models exhibited socially (for example, in the media, on television or on film), or as a consequence of a misunderstood permissiveness."

- *The social learning theory.* The main representative of this theory is Bandura [Bandura]. This author has underlined the importance of imitation in people's acquisition of aggressive ways of behaving.

C) Social teaching to combat aggression

One of the most effective ways (and surely one of the most efficient in the long run) to combat aggression in society is that using educational principles and norms. Among these the following stand out:

- Avoid reinforcing the violent behaviour (in other words, with rewards, justification or praise) and do reinforce behaviour which is incompatible with violence, for example: an understanding attitude towards others, collaboration, etc.

- Systematically provide information about the mechanisms which provoke aggression and collective violence.

- Develop a sense for looking critically at a social situation so as not to take everything done and seen as acceptable.

- Educate younger generations about tolerance.

- Place importance on self-satisfying experiences which are based on affection and warmth, starting in the family home and particular in parent-child relationships.

As we can see, the behavioural reaction of a person is very complex in origin and, in order to be able to understand it a little better, the principal psychophysiological factors which are involved in these reactions need to be considered:

---

[4] Cessare Lombroso (Verona 06.11.1835, Turin 1909). Considered the father of Criminology.

A. Personality

This refers to everything we have already seen about personality as well as the learning aspect, which includes, not only the information we have received via any media and which we have retained, but also all behaviour which has its origins in associations with life experiences of the person in question and which have been reinforced (positively or negatively) by the consequences of their actions, or fantasies, surrounding that experience.

Opening up the concept of personality a little further, it is worth including some primary components of temperament such as: *traits*, for example, psychopathy, obsession, impulsiveness, hysteria, depression, hypochondria, apathy, phobia, etc.

A human being's personality contains all these traits, but an individual's temperament will be characterised by one or more of these traits.

This means that we can have a person, for example, with a slight trait of obsession combined with a distinct trait of stability in their character, thereby creating a person with good powers of observation who will quickly identify warning signs in an emergency situation and will be able to react positively and quickly. This person's final course of action will, of course, depend on more aspects (regarding the situation itself), such as:

- Their IQ (they will think of solutions).
- Their age (which affects reaction time).
- Their physical condition (regarding mobility, for example).
- The conditions of the place (if it is an enclosed space, an open one, if it is a busy area, if it has natural obstacles, if there is good visibility).
-Sex (women tend to be more practical, for example); and many more aspects which we will look at further on.

The personality traits which are most interesting to study in emergency situations are:

a) *Hysteria*: This trait is characterised by loudness and exaggerated, childish and primitive behaviour.

The danger of hysteria is the high risk of it spreading to others. There are several characteristics through which it can be recognised:

- Excessive colour of facial skin only to be lost in a sudden and brusque way (the vascularisation is altered).
- Exaggerated and agitated gesticulation
- Verbal diarrhoea
- Dystonia affecting the voice (alternating between shrieks and whispers)
- Hyper- or hypo-activity (great agitation or absolute paralysis)

The way to avoid this behaviour appearing is to isolate the subject if the problem is detected in time. This way there will be no spectators and the spread to others will be avoided. If the subject is already showing signs of the behaviour, the best tactic is to show them that they are not going to be the centre of attention.

b) *Depression*: The characteristics of this trait are pessimism and demoralising behaviour which affects the both the individual themselves and everyone else.

The harm lies in the high level of explicit or implicit suicidal behaviour as the individual considers it the only method of salvation possible; they can influence others to increase their susceptibility to show this trait.

Depression can be recognised by the following actions:

> - Slow movements.
> - Speaking in a disheartening and despairing way.
> - Apathetic behaviour.
> - Weak and limp gesticulations.
> - Whispering and wailing.

The way to avoid the appearance of this behaviour is to provide plenty of support and kindness, transmitting calm and positive ideas regarding being saved.

It is important to make sure this person is one of the first evacuated.

c) *Obsession*: The main characteristic is the constant presence of fixed ideas which are impossible to refute.

The harm depends on the idea itself (these can be about being saved, or about destruction).

Recognition is based on the fact these are quite tiresome people who insist on something and are excessively repetitive as well as being perfectionists.

In some cases they can be very useful (for example, in organising evacuations), whilst in others they can be dangerous as it is impossible to dissuade them from doing something (going back to the scene of the accident, for example).

d) *Self control*: This is a very noticeable trait characterised by strict, but organisational, behaviour, which is very useful in this type of situation. These people will only need attention after the evacuation.

e) *Introversion*: This is characterised by a lack of cooperation in general.

f) *Hyper-reactivity*, which when linked to *impulsiveness* can lead to thoughtless behaviour and unwise actions.

g) *Inhibition*, which when coupled with *apathy* can lead to people not acting at all and putting themselves in the hands of fate.

h) *Guilt and distress*: Together these can give rise to imprudent heroic and altruistic acts (going back in to save others in spite of the presence of the fire service, for example).

The actual number of different attitudes is endless, which is why only the most relevant and frequently observed have been described. The aforementioned factors of the emergency should be combined with these attitudes.

B. Level of education

It has been observed that people with a higher level of education show more self-control and calmer or more introvert behaviour, as well as being more altruistic and supportive in cases of inability to move, for example.

They show a greater self-confidence and better control of their initial impulses. For this reason they mange to keep others calm.

They tend to show highly organisational attitudes and take control of the situation with leadership roles. This is providing the person in question does not have one of the aforementioned temperamental traits predominant in their personality.

The opposite is true of people with low levels of education. The behaviour of these individuals frequently shows insecurity, confusion, hysteria or depression, as well as causing them to scatter or stampede (causing accidents where people are knocked over and crushed). They are also likely to act as a herd, causing overcrowding and to be less cooperative.

C. Sex

The results of a study regarding the behaviour of people when accidents occur have shown that women tend to pay more attention to the warning signs (smoke, noise, shouting, etc.) than men. Men, on the other hand, tend to pay more attention to information which they perceive could indicate possible and subjective warning signs. In other words, in this case women are led more by a practical sense of the situation and men by foresight. Although in extreme situations women tend to show hysterical behaviour more then men, men do tend to be more impulsive.

Women tend to stop to collect their valuables and, although this is practical, it always involves wasting precious evacuation time or causing an obstacle in the evacuation routes.5

D. Age

This factor becomes important when the occupants of a certain area are all of a similar age and have to be evacuated.

- the amount of decibels produced by the acoustic systems (which is a powerful stimulant of the nervous system)
- the psychological characteristics typical of youth (instability, impulsiveness, extroversion and collective hysteria)
- the probable consumption of stimulants (alcohol, drugs, etc.)

These factors make it more likely that an emergency situation will arise as a result of general uninhibited behaviour linked to primary instincts. This could lead to a mass panic situation as there is a great deal of tension in the air coupled with the suggestibility of the subjects.

If, on the other hand, the group of people is of a mature average age, the risk of uncontrolled mass behaviour drops quite considerably. In this case the emergency situation will probably be dealt with far more calmly, with self-control and with cooperative behaviour and greater organisation leading to a quick evacuation.

However, it is possible that the average age of the subjects places them in old age bracket, so we need to take into account the fact we are looking at a group with the following main characteristics:

- slow reaction time
- slowness of movements and even inhibited movement
- stupor, confusion and disorientation as to time and place
- insecurity in movement and insecure behaviour
- certain suicidal tendencies shown by giving up.

---

5 John L. BRYAN: "An examinination análisis of the dynamics of the human behavior in the MGM Grand Hotel FIRE", Clark County, Nevada, November 21, 1980. NATIONAL FIRE PROTECTION ASSOCIATION.

Finally, a group of children is very difficult to control because the children are highly suggestible and irrational, they are also highly mobile and less controlled. They cannot be expected to cooperate, help with evacuation and be altruistic. All messages given to them have to be simple and understandable, as well as persuasive and calming.

If the occupants in the area of the accident are of a heterogeneous age, then the evacuation should be directed by strategically placed persons with the characteristic personality of a good leader with charismatic qualities: clear ideas, organisational ability, self-control, calmness, security, able to impose authority, understanding of the situation, prior training, etc.

E. Physical condition of people

Apart from the aforementioned characteristics, it is important to take into account those linked to old age, illness (physical or mental), physical disabilities, deformities and physical defects.

The following can be considered especially important in emergency situations on board:

- difficulties with mobility
- apathy towards life
- impaired sight, hearing, etc.
- slowness in reasoning
- short attention spans or low levels of concentration

All the above can complicate evacuation enormously, as can the unlikely appearance of collective panic.

Regarding ill patients on board, one of the first steps to be taken is to avoid hysterical reactions and distress.

F. Civil status

As a result of the aforementioned study, it was observed that significant differences in behaviour exist, (regarding prevention and evacuation) depending on the civil status of the guests and the company they keep.

Persons in the company of their spouses were much more organised, cooperative (including with their fellow guests) and calm than lone guests.

From this we can draw the conclusion that the mere fact of enjoying the company of someone familiar to and loved by them is support for the person and makes them show behaviour which is much better adapted to the situation, and they are far calmer and show a greater degree of self-control in their actions. In other words, being alone can act as a contributing factor to feelings of insecurity and uncertainty which may then lead to uncontrolled actions.

G. Tolerating frustration

It is a proven fact that all frustration produces aggressive behaviour and is the ideal breeding ground for selfish, and even violent, behaviour. It is one of the main causes of acts of vandalism as well as causing people to knock others over and crush them, or for subjects to attack each other.

Frustration is the personal feeling that arises from being prevented from doing something because there is some kind of obstacle and, therefore it makes it impossible for a need to be satisfied.

10.8 Conclusions

People react according to their personality from a specific moment (response time), and according to their character and ability to overcome their phobias, fears and insecurities which can vary from one person to another.

BEHAVIOUR	EXAMPLE
Strange or bizarre behaviour	• Speaking out of context • Strange facial expressions • Unkempt appearance • Behaviour not appropriate to the situation.
Decrease in ability to function	• Difficulty carrying out tasks which are generally carried out without any problem • Low self-esteem.
Difficulties with perception. Confusion	• Confused, disorganised thoughts. Lack of concentration.
Loneliness	• Introvert, no friends, sad, does not create a bond with people and surroundings.
Physical complaints	• Large amount of physical complaints with no evidence of any clear pathology. Fainting, weakness, difficulty breathing, enuresis, stuttering.
Depression	• Feeling really low, sudden mood swings, sadness • Difficulty sleeping, loss of appetite, apathy, crying.
Fears	• Fear of handling weapons • Fear of the dark • Fear of being in enclosed spaces, of being in public, of high places.
Behaviour which suggests a suicide attempt	• Handing out personal belongings to friends • Playing with weapons • Philosophical discussions about life, death and the meaning of life. • Saying goodbye, "inheritance"
Suicidal behaviour	• "Verbal" threats of suicide • Suicide attempts: taking substances or medicines, cuts, use of firearms, suffocation

People with a normal personality and also have stability of character are characterised as observers and can react well in an emergency situation as long as their physical condition allows them to.

The factors that make it more likely that an emergency situation will arise are a result of general uninhibited behaviour linked to primary instincts. This could lead to a *mass panic* situation as there is a great deal of tension in the air coupled with the suggestibility of the subjects.

If, on the other hand, the group of people is of a mature average age, the risk of uncontrolled mass behaviour drops given that there is a greater calmness, self-control and cooperative behaviour and greater organisation leading to a quick evacuation.

However, if the average age of the passengers places them in what is considered to be "old age", the visible characteristics will be those described earlier.

If the group is of children, it will be more difficult to control because the children are highly irrational, highly mobile and less controlled. They cannot be expected to cooperate and collaborate. All messages given to them have to be simple and understandable, as well as persuasive and calming.

The physical condition of the people may be affected by old age, illness (physical or mental), they may have physical disabilities, etc. all of which may include difficulty walking, apathy towards life, impaired sight and hearing, slowness in reasoning, short attention span and low levels of concentration, etc. Given the social improvements in developed countries and the increase in the average age of the population, it is becoming more and more common for groups with these characteristics to be travelling on board passenger ships, and this can present an additional problem to the normal evacuation process in emergency situations.

In emergency situations other aspects which can provoke these types of behaviour should be taken into account:

The characteristics of the place:

    a.   Which area may be the scene of an emergency situation: whether it is an open or closed space, horizontal (in a long line or broken up) and/or vertical (height or number of decks), layout, orientation and formation of the stairs.
    b.   Signposting of the evacuation routes (location, colour, acoustics)
    c.   Distribution of the rules to follow in case of emergency (cabins, screens in busy areas)
    d.   Clear signposting of safe areas (areas with cameras, decks, meeting areas) in case of accident

Passenger characteristics:

    e.   Personality types and behaviour which is most likely to appear: shock, panic, aggression, and active or passive attitudes
    f.   The average age and physical condition of the passengers: age, physical disabilities, blindness, deafness
    g.   Time of day

Characteristics of the crew members in charge of leading the passengers:

    h.   Leadership qualities
    i.   Prior input and training
    j.   Efficient, permanent and lasting communication

11 Investigation procedures

11.1 Protection procedures

This chapter aims to explain the basic conduct and procedures which will help reconstruct, and discover the origins of, specific events for their analysis, investigation and to help establish new measures for dealing with similar situations in the future.

As a general rule, if the area is an enclosed space then all that is needed is access control. If, however, the location is an open space then it will need to be cordoned off.

This must be done, not only to avoid damage to trails or prints left by the perpetrator, but also to avoid false prints or trails being introduced to the scene, which would lead the investigators to make a mistake. The guards in charge of the security of the object in question must immediately put the criminals in a controlled secure area, as well as secure any instruments, effects, or evidence of the crimes.

In order to protect evidence, the following rules should be observed:

- Do not walk on the crime scene and prevent others from doing so.

- Do not touch objects or places that may have been touched by the criminals and prevent others from doing so.

- Do not pick up objects that seem out of place and do not allow others to do so.

- Do not allow blood stains to be cleaned up or windows to be cleaned, etc.

- Places where prints, bullet holes and casings are found should be labelled without interference, or the precise location noted down.

- If you are obliged to alter the crime scene for reasons out of your control, the officials making the visual inspection of the scene should be informed of this. It is important to remember that in some circumstances, action will have to be taken in the area itself to avoid possible dangers, such as cutting off the gas, the electricity or connecting alarms, etc.

- In the case of papers which have been set alight, the fire should not be put out with water or air. It is preferable to close off the current or the flue if the fire is in a stove or a fireplace. When they have been burnt, they must be taken to the laboratory in packaging which will prevent their further deterioration (a cardboard box). There they will be exposed to a hydration treatment which make it easier for them to be read.

- The protection measures for ballistic evidence should be considered on two levels:

> a) As a means of self-protection as weapons held by suspects or found may be loaded and their safety catches off. It is important to remember that obviously placed weapons may be used as possible triggers for bombs.
>
> b) As protection of evidence, to prevent them being stolen, being moved or having their value as evidence changed either intentionally or accidentally. It is also to protect them from the atmospheric conditions if need be.

- Finally all details must be noted down which may help the investigation (special smells that are noticed, specific noises, etc.).

11.2 Definitions of proof/evidence, trace and clues

11.2.1 Proof/evidence

From a legal point of view, proof is the justification of the truth of controversial facts proven by means authorised by law and recognised as effective.

However police proof, known as evidence[1], is used in a much wider sense than legal proof, because it is justified by the same legal function and activity and because, in practice, it is the judge (when hearing the summary), or the jury (in the oral proceedings) who values the evidence either accepting it or rejecting it depending on the case.

Police evidence, itself, is divided into:

> a) Material or objective evidence:
>
> > - Irrefutable: evidence which will stand up in court.
> > - Circumstantial: evidence which, although it has no value whatsoever, nevertheless helps the investigation by proving the facts or identifying the criminals.
>
> b) Immaterial or subjective evidence:
>
> > -Verbal: evidence in the form of statements made by the accused, the witnesses, etc.
> > - Moral evidence: the suppositions which are established during the investigation.
>
> c) Counter-evidence: Evidence which annuls or destroys the values of previous evidence.
>
> d) Alibi: The justification, whether true or false, presented by the accused or the suspect to try and prove that they were elsewhere at the time of the crime.

11.2.2 Clues

This is a clear and known fact which leads to another, unknown fact being discovered.

Evidence proves something, whilst a clue indicates the route to follow in order to find that thing.

---

[1] The Word 'prueba' in Spanish is used for both 'proof' and 'evidence'. – Translator's note.

Clues do not have the same value as evidence, but they help obtain it and, above all, they are a great help in determining the direction the investigation should take. This is why they are such an important part of criminal investigation.

11.2.3 Trace

Trace evidence is a mark or sign left by an object after having been in a specific place.

It is important to remember Locard's Exchange Principle which states: "Every contact leaves a trace".

The trace does not always identify the person or thing of interest, but, as with the clue, it helps direct the investigation.

11.3 Search procedures

It is advisable to insist that personnel who are not experts do not carry out searches. However, it is advisable that staff are trained in search techniques so that in exceptional circumstances (where the police are not available, for example) they may carry out the search themselves.

In the search for evidence, clues and trace evidence, an exhaustive search should be made of specific areas where objects have been handled by the criminal, or where they have left signs of their presence.

It is important to find and collect all evidence, instruments and any object of interest, no matter how small (a match, a cigarette end, a button, strands of hair, etc.), as everything may be useful in the investigation.

11.3.1 How to carry out the search of an area

As has already been mentioned, in a search even the most trivial thing must not be overlooked. This means that the search has to be carried out systematically and in such a way that the persons carrying it out do not disturb each other. The normal methods used are similar to those used in Search and Rescue (SAR) missions at sea.

Although the ship may comprise a large number of areas (on different decks or including several of them), the surface areas to be searched will not be very large, except in restaurants, cinemas, holds and garages. The method used will be adapted to the requirements and peculiarities of the space to be looked at in each case.

There are two ways to carry out a systematic search:

• Circle or spiral search: This system is used when the area to be searched is small. It consists of moving in a spiral pattern inwards, either clockwise or anti-clockwise (Fig. 11.1).

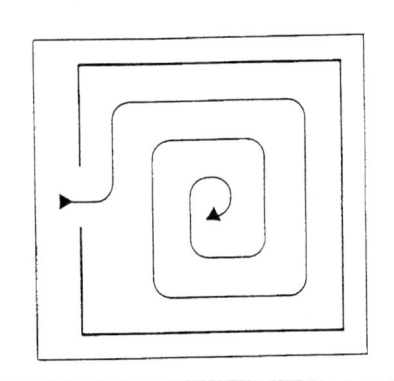

Fig. 11.1

• Search by area: When the area is large and several people are involved in carrying out the search, the following methods can be used:

a)   Zone search. The area is divided up into as many zones as there are people searching. Each person then carries out a spiral search within their assigned zone (Fig. 11.2).

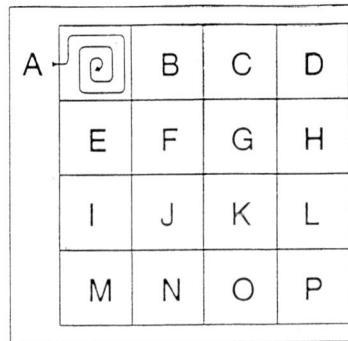

Fig. 11.2

b)   Circle method. Each person searches the area in concentric circles (Fig. 11.3).

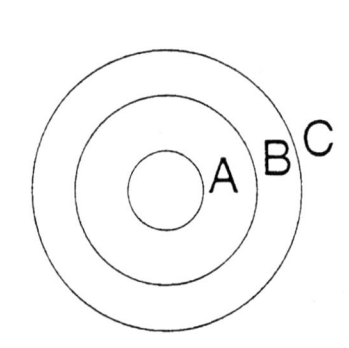

Fig. 11.3

c) Grid search (Fig. 11.4).

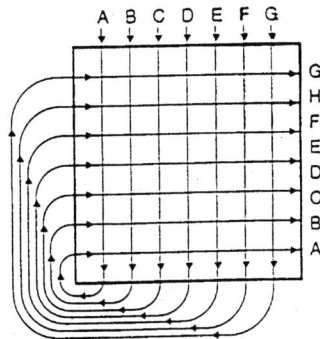

Fig. 11.4

The path followed by each of the people carrying out the search corresponds to an imaginary grid traced over the area to be searched. The first person follows their vertical line and, at the end, turns to the right and continue on the first horizontal line. The second person starts on the second vertical line and, at the end, turns right to continue on the second horizontal line, etc.

11.4 Transfer theory

It is important to take into account transfer theory when searching for evidence, clues and trace. Transfer theory refers to the fact that when objects touch, each one of them leaves part of itself on the other.

When there is contact between the criminal and the victim or the crime scene, physical changes occur and there is a transfer of materials.

Physical changes:

a) In the condition of the victim:

- Physical injury caused by weapons (guns, knives, etc.)
- Chemical products (poisons, acids, drugs, etc.)
- Vehicles crashes, etc., these cause loss of blood, skin, etc.

b) In the condition of the suspect:

- Physical injury caused by a struggle with the victim (scratches, injuries, etc.)
- The effect of a collision or other accidents (cuts from broken glass, etc.).

c) The condition of the crime scene:

- Broken objects such as windows, locks, doors, car headlights, bumpers
- Objects ripped off or marked, such as fenders, fresh paint, etc.
- Objects that have been moved, such as furniture, blinds, curtains, etc.

• Material transfer:

a) Objects taken from the scene or from the victim

> - Deliberately: tools used to commit the crime.
> - Accidentally:
>> - from the victim: blood, hair, textile fibres, etc. or
>> - from the crime scene: fibre from rugs, dust, hair from animals, etc.

b) Objects left by the criminal at the crime scene or on the victim, either deliberately or unintentionally

> - Cheques that bounce or other fraudulent documents, bullets, tools, weapons, cigarette ends, matches, ransom notes, traces of accidents, clothes, semen, fingerprints, footprints, textile fibres, etc.

11.5 Signs of violence on things

Normally, when a robbery has been committed, the doors, gates, furniture, locks, etc. show signs of having been forced. In the majority of cases this provides information on the modus operandi of the criminals.

There are three types of signs of violence or force on things:

• From compression: Signs of compression are produced when a surface is hit or pressed hard. For example, these signs appear when a surface has been hit to break it, or a jack has been used to separate the bars on a window,
• From slipping: These signs are produced when a something is not able to be hit vertically (in the case of compression), or accidentally when the tool is used to force locks or drawers.
• From cutting: These signs appear when cutting objects are used to reduce the wood around a lock, or when an attempt is made to use them as a lever.

Contrary to popular belief, robbers do not generally use specialised tools to commit their crimes. Instead, they tend to use common objects such as wheel jacks, screwdrivers, chisels, etc.

11.5.1 Forcing locks

The most commonly used systems for opening locks are:

> - With jacks
> - Banging a door until the screws holding the lock are freed
> - Using a picklock, false keys or copies of the real ones

The first two systems leave the aforementioned signs of double compression, slipping or cutting, whilst the third system leaves no visible signs at all, at first sight. For this reason it is necessary to examine the inside of the lock closely, even with the aid of a magnifying glass.

If the lock has been picked then there will be signs of scraping or scratching on the inside made by the picklock.

If a false key has been used, then there will be tiny pieces of wax or Plasticine stuck inside the lock. These will be from when the mould of the key was made.

The mould is made by introducing a very thin stick with a small ball of wax or Plasticine on one end into the lock. When the stick is taken out again, the inner pins will have left an impression, allowing the corresponding key to be made.

If, when the interior of the lock is examined, none of the aforementioned signs (scratches or pieces of Plasticine of wax) are apparent, then we must presume the lock has been opened with a duplicate key. This duplicate can be made pressing the original key hard into wax, soap, Plasticine, etc. to ensure it creates a mould for the duplicate to be made from.

11.5.2 Forcing safes

Safes are normally forced:

- With an oxyacetylene torch (if it is reinforced wood or metal), both from the front and behind
- By hitting the back plate of it with an axe (in cases of safes made from reinforced wood), muffling the sound with sacks
- With explosives (gunpowder, dynamite o nitroglycerine)
- With the safe's key (stolen or copied)
- Using the numerical combination (specialists)
- With a thermal lance

11.5.3 Investigating the signs

Reiterating once again the exceptional circumstances in which all these tasks will be being carried out, it is important to note that signs produced by slipping, compression or cutting always have specific characteristics (caused by irregularities or imperfections in the tool used) which should be photographed, as well as a cast made of the marks with silicone paste or Plasticine.

If the tool is found which it is presumed caused the marks, the following should be done: an impression of the instrument should be made in a block of Plasticine to show the marks left by it. These marks should be photographed and compared with those on the object that has been forced, a close study being made of the characteristic points of both marks.

All this should be either carried out or handed over to the specialised unit of the police force.

11.6 Blood stains

11.6.1 Chemical-biological appearance

With this study, carried out in a laboratory, it can be determined whether the stain is blood or not, if it is human or animal blood, if it belongs to the victim, etc.

11.6.2 Morphological appearance

Blood stains at a crime scene can be of a variety of shapes, and from them we can reach some very interesting conclusions which, when added to the details of the medical report, can help us form opinions regarding the phases of the attack and the circumstances surrounding it.

Blood stains are divided into the following groups:

1. Blood stains on horizontal surfaces

a) Drops. These are almost always small quantities of blood which have dropped perpendicularly onto a horizontal surface.

The shape and volume of the drop depends on the amount of blood spilt, the height from which it has fallen and the type of surface onto which it has fallen. The latter is of significance because if the surface is porous then the drop is hardly deformed at all and keeps an almost circular shape. If the surface is hard, however, the blood hits the surface and breaks up, producing splatters which are closer to or farther away from the nucleus depending on the height from which the drop has fallen (Fig. 11.5).

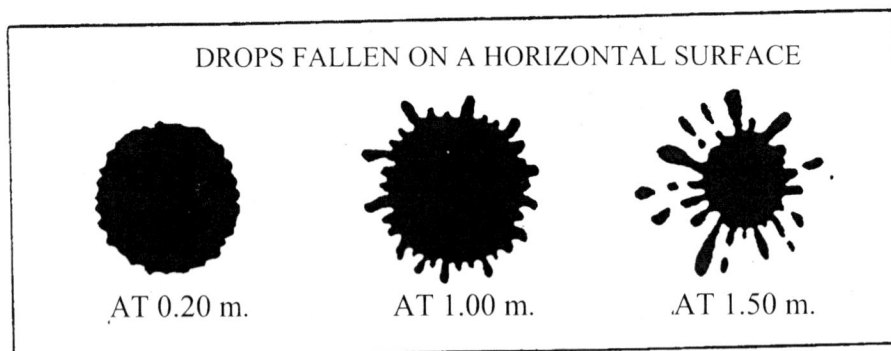

Fig. 11.5

b) Pool. This is a quantity of accumulated blood on a horizontal surface produced by a serious haemorrhage or by drops falling successively in the same place (Fig. 11.6).

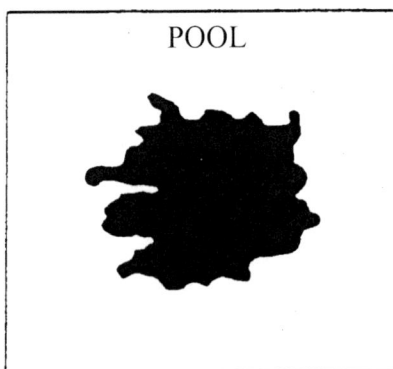

Fig. 11.6

There are often foreign bodies mixed into pools of blood such as hair, textile fibres, splinters of bone, etc., which are not normally detected at first glance. For this reason it important to study them in good light and with a magnifying glass.

c) Trail. This is a series of drops which have fallen or been cast from a moving body (Fig. 11.7).

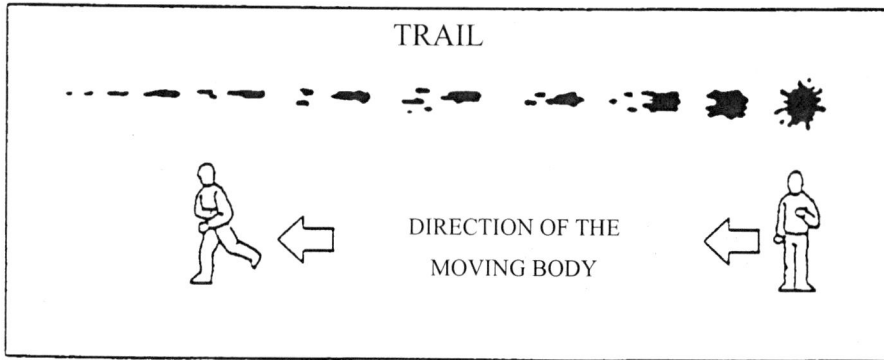

Fig. 11.7

From the morphology of the drops forming the trail and the distance between them we can deduce the direction the injured body was moving in, as well as the speed at which the bleeding person was travelling and how intensely they were bleeding.

d) Dragging. When a person is dragged they leave an irregular blood stain from which we can determine the direction the body was taken (Fig. 11.8).

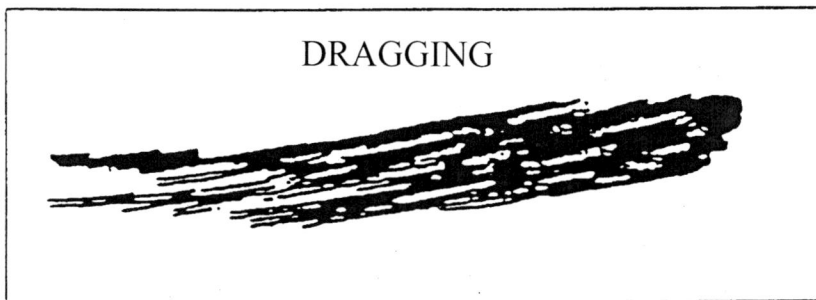

Fig. 11.8

This dragging may be due to the victim, still alive, dragging themselves along the floor to find help or to the perpetrator of the crime dragging the body by its hand or feet to try and hide the it or move it to another place.

2. Blood stains on vertical surfaces:

a) Splatters. These are produced by blood exiting a wound violently and are usually found on vertical surfaces (walls, doors, etc.), although they can appear on ceilings if the blood spurts out under great pressure.

Splatters not only come from a wound, but can also be created by the sudden movement of a limb or body part which is covered in blood.

These splatters can take on different shapes depending on the distance between the wound and the object on which the blood lands (Fig. 11.9).

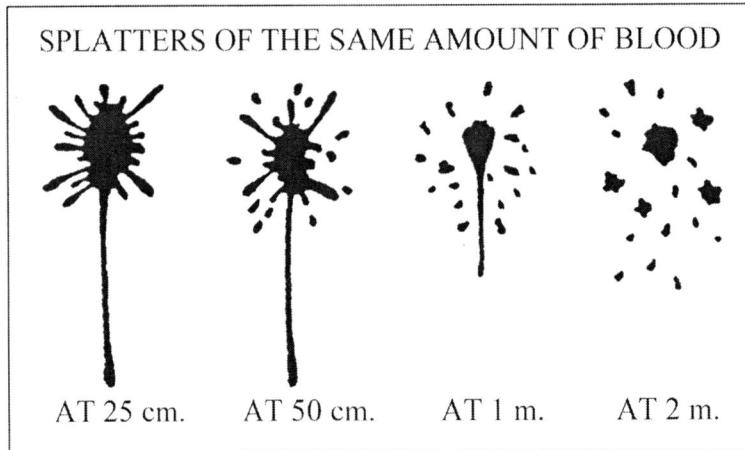

Fig. 11.9

c) Projection of drops. These are blood stains which are similar to the splatters produced by drops which fall or are projected onto vertical surfaces. They take on different shapes depending on the height of the wound and the angle of the fall (Fig. 11.10).

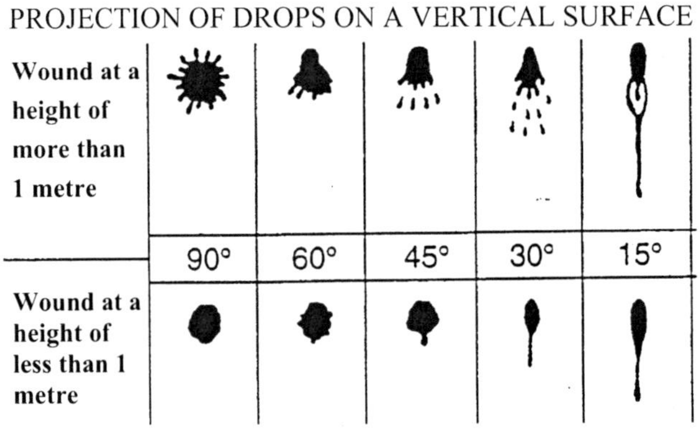

PROJECTION OF DROPS ON A VERTICAL SURFACE

Wound at a height of more than 1 metre					
	90°	60°	45°	30°	15°
Wound at a height of less than 1 metre					

Fig.11.10

d) Rubbing. Rubbing refers to small blood stains which can be seen on vertical surfaces and are produced by the brushing past of a blood-stained body or an injured limb (Fig. 11.11).

Fig. 11.11

Colour

The colour of the blood stains can vary from bright red to grey, and include dark brown and near black, depending on factors such as:

• the time since the blood was spilt

• the amount of blood in the stain

• the surface the stain is on

There are certain products which can be confused with blood stains due to their colour tone. This is the case with red, brown, black, sepia and grey; fresh fruit juice stains (lemon, orange, etc.) rust stains; nicotine stains; faeces stains; black coffee stains; etc.

For this reason, every stain suspected to be blood should be noted down, photographed and a sample should be taken to be sent to the Police Technical Laboratory for a chemical-biological analysis.

Search for the stains

The search for blood stains has to be carried out, not only at the scene of the crime, but also in other places, such as:

- On objects found close to the victim, as it is possible that one of them could be the murder weapon.

- On the decks, doors, timbers, screens, etc.

11.7 Collection procedures

Once the evidence and clues have been located (and still finding ourselves in the exceptional situation of having to collect them) the greatest care must be taken when collecting them to avoid destroying or cancelling any of them out, or creating false evidence by leaving our own prints on them (Fig. 11.12).

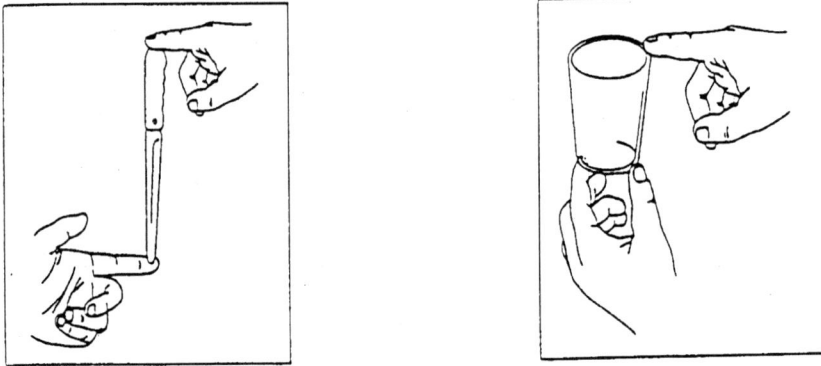

Fig. 11.12

To prevent this happening, some measures need to be taken, such as those in (Fig. 11.13):

    - Use rubber gloves if possible.

    - Do not fully touch any item that has the criminals' prints on it.

    - Use tweezers, if available, to touch the absolute minimum surface area of the objects.

    - Use string or thread to pass through holes, handles, etc. of the objects.

    - Put very small objects in envelopes.

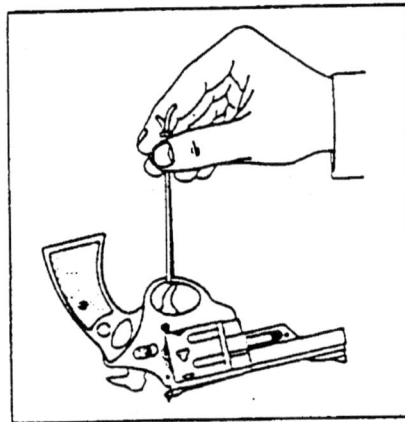

Fig. 11.13

11.8 Creating plans and sketches ·

Once the evidence and clues have been collected, these should be handed over or sent to the security forces to help them with their investigation and later to be handed to the judicial body responsible.

These pieces of evidence or clues should be accompanied by a report detailing the procedures used in this exceptional collection of evidence. It should explain where the pieces of evidence were located and should include photographs or drawings of the area for a clearer picture, and on these the location of the objects should be marked.

These drawings may be made in different ways, depending on if they are plans or sketches.

Plans

A plan is a scale representation of a place. On it all the measurements will be represented exactly, even though they may not be directly reflected on the drawing.

To make a plan, all the measurements of the area and the objects need to be taken and drawn to the chosen scale. This procedure gives us a very exact idea of the place in regard to its proportions and measurements. However, a plan is not useful for such a situation as ours as it is complicated and slow to do.

Sketches

These are freehand drawings on paper made by continuously comparing the drawing to the scene. If any changes have to be made to the sketch then they must always be made at the scene and never from memory.

Sketches are easier and quicker to make than plans and are, therefore, used more frequently, even to accompany and help the photographs to be understood.

When making a sketch, the following should be taken into account:

- In open spaces, north should be marked with an arrow and the letter "N".

- The objects at the scene should be drawn in the correct place and position, including only the essential ones and excluding those that are not important.

- The sketch should have notes reflecting the most representative or important measurements. These measurements should be taken exactly with a tape measure or similar, never with steps or using the hands, etc.

- It is essential that symbols, letters and numbers are used to identify the objects on the sketch, and that the key to the symbols is put in one of the corners.

- If photographs are taken, the position of the camera should be indicated on the sketch.

- The objects should be described in the footnotes of the sketch to avoid covering the drawing with measurements that will make it difficult to understand.

To place an object or body in its correct position, the following techniques are used:

- Location by coordinates. This involves identifying the location of the object with pairs of coordinates.

- Location by triangulation. With this system two fixed points are used as reference points (if there are no permanent reference objects, two spots can be painted on the floor) then the distance between these two points is measured and then the distance from each of those points to the object that is to be placed.

11.9 Documents reporting illegal acts

To safeguard maritime interests from illegal acts that threaten the safety of passengers and crew aboard passenger ships, the incident reports, and measures taken to prevent the same incident happening again, should be given to the corresponding authorities as soon as possible.

We recommend the use of the following as a model for a form for reporting illegal acts. The simplicity of the form should not necessarily be adhered to, as the maximum objective and proven information should be noted down, and the statements of the people who most directly saw the incident should be included as should photographs, diagrams and examples of everything which best leads to the motive of the crime being discovered.

The report should contain the following details as in this model:

ILLEGAL ACTS REPORT

Date: ....

1. DESCRIPTION OF SHIP OR PORT AREA

> Name of the ship ....
> Flying the flag of ....
> Captain ....
> Port security official ....

2. DESCRIPTION OF THE INCIDENT OR THREAT

> Date, time and place of incident or threat ....

3. NUMBER OF STATEMENTS

> Passengers .... Crew .... Others ....

4. METHOD USED TO INTRODUCE HAZARDOUS SUBSTANCES OR DANGEROUS MECHANISMS INTO THE PORT OR THE SHIP

> People ....
>
> Luggage .... Cargo .... Cargo hold .... Other ....

5. TYPE OF HAZARDOUS SUBSTANCES OR DANGEROUS MECHANISMS USED, WITH A FULL DESCRIPTION

> Weapons ....
> Explosives ....
> Others ....

6. WHAT MEASURES AND FURHTER ACTION DO YOU RECOMMEND SHOULD BE TAKEN TO PREVENT A SIMILAR EVENT RECURRING?

7. OTHER IMPORTANT DETAILS

12 Negotiation

We know that in our relationships with others we have a certain degree of influence on people, with some people being influenced more than others; quite another question is how and why we influence them. Nevertheless, it is clear that some influences are absolutely necessary. The use of influence to educate and, in particular, to impose authority, are two clear examples.

How strong our influence over others can be depends on these main factors:

- Relationships based on affection: Closeness in a relationship reinforces interpersonal influence. We all accept advice or suggestions better from someone who loves us or whom we love.

- Relationships based on strength: People who are sure of themselves dominate situations and end up imposing their will. In certain professions it is requirement to have a strong personality, something that is not to be confused with the imposing personality of a person who will dominate at all costs. People with strong personalities are people who are convinced and sure of their opinions and criteria. They are coherent and they exude a strength which is transmitted in their relationships with others.

- Relationships based on authority: Authority has an influence on everybody who is subject to it. There are *natural* authorities, such as the authority parents have over their children, or those commanded by position, such as the Captain of a ship or the use of a uniform. There are authorities based on competence or specialisation, for example when a doctor gives and opinion or makes suggestions related to health. And there is a *moral* authority which is equal to prestige. This is demonstrated by certain people whose personal qualities are well-balanced and outstanding in comparison to others. These personal qualities make a person's opinions, attitudes and behaviour, etc. have a positive influence on others. Without intending to, these individuals influence people and are respected. This is the case of the wise man, the true maestro, or one who deserves the title of statesman or stateswoman, or someone who has been of a real service to society, etc.

12.1 Leadership as a form of social relationship and of influence

One of the forms of social relationship and of influence on others is leadership. The leader within a group or in society itself is a *born leader*. This leader is above everybody else; they have a greater capacity for commanding and influencing people. They are respected and loved by others and find themselves in this role thanks to a certain set of personal qualities.

They are normally intelligent people, perhaps more so than the others in their group, but not overly so. They are self-confident, able to make decisions and run greater risks. The leader is the person who binds the group together and who can summarise and express their needs and aspirations better than any of the others.

The leader is, therefore, the representative of the group and as such has several roles to play and duties to carry out either simultaneously or consecutively: they lead and give value to the group, etc. Sometimes, when things are not going well for the group, the blame falls on the leader and they are made a scapegoat and reviled by the very same people who established them as leader. A leader is a reality and a role created by the group because the group needs it.

There are generally two types of leader, depending on the characteristics of their personality. However, the type of leader a person is is also based on the way they act and on the characteristics of the group they belong to. The following types of leadership are relevant here:

- The doctrinarian: This person has a logical way of thinking and tries to fit everything they do into it.

- The opportunist: This person adapts their behaviour to the circumstances, without adhering to any system in particular.

- The fighter: This person sets themselves specific goals in a pragmatic way and focuses on achieving them.

- The peacemaker: This person is a mediator, a person who smoothes things over and reconciles differences between members of the group.

- The idealist: This person promotes a certain set of values and others feel attracted to this.

- The cynic: This person is not a true leader, they are a negative one. Deep down they are only interested in personal gain.

- The strict leader: This person lack flexibility. They usually establish objectives from which they will not sway and which they will not change, no matter how advisable it is for them to do so in the circumstances.

- The imaginative leader: This person is creative. They are not phased by new circumstances and they know how to come up with solutions to new problems.

- The player: This person is a risk-taker. They confront danger and are quick to make decisions.

- The prudent leader: This person does not like risks so they do not take them. They are slow to make decisions, but end up dominating the situation.

The importance that the leader figure acquires, especially when the leader is a crew member, can create certain negative reactions if authority is imposed in an unfair, partial or intentional way. This creates negative resistance to complying with the instructions given, almost always because people consider they have the right to resist and to question the instructions in such extreme situations.

A leader should always avoid only partial leadership, and try to include the largest number of passengers possible to avoid division within the group, or small breakaway groups which do not agree with the unfair authority as they see it. In these circumstances, resistance to obeying orders can be shown through passive attitudes, which do not favour the uniformity of passengers' behaviour; or legal active resistance, when the objections are based on legal principles and rules, thereby creating a situation of negative leadership as the person is exposed in front of others. This resistance can be justified by filling in complaint forms. There is also a peaceful illegal active resistance, where specific groups of passengers unite in angry protest and try to convince all the others of their argument by shouting and vociferating. Last but not least, there is violent illegal active resistance which crosses boundaries, not only as regards procedure, but also because it involves threats and violence and, as a result, possible damage or injury, passive groups joining active ones, all of which results in a general chaos which the leader was specifically hoping to avoid. A leader should have the following characteristics: clarity of thought, organisational ability, self-control, calmness, self-confidence, the ability to be authoritative, an understanding of the situations, prior training, etc.

12.2 Non-verbal communication

People send out infinite non-verbal messages without even being aware they are doing so. This collection of gestures, attitudes, positions, body movements, etc. is known as *non-verbal communication* (N.V.C.). It is very important to observe a person's N.V.C. if we want to obtain a full picture of a person, as well as to determine their true intentions.

N.V.C. becomes more important when the success of the crisis control measures depends on communication and dialogue. Nevertheless, it is all about trying to interact with a person, because by observing their body language in response to questions we can obtain far more trustworthy information than by listening to their words. Someone who knows how to interpret the signs properly will be able to use their knowledge to ensure no counterproductive or contradictory decisions are made due to the suspect disguising the truth with his words, as their body will show these words to be false.

The understanding of clues provided in non-verbal communication should be used to help improve the leaders' negotiating ability. It should substantially improve their ideas for resolving crises generated by human factors and, in general, it should improve working relationships on the ship on a day-to-day basis, with a view to preventing tense situations which may lead to a crisis.

It is a well-known fact that 10% of our information comes from reading; 20% comes from the tone of voice used when speaking, whilst 70% comes from observing the body language of the person we are speaking to. This is why a correct interpretation of non-verbal communication is so important.

In negotiation, body language informs us of the intentions of the conflictive person or attacker. It lets us know the person's state of mind with regard to levels of aggression, fear or insecurity, as well as helping us detect any crew members experiencing problems in dealing with the threatening situation. This is all designed to boost the capacity of the leader during the difficult negotiating phase, to help them be absolutely clear about their approach and, in general, to build and create an excellent interpersonal relationship which will help reach a successful outcome in the negotiation.

The fundamental basics of non-verbal communication are that:

a. Everything a human being externalises comes from within, although not everything that is within externalised.

b. A body is not master of itself as far as image and presentation are concerned, because it shows and expresses its own inner situation. Such signs are shown at all moments in life.

The five senses are only instruments for transmitting impulses to the brain so that they can be translated into something that a human can understand. They may be more or less intense or beneficial depending on the experience and practice already in our consciousness.

It is difficult to understand what we are seeing if we do not learn what to look for. In this sense, techniques for developing and improving vision and powers of observation should be used.

12.3 Gestures and postures

When observing gestures and attitudes, it is important to remember certain aspects which will help avoid the wrong conclusions being drawn. The most relevant are:

- There are no universal gestures. There is not one facial expression, one attitude or one posture that means the same in all cultures. For example, Latin people gesticulate more than Saxons.
- The meaning of a message always depends on the context, never is it just in an isolated movement of the body.
- Non-verbal behaviour does not always support what is being said, in fact it quite often contradicts it.
- Each gesture is just one element forming part of a message, it is not the message itself.
- There are gestures which have been carried out for many years as part of a ritual and yet the meaning of them is often not known. An example of this is when two rivals are going to fight: one of them spits on their hands and then rubs them together. The meaning here is that the opponent sees that the other one has saliva, meaning they are not afraid. If they were afraid, they would not have been able to do this as it is normal for a person who finds themselves in a difficult situation (one of fear) to have a dry throat.

When a person does something risky, or finds themselves in a risky situation, their inner tension increases, and this shows on the outside with recognisable symptoms or signs. When this is observed in a suspect, the external signs may show their true intentions or their inner level of negativity. Preventive measures can be taken in response to this.

The best procedure for discovering contradictions and bringing suspicious signs to the fore is to put the person in conflict under pressure. As the pressure is applied, the signs will increase, both in quantity and intensity.

A minimal detection procedure could be the observation of:

a. Physiological changes such as sweating, changes in rhythm of their breathing and their heart rate.
b. Volitive signs: slight tapping of foot and swinging legs is a circular motion.
c. Corporal signs: a concentrating person sits forward, a tired person sits back, a tense person sits up straight and a desperate one will sink into the chair.
d. Signs made by hands: kind or nice words whilst accompanied by closed fists, affirmative movements made whilst moving the head from side to side, or signs of triumph given whilst showing obvious tiredness.
e. Facial and muscular movements: the easiest to identify are the smile, anger, laughter, crying, etc., whilst the most difficult to spot are tension shown in the brow, the lips, the hands and the jaw, etc.

The classification of mental states that can be detected is as follows:

a. Defensive, with barrier. Arms crossed over chest (closed fists), head bowed or raised shoulders (protecting the neck), crossed legs, pursed lips, hands hidden (in pockets, behind the back), hands hiding or covering parts of the body, territorial limitations (sitting only partially on the chair, leaning on the wall, totally or partially hiding behind an object or person).
b. Tension. Tense limbs and frozen features, body positioned facing the door, fleeting glances or avoiding looking directly at something, touching ears (doubting), holding their breath and letting it out subtly, shallow breathing, scratching parts of the body (mainly the head), hands strongly locked or fingers strongly crossed, glazed eyes, lack of coordination in movements (out of context), eyes half open, tense neck, lack of flexibility.
c. Nervousness. Quick and nervous steps, they sit away from the negotiator, wait to be invited to sit down, cross their hands and arms, and gaze at the window (looking for a way out), coughing, sighing and frequent whistling (releasing tension), half-smoked cigarettes, they move whilst sitting, when standing they frequently shift their weight from one foot to the other, they only partially move their lips when speaking (mouth at an angle), whilst they are speaking they touch their trousers with their hands (they do not know what to do with their hands), they clean marks off objects or off their clothes, they play with coins or keys (in or out of their pocket), they constantly touch their ears.
d. Insecurity. Drooping shoulders, hunched back and sunken chest. Constant opening and shutting of eyes, nervous hand movements and brief contact with objects (they do not know what to do with their hands), chin down, small hand and arm movements close to the body, lack of energy in their movements, body supported by hands or elbows, short steps with many head movements (fear), movements are indecisive and weak.
e. Contradictory. Broken speech and lack of fluidity. Incomplete smile, threatening facial features and legs pulled back (fear). They smile but keep the body frozen, they smile but their eyes are cold.
f. Intensity of the tension. In sudden reactions, large movements and tone of voice.
g. Retraction of position and approach. Change of subject, coughing, looking down, etc.

12.4 Personal space

Everybody moves around in their own kind of *private bubble*, the limits of which are defined by the *individual self* and in which they feel comfortable. This is a territorial concept.

- o *Status*: the distance between persons of a different *status* is greater.
- o Attitude: the more people like each other, the lesser the distance between them will be.
- o For competing: a greater distance and confrontational positions.
- o For cooperating: a lesser distance and standing side by side.
- o For conversing: at right angles to one another.

If another person invades this personal space, tensions may arise and reach a point where, because of the closeness, messages more subtle than threats can be transmitted.

12.4.1 Concept of territoriality

This concept is important on land, but aboard ship it influences people's behaviour even more. This has a very negative influence on people's behaviour aboard a ferry or cruise ship transporting a large number of passengers in an enclosed and isolated space at sea, with no means of escape.

Animals and even people have a very intimate and unconscious awareness of what is their territory. In other words, the territorial space that is vital for them to maintain their mental stability, and that gives us security because it is part of our being and is not shared with anybody. This is why when somebody invades this "space" that we consider ours, we immediately tend to defend it by showing aggressive and even violent behaviour. This is one of the things that send our *stress* levels shooting to disaster level, as well as those of our attacker.

This "vital territory" or personal space can vary in size according to the character of each person and their circumstances. Under no circumstances should we invade this space during negotiations in a hostage situation, if we do not want to fail through increasing the stress levels of the attacker.

Several authors have tried to establish a specific space to create a rule. There are too many factors to take into consideration, but when building a ship some rule of thumb is necessary for them to be habitable. The minimum dimensions for a living area (LA) for one person is the sum total of the dimensions occupied by the body itself in the space (D) and the imaginary projection of the body outwards in all directions; this may be an average distance of 59 cm. Therefore the formula could be the following: LA = D + 50.

It is as if each person had a bubble surrounding them and when another person enters that bubble it creates a feeling of uncomfortableness and irritation, thereby provoking an immediate aggressive reaction of self-defence that can be controlled to a greater or lesser extent.

This is a very significant aspect in situations of herding or overcrowding, which is why it is so significant and influential on the behaviour of people in emergency situations or in larges group.

For example, imagine the disagreeable situation that arises in the simple situation of an almost full lift, or of a bar on deck where there are a large number of passengers invading the personal space of others.

Of course, this personal space experience depends on the circumstances. In open spaces, the territorial bubble expands, and it contracts in enclosed spaces. On board ship the crew is used to small spaces and living with others in very confined areas. The passengers are not used to it and when they are on board they have to drastically reduce their personal space, causing numerous conflicts.

In a large building with many floors: the "invasion" of personal space is made worse by the unconscious feeling of oppression coming from the roof; especially when one is on one of the lower floors. Due to social circumstances, some people have the right to enter our intimate space, such as family members. In our personal relationships, the conversation zone tends to be between 40 and 50 centimetres. With strangers and in public places a person extends "their bubble" and tends to increase the separation from the people surrounding them. In all these cases a person will often even mark their territory with personal objects.

The same dimensions of personal space found in intimate or personal circumstances can also apply in areas dedicated to leisure pastimes, such as night clubs or football stadiums, etc. In a work environment the areas of personal space will be strictly imposed and respected, with even the smallest of "invasions" leading to interpersonal conflicts. This is a well-recognised problem on board ship.

In disaster situations a person will not, under any circumstances, tolerate an invasion of their personal space. This is especially true in long-lasting situations where people will violently defend their space.

All the aforementioned aspects can occur in combination, often becoming a serious aggravating circumstance in both the individual and of group reactions. Of course it is always far easier to control one person than a whole group.

This feeling of tension and uncomfortableness provoked by an invasion of personal space often arises, for example, in enclosed areas full of people, such as on underground trains, in a lift, etc. where we can see how people tend to move away from each other in search of their own *private bubble*. The area within which this reaction is provoked is known as *flight distance*.

There is a *critical distance* which, if breached, can provoke an aggressive response. The larger this critical distance is, the more aggressive the person.

It is important to understand this need for this tiny space in order to avoid misunderstandings which may lead to false impressions of a person's character.

For example, for North Americans a comfortable distance for conversing is 60 cm, whilst for South Americans the comfortable distance for conversing is 40 cm.

If a North American and a South American come together for a conversation, both will try to place themselves at the distance that is comfortable for them. The North American will step back giving the other the impression that they are *conceited*, whilst the South American will get closer and come across as *aggressive*.

Personal space is determined by factors such as the following:

- culture: the North American and the South American, for example.

- sex: The distance between women is less than that between men.

- character: Introverts have a larger bubble than extroverts.

12.5 Formal and informal communication channels

Handling information is essential for all human organisations, whatever kind they are.

For an organisation to work every one of its members has to be able to receive and supply the necessary and sufficient information to be able to act correctly at all times.

This implies the need to establish certain channels for the flow of information which will ensure that every member of the organisation can give and receive this information, as and when needed, in order to fulfil their tasks.

Communication channels structured in this way are known as *formal communication channels*.

In the case of a structured hierarchy, such as the organisational structure of a civilian ship, the information channels coincide with the hierarchical strata so that each member of the structure:

- Receives the information from their immediate superior and relays it to those immediately under them. The same procedure also works in the opposite direction.

- Should not let themselves be influenced by any gesture they observe, however clear it may seem.

- Must start by interpreting the easy-to-recognise gestures which appear more frequently.

- Emotionally provoked movements can be detected by their contrast to recurrent behaviour.

12.5.1 The face and the eyes

People can fake expressions by controlling their face and using it to send out messages. If it is forced, however, an expression does not disappear as quickly as it does when it is natural.

It is not easy to capture the meaning of a facial expression, as we are not trained to do so because our culture has taught us not to stare at the faces of others out of politeness. In other cultures exactly the opposite occurs. However, nobody can prevent their face showing some expression.

The same happens with the eyes. These are seen as *an extension of the brain* and, therefore, they can give a good indication of emotional state. For example:

-   Brazenly holding a stare can mean aggressiveness or provocation.
-   Looking away can mean the person does not agree with what is being said.
-   Repeatedly looking away and then back to the negotiator is a sign that they are going to change their mind.
-   A person's pupils will dilate when something interests them.

In the same way we can detect when someone is not telling the truth when:

-   They lick their lips constantly.
-   Their blinking becomes more pronounced.
-   They rub their eyes.
-   They glance quickly to the side
-   They blush.
-   The maintain eye-contact excessively and continually (they are trying to convince us of their innocence).
-   The gestures used do not correspond to what is being said.
-   They make quick and nervous movements.

12.5.2 The handshake

The way a person shakes hands is also a good indicator for understanding a person as it tells us about: the person's character, how interested they are in the situation, the non-spoken message that they are sending us.

Regarding character:

-   o   A strong handshake means a determined character.
-   o   A weak handshake means an indecisive character.
-   o   A stiff handshake means indifference.
-   o   A damp handshake means anxiety and nervousness.
-   o   A gentle handshake means shyness and withdrawal.

Plus, we should identify ourselves and state our position and rank, something we should always do before they ask us when it is us who have made the call.

Regarding interest:
-   o   A prolonged handshake means a strong character and interest in the situation.
-   o   A quick, stiff handshake means a strong handshake but no interest in the situation.

o A prolonged but uncomfortable handshake means a weak character but interest in the situation.
o A mere brush of the hands means a weak character and no interest in the situation.

Regarding the message:

The following behaviour represents negation:
o Hand extended automatically without looking: out of habit.
o Passivity, leaving the initiative to the other person.
o Stiff arm stuck to the body, elbow stuck to the body and forearm perpendicular to it.

12.6 Verbal communication

Whatever the situation, communication should be kept open and fluid between the two parties in confrontation in a crisis situation. When this communication is interrupted, the negotiation and possibility of reaching an agreement are also broken, resulting in each opponent continuing with their own objectives. This increases the possibility of damage and a solution to the abnormal situation not being found.

When the telephone is the means used to transmit the voice in the communication, the priority is to keep the conversation going so that we receive the whole message the other person is trying to convey about the crime in hand, and also to allow us to ask questions about the areas we are not clear on and to help us reach the person causing the situation to try and convince them to desist.

The main rules when using the telephone have to do with courtesy, rhythm of voice, clarity and diction, the ability to listen, the ability to respond, confidence, organisation, concentration, identifying the persons you are communicating with, not revealing private information about employees and executives (address, telephone number, etc), as these cannot be given out to third persons without authorisation of the people themselves.

12.6.1 Tips for improving communication

Whatever the means used for communicating with a negotiator, this communication can be improved if the following are taken into account:

- Tolerance of the feelings of others.
- The intention of the addresser to instil feelings of safety and security in the addressee.
- The intention, as an addressee, to listen to the addresser instead of evaluating the communication from an addressee's point of view.
- Willingness of both the addresser and addressee.
- Feedback should be given on all communication.
- Trust should be established between addresser and addressee.
- Do not take or provoke a defensive position.
- Bear in mind that listening is an active and not a passive function.

Consequentially, effective communication is not just one-way communication. It requires reciprocal action between the person speaking and the person listening, and both have to take on this responsibility.

To look more deeply at the psychological behaviour of people in emergency situations we need to take into account other details that are of particular relevance, such as contributing factors to this behaviour which include the following:

Characteristics of the area or place: The location of the area where an emergency situation may take place, taking into account whether it is an open or enclosed space. The horizontal layout of the area (long and straight, angular), the vertical layout (width of decks, number of decks), and mixed. Layout and formation of the stairways. Signposting of the emergency exits (location, colour, acoustics). Circulation of rules on first steps to take in case of emergency. Clear signposting of areas of refuge (terraces, watertight compartments,) in case of accident.

Characteristics of the population using the area where a disaster may occur, taking into account the type of personality and behaviours which are most likely to surface in the event (avoidance, escape and people camouflaging the problem). Average age and physical condition (old age, paralysis, blindness, deafness, state of awareness). Predominant sex (men, women). Time of day (awake) or night (sleeping/tiredness). Previous experience of disaster situations and evacuation training.

Types of disaster that can cause an emergency situation: flooding, fire, explosion, mass disorderly behaviour, etc.

Material available to use in case of emergency; whether specifically designed for the situation or improvised (e.g. towels).

Factors which most influence the behaviour of people in emergency situations. These especially include external factors (visibility, atmospheric pressure, acoustic aspects), internal factors (sense of direction, loneliness, despair, levels of toxicity) and access to information about the incident (rescue personnel, media).

Phases of intervention during the disaster. Consideration of adaptive and preventive behaviour as well as behaviour aiding evacuation (organised, altruistic behaviour), and maladaptive behaviour such as that shown by a selfish person (aggressive), re-entering the scene of the incident, vandalism, intolerance of the invasion of personal space.

As regards the crew or the security guards: leadership ability, organisation of the evacuation, efficiency and speed of action, and crowd control.

12.7 Guidelines for the negotiation process

All negotiation should follow these basic principles:

1. Have a good and fitting idea of the emotional state of the person to be negotiated with. This will principally be obtained from the outward signs of non-verbal communication shown through symptoms and gestures.

2. Pay special attention to identifying the causes which have given rise to the incident and which show the stress levels of the person in conflict. Evaluate the level of activity (whilst showing an appreciation of proximity to the boundaries of normality and disaster), and their emotional reaction.

3. Monitor the emotional state and the stress suffered by the negotiators themselves. It should be remembered that, any attitude that could spark further events should be avoided.

4. Have two negotiators available for every group or area that may hold a large group of people. This means that several possible negotiators should be appointed among the crew based on their knowledge, their ability to get on with people, their conversational skills, their rank or position of employment.

5. One negotiator should act first and try to reach an agreement and stabilise the situation. If the negotiation does not appear to be taking the positive course hoped for, the second negotiator should intervene and change tack, as far as is prudent or necessary. This should always be done with the aim of improving the willingness of the interlocutor to start communicating and accept the standard procedures.

6. The procedures which achieve the best results are as follows:

    a. The negotiator should try to put themselves physically on a similar level to their interlocutor (this could be either sitting or standing), they should adopt body positions not dissimilar to their interlocutor's own, and use similar language in both words and physical expression. They should keep the jacket (of their uniform) open and not wear a tie when they are negotiating with someone wearing trousers a shirt and sandals. This is to avoid an increase in the scale of activity when the interlocutor is faced with an impeccable uniform which represents authority and which diminishes the authority they themselves were hoping to achieve.

    b. In a cautious, but determined manner, analyse the mood of the interlocutor and the truth of their claims as well as their real intentions. It may be enough to just pose questions which, using the same sentiment expressed by the interlocutor, transmit understanding, interest, and willingness to find a solution involving the least human and moral cost to both parties. Any questions which make the other person nervous, are negative (avoid using the word NO), or lead to a complicated or unclear solution should be avoided. The interlocutor bases their action on a proposal, involving violence to a greater or lesser extent, which represents a certain cost to the ship (physical harm to persons, damage to objects, etc.).

    c. As the first negotiator continues to advance in the process of neutralisation and control of the situation, the second negotiator should be observing and following the procedure so they can intervene as soon as they detect signs that things are going badly and that there may be a break down in negotiations due to nervousness, the fact they are heading down a dead end making the situation more complicated, or when the first negotiator is eliminated from proceedings by the actual actions or words used in negotiating.

    d. Forethought should be given to the use of bribes and exchanges, and consideration should be given to each and every one of the courses of action which may be taken and of any changes in proceedings, i.e. when would be a good time for the second negotiator to appear on the scene, etc.

Discussing all this means a communication process between the crew members involved is created, their points of view are made known, ideas and possible solutions are offered, skills are generated in little-discussed areas or areas only dealt with on a personal level and on isolated occasions, the an open and unrestricted atmosphere of intervention is created, leading to true threats being detected (weak points in the system) and the resources available for each case (strong points) being made known.

It is during this phase of routine activity (always before the event, with the crew in a stable, emotionally calm state, and with the support of their colleagues, and in similar conditions to the preparation and carrying out of simulations (exercises)), when effective reactions are available, that several alternatives to different negotiation situations should be prepared. The worst possible case scenarios should always be considered, for example; negotiation processes for cases of angry protests by passengers, arguments caused by drunks or drug addicts, conflicts caused by urban gangs, acts of vandalism, physical threats to people, hostages taken, piracy with possession of the ship, acts of terrorism, prisoners having escaped from their secure cells, the use of different types of weapons, etc.

13 Principles for intervention in emergency situations

13.1 Intervention in incidents on board

Incidents on board are the situations that require the least intervention as initially they are easily controllable. However, if a logical and organised response procedure is not put into practice by personnel with the correct training then the situation can get out of control and reach a serious level which would then constitute an emergency.

The response to the emergency should follow specific steps as strictly as possible. These steps should be a result of a process of identifying emergency situations, planning and training the personnel involved. Given the isolated condition of a ship, an emergency on board, more than in any other place, must basically be dealt with using the ship's own resources. Any help from outside resources will involve waiting, and it may take quite some time and be quite difficult for external help to reach the ship.

13.2 Duties in an emergency situation

The duties required in an emergency situation and which should form the basis of an effective and, if possible, efficient response structure are: command, coordination, execution and support.

The structure that is considered classic in reference to the aforementioned duties is:

Captain: Maintains command of the ship and the emergency situation at all times. External help is requested through him and he makes all the decisions affecting the ship as a whole. The Captain informs the ship's owner and the consignee of the situation and maintains communication with the corresponding authorities.

Emergency Manager: This person is delegated the responsibility of resolving the emergency situation by the Captain. They are also responsible for coordinating intervention internally as well as any help that may come from outside. They activate the internal information plan.

Intervention Manager: This person leads the intervention group made up of internal teams, keeping the Emergency Manager informed at all times and requesting further intervention as support or for manoeuvres. They substitute for the Emergency Manager if need be.

Intervention Group: The composition of this group may vary depending on the circumstances of the situation. It is normally made up of an indeterminate number of teams corresponding to two different categories: primary intervention teams (P.I.T.) and secondary intervention teams (S.I.T.).

The first are on the scene when the situation first arises and they carry out duties which can be considered basic. The teams in the second category are made up of specialised personnel and they intervene when the primary teams are not enough or the situation requires intervention to avoid a disagreeable outcome even if it is not possible to return to normality.

These groups carry out what is technically known as a *step up*. The intervention of outside resources would be a further step up.

The personnel in these teams must be adequately trained to respond to all the possible risks they may face. This is in addition to the every day knowledge they need for their professional contracted positions.

Order Group: Members of this group have two main duties which come one after the other: to keep the area cordoned off and to help with the evacuation of people from one area to another within the ship, or the abandoning of it altogether. This is mainly done through directing the evacuees and transmitting calm to them.

Health Group: Members of this group move affected people to the first aid post, categorising them according to levels of seriousness and providing the necessary medical care.

Logistical Support Group: The duties of this group can be very varied, but can be divided into two main areas. Logistical support to the rest of the groups. Logistical support to all the people on the ship, moving cargo, removing objects, preparation of lifeboats, etc.

13.3 Emergency committee

The Captain may also create an emergency committee which is independent from the established emergency structure. The main characteristic of this committee is that it is internal; its objective is to resolve the emergency situation.

This committee is formed by:

- The Captain, who chairs it

- The bridge officials. One of these will also be the Emergency Manager

- The Engineering Manager

- The Purser

- Others

Here 'others' may include passengers who are specialised in the specific type of emergency. For example, an emergency involving a biological or chemical agent, food in bad condition, mass illness, etc.

13. 4 External help

13.4.1 In the port

Security forces and bodies:

Preferably the State Security Forces (the National Police Force and the Civil Guard) will intervene in cases of public order, antisocial behaviour, bomb threats, illegal immigration and stowaways, etc.

Fire and rescue services. These will mainly intervene in fire and rescue situations.

Port Authorities. All the help in port-related matters that come from contractors and subcontractors is channelled through these authorities.

Tug boats and pilots. Especially in fire situations and any other situations that require the ship to leave the dock.

13.4.2 At sea

- Other ships and the navy
- Maritime branch of the Civil Guard and Customs
- Environmental Authorities and their organisations
- Air rescue service
- Naval Captain – Control Tower
- Maritime rescue and safety society
- The Red Cross

13.5 Control and alarm systems

Security control

A basic function of a ship's security control system should be to provide a sufficient amount of information to the Captain in large blocks of content that in turn give access to more specific details of each situation. Diagram 1 shows the following blocks of content:

Monitoring parameters

Monitoring the parameters allows an abnormal situation to be identified, and means the primary course of action may be taken once the need for it has been confirmed.

Progress analysis

Continuous evaluations of people and the environment should be made to monitor the progress of the blocks corresponding to the ship and to find the best solutions to the situations which arise.

Diagram 1

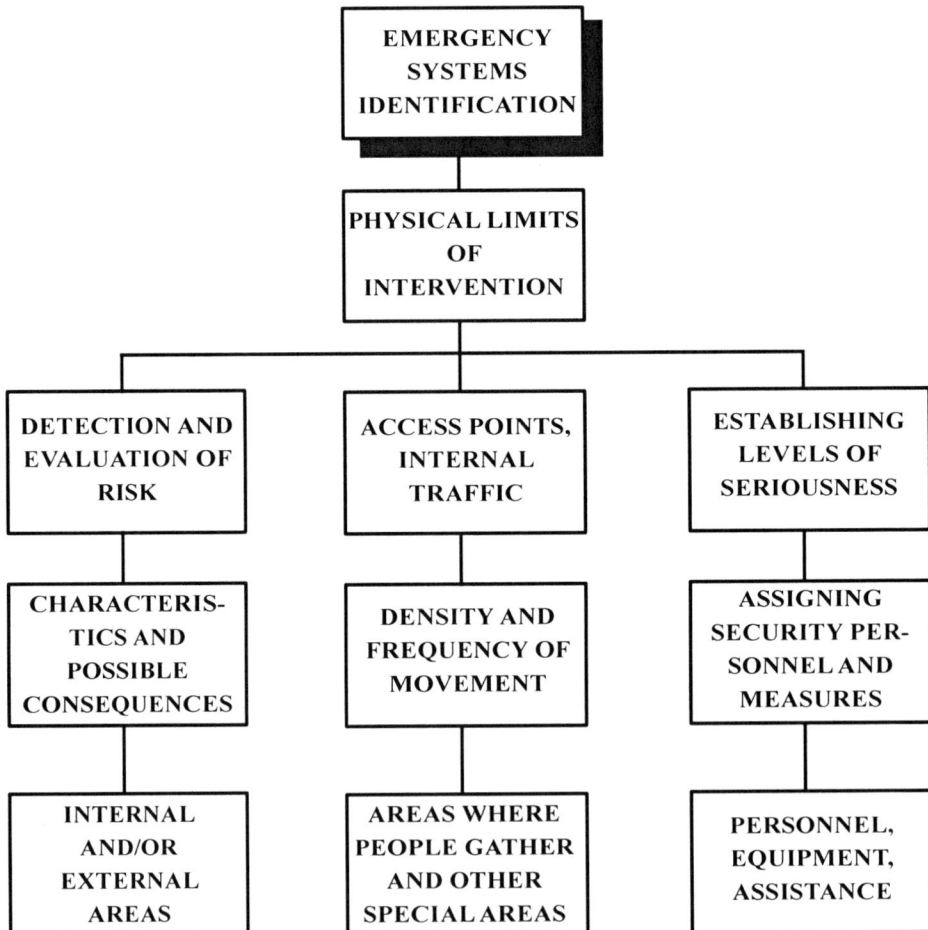

In diagram 2 we can see the blocks which determine the risk and make it easier to evaluate the level of security.

Engine room vulnerability

The analysis of an alarm situation and the courses of action to be taken anywhere on board, especially in the engine room, require a complete model of the internal and external relationships which will bring about the final control of the situation.

Diagram 2

```
                        ┌─────────────────┐
                        │    PROGRESS     │
                        │    ANALYSIS     │
                        └────────┬────────┘
                                 │
                        ┌────────┴────────┐
                        │    FOLLOW-UP    │
                        │   STRATEGIES    │
                        └────────┬────────┘
         ┌───────────────┬───────┴───────┬───────────────┐
┌────────────────┐┌────────────────┐┌──────────────┐┌──────────────┐
│   FOR AREAS    ││  RELATED TO    ││   EXTERNAL   ││   INTERNAL   │
│    AT RISK     ││      THE       ││   ASPECTS    ││   ASPECTS    │
│                ││   PERSONNEL    ││              ││              │
└────────┬───────┘└────────┬───────┘└──────┬───────┘└──────┬───────┘
┌────────────────┐┌────────────────┐┌──────────────┐┌──────────────┐
│   AVAILABLE    ││   RESPONSE     ││  ENVIRON-    ││   SUPPORT    │
│      AND       ││   OBTAINED     ││    MENT      ││  RESOURCES   │
│    APPLIED     ││     FROM       ││   AFFECTED   ││              │
│   RESOURCES    ││   TRAINING     ││              ││              │
└────────┬───────┘└────────┬───────┘└──────┬───────┘└──────┬───────┘
┌────────────────┐┌────────────────┐┌──────────────┐┌──────────────┐
│                ││   ADEQUATE     ││  EFFICIENCY  ││  COMMUNI-    │
│   RESULTING    ││   FOR THE      ││     OF       ││   CATION     │
│     NEEDS      ││ TYPE OF SHIP   ││  RESOURCES   ││  RESOURCES   │
│                ││ AND N°. PAX    ││    USED      ││              │
└────────┬───────┘└────────┬───────┘└──────┬───────┘└──────┬───────┘
┌────────────────┐┌────────────────┐┌──────────────┐┌──────────────┐
│   EFFICIENCY   ││                ││              ││ ORGANISA-    │
│      OF        ││   PERSONAL     ││   EXTERNAL   ││  TION OF     │
│   PREVENTIVE   ││    SAFETY      ││  RESOURCES   ││  EXTERNAL    │
│    MEASURES    ││  EQUIPMENT     ││  REQUESTED   ││  RESOURCES   │
└────────────────┘└────────────────┘└──────────────┘└──────────────┘
```

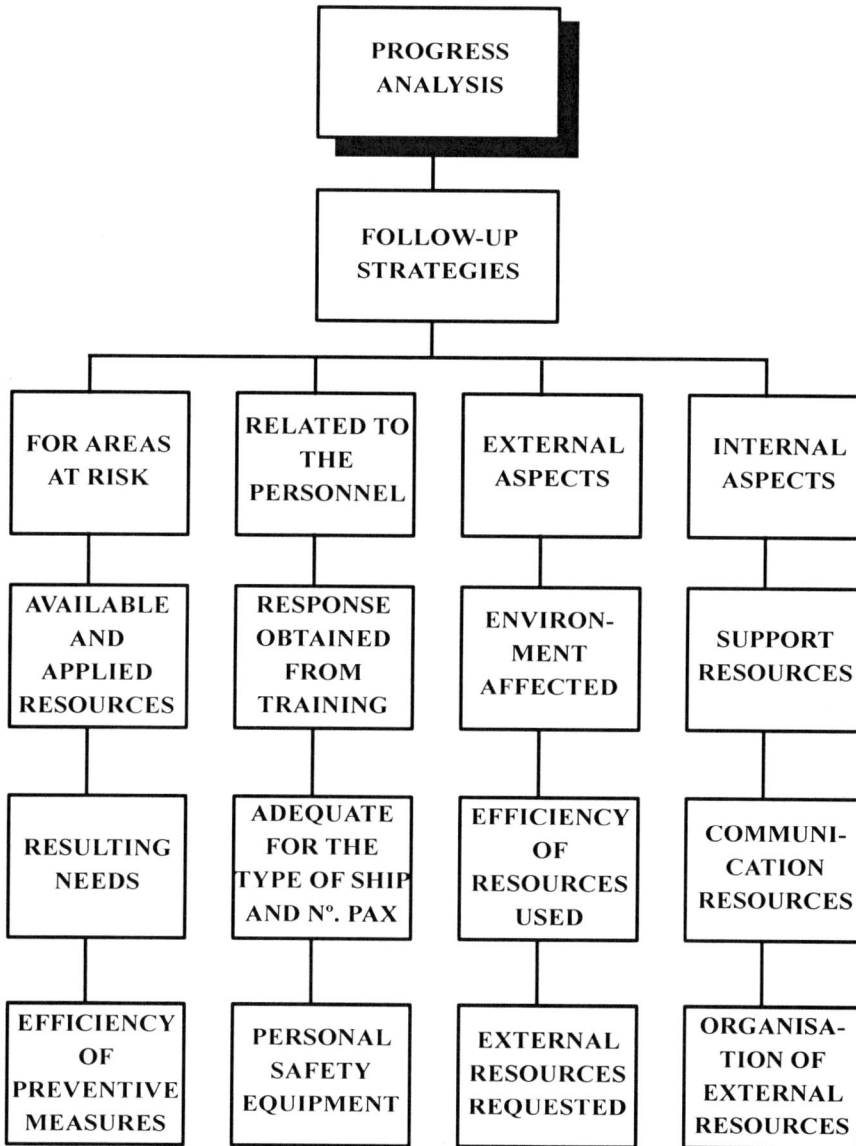

For this reason the system should incorporate information of all kinds, whether intrinsic to the department or coming from anomalies elsewhere. All aspects should be taken into consideration, all courses of action should be covered and the crew should be mobilised to carry them out.

The consequences of any action carried out on board should be considered with regard to the environment and linked to the respective pollution prevention plan or those created outside.

13.6 Comprehensive security plans

The technical and planning departments of the shipping companies will be in charge of the organisation and procedures of a comprehensive security plan, based on the analysis and study of:

- The vulnerability of the people and ships under protection
- Threats affecting the people and ships under protection
- Risk factors which could have an influence on protection
- The required level of security
- Security measures to be adopted
- The cost of the security measures and resources and of their maintenance in the short, medium and long term

The ultimate aim of a comprehensive security system is to detect danger and quickly relay the information to the control centre so that the best response can be organised.

13.7 Control systems

A wide variety of systems are available which cover a wide range of services, such as:

- Controlling the connection and disconnection of security systems
- Opening and closing of centres selling to the passengers, special retail units
- Custody of keys
- Monitoring the flow of personnel traffic in restricted areas
- Coordination with technical services in case of urgent intervention
- Access control according to a timetable
- Nighttime working of the product vending machines
- Monitoring the rounds made

13.8 Alarm reaction procedure

The first step that should be taken in the control room when an alarm is detected it to verify it via the resources it has available.

The basics of safe action

Although in the majority of cases neither the integrity or security of the ship is affected, there are occasions when its integrity and security can be threatened by the presence of people who seem suspicious for various reasons including:

- Being in a non-authorised area
- Acting suspiciously in the presence of the security guard
- The outward appearance of the suspect
- Strange behaviour
- Carrying luggage or packages that are not normal for that area

In these circumstances security in the area where the person is located will have to be re-established via two courses of action:

13.9 Security checks

This is the course of action taken to try and classify the situation which has arisen due to the presence of a suspicious person or people. It can be classified as: a normal situation, an alert, an alarm situation.

The security check can consist of simply observing the behaviour of the person to asking them to undo their jacket, anorak or coat, put their bags, packages or suitcases on the floor and turn right round slowly so that their body can be observed fully.

This will always be carried out wherever possible by two crew members, one of whom should carry out the intervention whilst the other provides protection, making sure the procedure does not take place on a dark area, an area where there is little visibility, among crowds, etc., in other words, choosing the ideal place as regards the safety of the crew members intervening.

As a result of the check, the classification of a situation that was normal can be changed to an alert or an alarm situation, or vice versa. The procedure to be followed by the security guards in each of the situations mentioned above should be as follows:

a) A normal situation. In this situation a person should only be asked to identify themselves or be informed of our intention or wishes, i.e. that they should leave the area they are in to inform them of some kind of prohibition. The questioning or communication will be done by the intervening crew member who should situate themselves half to one side of the person to be questioned and at approximately an arm's length. Meanwhile, the other crew member, as protection, will situate themselves further away from the subject thereby giving themselves the widest possible field of vision, not only covering the situation itself, but also the surrounding area. This distance can be around 2 to 3 m, and they should remain fully alert and ready to help their colleague if necessary.

b) An alert. The same form of questioning as above should be used, but in such cases there are indications that some extra precautions should be taken. These include carrying out a full security check as mentioned previously: undo clothes, turn around, etc. and, if a dangerous object is found or any difficulties are encountered, the crew member in charge of protection should be alerted and the suspect neutralised. The protecting crew member must be ready to intervene.

c) An alarm situation. This is a serious situation, prior to an arrest, or in which there is an imminent and real danger that could lead to confrontation. The crew members should work in a calm but energetic manner, ordering the suspect to remain still unless otherwise indicated and then handcuffing them, if deemed the necessary, and frisking them thoroughly. The protecting security guard (located in the same position as in the previous situations) should be in possession of a dissuasive object, keeping it discretely down the side of their leg, and should be ready to defend their colleague. Particular attention must be paid to the surrounding area and the movements made by the suspect.

13.9.1 Identifying people

Identifying a person is an action used to prove that person is who they say they are. The first and most basic form of identifying a person is to check their National Identity Document or passport, and in normal situations this will be enough. In an alert or an alarm situation, this identity document will need to be checked against police files over the phone or via radio with the corresponding security force.

The identification should be done in one of the two following ways, depending on whether it is carried out by one or two crew members:

a) One crew member only. They should request the document politely but in a firm and decided manner, explaining that it is required for their own safety as well as that of others aboard the ship. They should remain alert to any possible hostile response from the subject. The photograph, the issue date and, therefore, the expiry date should be observed and the document should be checked for any signs of manipulation. The condition of the document could be used to hide signs of manipulation, and in an alert or an alarm situation the crew member should proceed with extreme caution or wait for the arrival of a second crew member.

b) Two crew members. As in the case of the security check one of the crew members should carry out the identification of the person whilst the other protects their colleague. This second crew member will be the one who calls to verify the identity of the person if need be, taking all the precautionary and preventive measures necessary depending on the place and the situation.

14 Bomb threats

Bomb threats on merchant ships have never been given much thought during peace time and, as a result, have not had much influence in the ship's design or the operating procedures, the purpose of which are to transport people and cargo at sea. Nothing has been specifically written about merchant ships and, due to the special nature of the subject, it cannot be dealt with according to the construction and operation criteria of the Navy because:

> a) the Navy has strict security checks, with all crew members on the ship being well-known
>
> b) its vulnerability is to attack from the outside and it has its own preventive and protective security measures in place. The possibility of military intervention also exists.

Bomb threats or attacks on ships are as well publicised as their consequences are serious, and their seriousness is measured in human lives or goods lost. However, it is very difficult to obtain the results of an investigation as, in many cases, they are carried out while the ship is still at sea. It is for this reason so little has been written about the subject in scientific terms, except reports by the military and State Security Forces on other operations in different operational areas (buildings and facilities, industries and transport, all of them land-based). This information, obtained from the Special Intervention Unit of the Civil Guard, forms the basis of the current scientific and technical knowledge which has to be used as a basis for intervention procedures on board ship.

The International Maritime Organisation (IMO) has also introduced several resolutions which provide more information on passenger safety, as regards crowds in a state of shock or panic in crisis situations [MSC 66(68) and MSC 67(68) approved on 04.06.97] and the structure of an integrated system of contingency plans for shipboard emergencies [Resolution A.852(20) dated 27.11.97]. In both cases precautions are required to prevent the effects of explosives on board allowing passengers to be evacuated to identified safe areas.

A terrorist attack on a civilian target constitutes a threat to society, the effects and consequences of which can only be lessened if efficient preventive action is planned. One of the greatest risks to the population is the activation of explosives in an occupied area. The efficiency of the preventive action will be directly related to the use of courses of action which objectively take into account the physical parameters generated by the use of explosives.

As things stand today, there are no known procedures which provide a simulation of the destructive effects of a bomb on a ship, especially one which is carrying a large number of passengers.

It would be advisable to use a physical model so that any preventive approaches and solutions could take into account the technical criteria and the resistance of the materials used in the construction of passenger ships thereby providing information regarding the destructive effects of terrorist attacks using explosives. This way, when faced with a bomb threat, the ship's crew can move the passengers to relative safety and, at the same time, the best means of protection for the bomb disposal units of the State security forces that may be involved in the deactivation would be known.

To reach such an objective information should be available, both on board and at the shipping company, on the following:

    a.   The physical parameters (pressure and temperature) generated by each of the different types of explosives in areas similar in volume to the areas and spaces that can be found on a passenger ship.

    b.   The relationship of the physical variables above with the structural resistance of the ship in general and of the individual materials used in the ship's construction (outer layer, screens, decks, etc.).

    c.   The procedures to be included in the ship's security plans and to be applied anywhere on the ship in immediate intervention by those responsible.

This information could result in:

    a.   The management of intervention plans for controlling crowds (approximately 1,200 people) based on much more realistic and objective criteria.

    b.   The improvement, and guarantee of external intervention by the security forces in anti-terrorist intervention operations aboard ship.

    c.   A new basis to be applied in ship building to improve ship safety and maritime safety in general.

To achieve this ambitious objective, the work must be carried out by a group of professionals from different fields comprising experts and professionals in industrial and naval engineering, maritime engineering, security and maritime transport.

Attacks by criminal organisations and terrorists on civilian targets are all too familiar for the damage they inflict on people as well as property. When warning is given of a bomb threat on land or in any form of public or private transport (air transport included), there is always the possibility that everybody has enough time to put themselves at a safe distance out of reach of the effects of a possible explosion and thereby avoiding tragic consequences.

When this happens on a ship, from the very moment the bomb threat is issued, especially when the ship is at sea, it can be enormously difficult to abandon ship. This can be due to:

    a) adverse weather conditions and the state of the sea which can make it very difficult for people of all ages and conditions to get into the lifeboats or life rafts which, as their name indicates, are a clear reference to the extreme situation generated when a person climbs from a ship into a small craft.

    b) the uncertainty of whether to direct the passengers and crew to the lifeboat deck to begin evacuation (where the explosive device may be located) or to another area of the ship where currently the resistance to a voluntarily provoked explosion is unknown.

The defencelessness experienced by the Captain of a ship with 1200 people on board (passengers and crew) in a bomb threat situation can only be eradicated if he has prior knowledge of the nature of the threat and of the places on the ship which are safest as regards to withstanding the effects of the blast. Of course these areas must first be checked according to the established procedures for these cases to ensure they are free of hostile devices. These spaces should be able to withstand, to a reasonable extent, the effects of an explosion outside the area considered safe, or at least be safe enough to minimise the effects of the blast on the people using them as a refuge.

It is interesting, although rather surprising, to note that the design and calculations of passenger ships do not take into account acts of sabotage. Until recently this was of no great consequence, but it has become very important point due to the proliferation of terrorist acts.

Taking into account the fact that the State Security Forces (S.S.F.) now have resources which allow them to travel quickly in the marine environment (speed boats and helicopters) and that they can intervene in high risk situations such as those resulting from terrorist acts of this type, then they should also have a thorough knowledge of the safe areas so that, by a process of elimination, they can work out which are the weak points in the ship's structure to be able to exercise greater control:

a) over the safety of the members of the intervention team, by establishing adequate preventive and protective measures outside the reach of the possible explosion, and

b) over where it is easiest to force access to the ship to intervene in specific situations, such as hostage situations (just one example of possible terrorist acts).

Until just a few years ago a terrorist attack was a remote possibility with very low levels of probability, although history confirms such attacks did exist (P/S "SANTA MARTA" in 1962, P/S "ACHILLE LAURO" in 1985). Recent information published in the press indicates that the probability of a terrorist attack being carried out on a passenger ship (P/S) has increased dramatically (ETA wanted to blow up a Transmediterranean ferry in the port of Valencia. El País, Saturday 21.10.2000). This fact has been absolutely confirmed by the conclusions reached in the United States: due to the high vulnerability of ships and the little control and few measures acting as deterrents which are still used as security filters for the detection of risk, we should expect terrorist attacks on ships rather than on means of air transport which are currently more numerous.

If these predictions were to come true, they would cause widespread alarm among the population, possibly due to the number of victims which, between passengers and crew members, would reach a number similar to that of the recent, sadly remembered attack in New York.

For the first time, due to the aforementioned reasons, and the knowledge needed about the structural vulnerability of the ship, we can keep ahead of the terrorists in the following ways:

a) Increasing the safety of people who may be involved, thereby reducing the number of victims. This is done by increasing their protection by locating them in an area of greater structural resistance.

b) Designing plans for intervention on board both for the Captain of the ship affected by the threat (who could then predict the effects and possible consequences and take the right course of action to get the greatest number of passengers to safety as possible) and the S.S.F. (who could objectively identify the strong and weak points of the structure and use them to their advantage in their intervention).

The improvement in the safety of people (passengers, crew and intervening forces) as a result of the investigation of the effects and consequences of the explosion of a device in the superstructure of the ship (inside or out), in other words, in the topside and upper works (above water level), where the areas usually used by the passengers are located, such as the cabins, chambers, cafés, cinemas, etc., would be of great use to those responsible for the ship.

Areas located below the waterline (in the underwater hull), although they could pose a more serious problem, are not dealt with in the area of bomb threat security for the following reasons:

a) they can be, and in fact are, more controlled by the crew: it is more difficult for someone who is not a crew member to access the nerve centres (passing control points).

b) because an explosion in an area of the ship below the water line will inevitably mean major leaks accompanied by the danger of flooding and severe listing of the ship, both of which are problems which are perfectly well-known and understood, as much on a naval engineering (design) level as by the professional seafarers (operation of the ship).

14.1 Explosive device threats

A bomb threat can be defined as an anonymous announcement, made by whatever means, of the existence of an activated explosive device ready to explode in a specific place.

From this definition we can take the essential elements which all need to coincide for us to be able to determine if this is a true threat. The elements are the following:

a)   An anonymous announcement. This is understood as the person not identifying themselves personally, although they may attribute the bomb to their group or organisation.

b)   Means of communication used. The most commonly used means of communication is the telephone, although there may be cases of threats sent by post.

c)   The existence of an explosive device. In the announcement we will be informed that a device which is ready to explode has been placed or is going to be placed.

d)   Specific place. If a specific place is not given, then we are faced with a general bomb threat which requires preventive action on a large scale.

When the threat contains all the elements listed above we can consider it a typical threat with the following type of response being required:

a)   Firstly, although the majority of bomb threats are hoaxes, the substantial amount of explosions which do actually take place oblige us to consider each threat as real until otherwise proven.

b)   Both the explosive itself and the prior warning, whether real or not, cause significant losses.

c)   A preventive security programme reduces the risk of bombs or artefacts being placed inside a ship, and as a result, the organisation can be fairly sure if it receives a bomb threat that it is a hoax, meaning the response can be minimal. With only 2% of threats being detected as real, preventive security has obvious advantages from a cost/efficiency point of view.

14.1.1 Causes

There are a variety of motivational reasons behind bomb threats based on certain causes which are related to the interest the informant has in making the announcement. The main causes are as follows:

a)   Terrorist cause. Issued by members of terrorist groups, these threats aim to create instability by altering the normality of a specific activity and thus making their objectives more widely publicised.

b) Social causes. These are usually based on abnormal work or social situations. They are aimed at disturbing the peace and tranquillity of a workplace or business by interfering in their work. These threats frequently take place during strikes and conflicts at work due to negotiating agreements, etc.

c) Psychological causes. These threats originate in abnormal psychological behaviour in adults. They make the announcements to satisfy a personal need, with no other aim than to disrupt an organisation, and all of it motivated by their own pathological personality.

It is of interest to note here the sharp increase in bomb threats in the aftermath of the explosion of a real device. Hoax callers make the most of the psychosis in society which will provoke a greater reaction to the threats: evacuations, police movement, etc.

d) Common causes. These refer to threats based on a person's specific interest which does not fall into any of the previous categories.

This group includes threats made to get an aeroplane delayed so that the person in question will arrive in time to board it; threats made shortly before the end of the working day to ensure the evacuation of the building so everyone leaves work early and, in general, all threats of a similar nature which are borne of personal interest.

14.1.2 Types of communication

A bomb threat is issued, primarily, in written form or by phone, with the latter being the most common. If a written threat is received then the following precautions should be taken: avoid handling the paper and the envelope and immediately make a photocopy of both to work with in the investigation. The originals should be handed in to the State Security Forces and Bodies for their investigation, and they should be informed of exactly how the communiqué was received and the course of action taken after its opening. As regards threats issued over the telephone, it is important to remember that the threat will normally be received by one of the operators manning the ship's telephone lines, the numbers of which appear on leaflets about the itineraries, departure dates and the services offered by the shipping company. They may also call the head office or the docks themselves, preferably speaking to the person in charge.

a) The few seconds duration of the call may be the only contact there is with the anonymous caller, which is why it is so important to record all the information relayed as accurately as possible.

b) If the person receiving the call has been instructed in how to deal with an emergency of this kind, they may be able to provide information of great value to the subsequent process. On the other hand, if the person loses control when they receive the call, then the terms of the message will most likely become distorted causing unease and even chaos.

14.1.3 Techniques for prolonging the call

The telephone can sometimes be used by strangers to warn us that an explosive device has been placed, or that another situation has arisen which requires us to obtain the maximum information. To do so we need to prolong the call as long as possible and keep the caller speaking to get all the information we need.

However, this situation may vary depending on the motivation the caller has to carry out the threat. A mentally disturbed person, or simply one who does not want to cause any casualties, only damage, will let the conversation be prolonged, especially if the operator receiving the call knows how to make the most of the fact.

To do so, the receiver must remain calm and remember that the caller:

- knows where the device is (exact place)

- when it will explode

- what it is like, in other words what the device looks like and what is inside it

The main objective will, of course, be to get answers to these questions, so they should be the first that are asked. These can then be followed by other questions to glean further information, although it important to remember that asking too many questions can make the caller nervous and make them hang up. The questions that could be asked are the following:

- How big is the device?

- Is it working now? (especially if it is a time bomb counting down)

- What do you want us to do?

- Why are you calling?

- What are your demands to stop the explosion?

- Why did you place the device?

- What explosive is in it?

- What is your job?

- Have you got family?

- Any other questions of a moral/charismatic type

Unless the caller is willing to collaborate, which is quite unlikely, it is possible that the answers to the questions above (if they were replied to) are not true. They may, however, be useful in determining if we are dealing with a traumatised person and, in the meantime, gaining time to figure out the best course of action to take.

It is important to try every way possible to keep the caller talking.

Given that the average number of words used in a threat over the telephone is between ten and twenty, some of the strategies that can be used to get the caller to talk as much as possible are:

-    Doubt the seriousness of the call. This is sure to infuriate the caller and keep them talking until they have convinced us to take them seriously.
-    Tell them about the possible presence of children or innocent people in the area affected by the threat and ask if they are that callous that they would let these people be victims too.
-    Ask if the device is located in a place which does not exist instead of asking for the exact location of the bomb. For example, ask if the bomb is on the 7th deck when we know the ship only has three, or ask if it in a place between two corridors, knowing that that place does not exist there.
     If they answer in the affirmative then it is most likely a hoax. If, on the other hand, they say know then we need to continue with the questioning.
-    Pretend the line is not working well to prolong the conversation further.

We do not need to play clean with someone who makes a call of this type as they do not.

As a consequence, we need to do everything we can to keep the caller on the line: lie without any qualms about it, give out false information, flatter them, provoke them or take pity on them. All this is will help gain time and information to try and stop the person before innocent victims are claimed.

Whatever happens, in a call of this type a tape recorder will be an advantage and will give us more details about the caller.

If there is no recorder available then the exact words spoken by the stranger must be written down immediately after the conversation has taken place and before they can be forgotten.

It would be of little use to have prolonged the call made by the stranger (and obtaining more information then they were intending to give in the first place) if, by not writing those details down immediately, they were lost due to being forgotten later on.

For this reason it is very useful that people in charge of receiving calls, or anyone who is in the position to receive information orally in some way, to have at hand and fill in a copy of a form similar to the one shown below.

14. 2 The characteristics of an explosive

The characteristics which define an explosive are:

a) *Power*: This is the energy that an explosive can create. It is measured by the mechanical effects it is able to produce.

b) *Sensitivity*: This is the measurement of the ease with which an explosive will enter a state of reaction.

c) *Stability*: This is the ability of an explosive to maintain its chemical composition unaltered for a certain length of time in normal conditions. The main causes of instability are the chemical composition of the explosive itself and the impurities it contains.

Highly explosive materials can detonate another explosive nearby without any direct contact or connection between the two.

This transmission is caused by an impact wave or shock wave passing from one mass to another.

14.3 Classification of explosives

Explosives can be classified in many different ways. Regarding the main substances they contain, they are classified as:

a) Chemical types: aromatic nitro-derivatives, nitroamines y nitroamides, etc.

b) Mixtures with an explosive base: of TNT, of ammonium nitrate, of nitrocellulose, or with an explosive exogenous base, etc.

c) Mixtures with a non active-explosive base: with nitro polyalcohol dynamite, of an energy-giving oxidant, of potassium nitrate.

d) Mixtures with a non inert-explosive base: with nitro polyalcohol dynamite, of an energy-giving oxidant, detonating mixtures.

Regarding their application and the characteristic effects, they are classified as:

a) Initiators: the burning or detonation of these is used to ignite another explosive.

b) Breakers: these are used to break or fragment the surface or object they are in contact with.

c) Propellants: the speed of transformation of these devices is used as a propulsion or projection charge.

Regarding the systems which cause the initiation of the explosive devices and, consequently, the explosion, they are classified as:

a) Timer or timed devices. Fundamentally those which cause an explosion at a specific time which was set beforehand. These include time bombs, electronic devices and pyrotechnical devices, depending on whether the mechanism is clockwork, radio-controlled or whether it is heat that activates the explosion process.

b) Movement, pendular or inertia devices. These are more selective devices and the ideal place to put them is in a car which, when started, will activate the mechanism that produces the explosion.

c) Victim operated. As the name suggests, these devices are activated when operated or handled in some way or another. The most obvious example is the "letter bomb", which is designed to explode when opened or when they are pressed in a certain way or subject to some kind of traction.

d) Incendiary devices. These can be made from a wide variety of products available on the market, and can use different types of containers, bottles being preferred. They are essentially made up of a liquid (acid) which is in contact with a solid (salts) next to flammable liquids. They have a very delayed point of ignition and their behaviour, as far as the possibility of causing accidents or victims goes, depends on how they are handled.

14.4 The effects of explosions

The main effects of an explosion can be divided into three types:

a) Heat. The heat produced will hardly have any effect unless it is an incendiary device, or there is flammable material in the area of the explosion, in which case we are confronted with a fire protection problem.

b) Mechanical. These are the results of the rapid expansion of gases at a high temperature in a small space, which creates pressure transmitted at high speed. In the area surrounding or close to the explosive device, this reaction causes other, purely mechanical, phenomena which are those that cause breakages, destruction, secondary explosions, etc. The main ones are the following:

    a. Blast of air. The gases from the explosion, travelling at approximately 25,000 km/h, hit the atmosphere around the explosive and, by transferring a good part of their movement, create a virtual hurricane. This phenomenon is only experienced a short distance from the source of the explosion (approximately 8 metres for 250 kg of explosive).

b. Shock wave. Due to the force of the hot gases from the explosion with the atmosphere surrounding the explosive, a shock wave is created which has all the characteristics of a sound wave (frequency, amplitude, etc.), although its speed is much greater. Its energy is absorbed by its speed which is in turn reduced over distance until, at the end of its journey, it becomes a true sound wave (it moves spherically from the centre of the explosion outwards, not dragging the atmosphere in which it is spreading behind it, but causing a vertical elevation of pressure.).

c. Suction wave. The compression produced in the air mass is followed by a quick sucking towards the centre of the explosion. As a consequence of the vacuum created, another wave is formed travelling in the opposite direction as the shock wave, which lasts longer and continues to break things, making the objects affected fall towards the centre of the explosion.

Both waves leave their mark on the obstacles they find in their way, and they can be sufficiently strong enough to inflict considerable damage even a long distance away through the combined effect of pressure and dragging. They can sometimes even affect the frequency of the objects themselves as, if they are close to the waves, they are violently shaken by reverberating vibrations.

c) Projectiles. At the same time as the other effects are taking place, and as a consequence of the pressure generated, everything in contact with the explosive and everything in its vicinity are thrown violently into the air. It is important to take care with regards to the possible consequences of flying fragments as shards of glass can fly quite a distance, so it is advisable to stay away from windows and similar. The ideal protection from the blast would be behind screens, cover, etc., or by remaining at a safe distance as indicated in tables 1 and 2:

Table 14.1

DATA	QUANTIFICATION		OBSERVATIONS
QUANTITY OF EXPLOSIVE IN RELATION TO THE EFFECTS PRODUCED BY THE PRESSURE WAVE	4 kg	25 m	At the distances stated considerable damage can be produced. If the circumstances vary the results can also vary considerably.
	10 kg	40 m	
	20 kg	100 m	

Table 14.2

DATA	QUANTIFICATION		OBSERVATIONS
QUANTITY OF EXPLOSIVE IN RELATION TO THE DISTANCE WHICH CAN BE PRESUMED SAFE	0,5 kg	100 m	These distances take into account the effects of any possible projecttiles thrown out as well as those produced by the pressure wave. Any special causes which may make the results vary noticeably are not taken into account.
	1 kg	175 m	
	5 kg	250 m	
	10 kg	300 m	
	20 kg	500 m	

14.5 Intervention in cases of explosive device threats

Once the threat has been received, intervention by the ship's security service begins by immediately communicating it:

a)   To the person responsible for security in the shipping company.

b)   To the State Security Forces: at sea via the shipping control tower, and in the port via the security system established by the port authorities. In both cases the police emergency numbers should also be called.

Whilst waiting for the intervention by the experts, both deferred (at sea) and that carried out by the police (in the port), all the areas of the ship where it is most likely a device would be placed should be searched. These areas may include the following, for example:

a.   Areas of passenger traffic

b.   Halls, entrances and toilets

c.   Corridors and stairwells, etc.

d.   Under the seats

e.   Car decks

Permanent communication with the S.S.F. will be established to inform them of the circumstances surrounding the threat, and the details known due to the guidelines for prolonging the call. They will be told of the procedure followed to find the explosive and the general inspection of the ship, as well as the success or failure of these actions.

If so requested, a crew member should accompany the intervening officers around the ship to carry out the inspection or any checks considered necessary.

When the security forces have finished the search and leave the ship, having found the threat to be a hoax, the people in charge of security at the shipping company must be notified and normal activity can be re-established.

If the evacuation of the ship was ordered as a result of the search, then the evacuation plan should be followed.

The following should be taken into consideration as general rules:

a)   The explosive device threat should not be revealed in an uncontrolled way so as to avoid panic situations which may make the whole scenario worse and inhibit the search and evacuation procedures.

b)   If it is decided that the evacuation plan should be followed, then it should be done in accordance with the established guidelines and in an orderly and calm fashion.

c)   It is important to remember that the officers of the State Security Forces do not know the ship or the place the threat refers to. For this reason it is essential that the crew help by acting as guides, answering any questions they are asked and helping in any way they can.

d)   If the decision is made to evacuate, a strict control of the entrances to the boat must be maintained with all the necessary precautions in place. This has the double aim of complying with the order to evacuate and also avoiding anyone entering.

e)   If this kind of incident happens fairly frequently, it is a good idea to keep a record of the threats made as regards number, the most common times they are made, any links to periods of seasonal activity and, in general, any circumstances which could help prevent damage.

14. 6 Search and detection

Once the explosive device threat is known about and communication has been established outside the ship and the correct courses of action have been taken, it is time to search for the device using very specific procedures.

A threat made about the existence of an explosive device sparks an investigation or search for the device itself. It is important to remember this and the heads of security on the ship must plan and create investigation or search teams, however difficult it may seem, to avoid the search being carried out in a disorganised way and end up being counterproductive because of the danger that may be involved.

To guarantee the success of these courses of action, it is a good idea to have carried out simulations previously. By simulating the situations and practising the procedures the teams become quicker and waste less time in their searches, although it is always better to carry out a slow search than a disorganised and hasty one.

The search for the device can be carried out by:

a)   The ship's crew. The staff who work in the affected department or area are ideal as they know the place well, allowing them to quickly detect any foreign object, or one which has been tampered with or is out of place. Due to the risk involved in the task, without taking anything else into consideration, the job has to be voluntary.

b)   If it is the case that among the ship's crew there are teams who are competent in search procedures, and who have specialist knowledge and resources for detection and protection, then they should be sent to search the areas where the probability of the device being located is higher.

c)   When the find is made, or rather, when a suspicious object has been found, the person or persons who found it should not touch it and should prevent anyone else from touching it. They should inform the leader of the search party immediately, clear the area of people and try and report as many details as possible.

d)   External security personnel may also carry out the search. In this case, bearing in mind the fact that they are probably well informed on the subject and are trained for this type of intervention, they will probably only need accompanying, with all the safety guarantees in place, by a member of the crew to identify the search area.

e)   The task of searching in all situations actually corresponds to the State Security Forces and Bodies who have a specially trained team and sophisticated equipment.

When the State Security Forces and Bodies take charge of the situation, the role of the personnel on board, specifically the search teams, will be one of collaboration. This does not mean it is any less positive, as the knowledge of the areas within the ship will be of great use in the search process.

14.7 Search areas

The search should be carried out in the following areas:

a)   Areas inside the ship. Starting with the assumption that a person placing an explosive device on a ship will look for a place that is accessible to the public and, at the same time, somewhere they can be as alone as possible, the following must be searched: toilets, plant pots, hallways, large ashtrays and bins, rooms of all types, behind and below radiators (if there are any), lifts, empty corridors, under stairs, etc. The search should be done in a logical way in all the rooms.

In the case of the cabins, the search should be based on the quantity and type of objects rather than on the area itself. A detailed search of all the objects, even those on the wall and the ceilings (such as air-conditioning apparatus or air vents) not forgetting the mouldings and false ceilings, should be made. Rugs must be folded, never rolled. The investigation of these areas should be based on logic and common sense.

Taking into account the fact that on the ship access to the nerve centres and control centres (engine room, bridge, storerooms and security booths, etc.) is very restricted and only authorised for crew members, these should not be considered areas with a high threat level. However, this criteria has to be weighed up alongside their true vulnerability, as regards risk analysis for such areas.

b) The outside areas of the ship itself. These vary according to the characteristics and design of the ship's superstructure, but the following are very important: entrances and exits, corners, cornices, windows, doors and hatches, decorations, drains and gutters, any possible hiding place, especially boxes for safety equipment, inside the open lifeboats, etc.

c) Areas outside the ship itself. The search of the area outside the ship should be done by the S.S.F., except in the case of the immediate access routes to the ship which need to be guaranteed as safe evacuation routes for if the ship needs to be evacuated. These include ramps and gangplanks used as connectors or for accessing the ship, and the immediate area around the ship which could be used as locations for possible explosive devices. All vehicles parked on the quay near the ship and which are not sufficiently identifiable will be investigated thoroughly.

The procedure will always be to search from bottom to top (from the deck to the ceiling), especially inside. In the area surrounding a building, the actual area to be searched will logically depend on the actual size of the area itself. The search should start at the building and work outwards, with special attention being paid to any earth that has been disturbed.

14.8 Search techniques

The search operations carried out by the crew must be directed and coordinated by the crisis manager located in the security control centre. This person must collect all the data and record all the incidents that occur, as these will later be of vital importance for the police Tedax (Spanish bomb disposal) teams.

To reduce the undisputable danger of the search, the teams should comprise a limited number of people, such as one or two people. One person would be the ideal, but a team of two has the advantage of being able to help each other as regards knowledge of the area and the ability to discern suspicious objects is concerned.

The search should be carried out in an orderly fashion so that it is not compromised. No object should be left uninspected and no area should be left unsearched and, above all, nobody should expose themselves to an accident for any reason.

There should be three phases to the search:

a) First phase, the observation of everything from the floor to waist height.
b) Second phase, the observation of everything from waist height to head height.
c) Third phase, the observation of everything left between head height and the ceiling, including the false ceiling.

Searches in rooms and bedrooms, carried out by two investigators, should be done in such a way that there is always a maximum distance between them wherever possible. This avoids both of them being exposed to the effects of an explosion. One of them should move to the farthest corner, while the other stays close to the door. They should begin their search from these positions.

The procedure for searching the decks should be similar. One of the investigators will go to the end of the area, remaining in sight, and the other will stay at the beginning. Starting in these positions, they will move in opposite directions, using a central corridor, for example, as an axis for their advance. Each of them should search to one side of the central corridor, and they should always try to keep as far away from each other as possible.

In outdoor areas the principle of the two searchers never being close together should be maintained. They should work parallel to one another, but one sufficiently further back from the other to create a safe distance in case the other finds the device.

Regarding the system used for the search, the strict order to be followed should be based on tried and tested systems, and always with the following general rule: searches should be made from the outside in and from the bottom upwards.

Searches need not only be made when there is a bomb threat. Preventive searches should be made to educate the personnel, to practise following the rules and guidelines, to try out the system and to regularly monitor the safety of the ship.

Another important rule, for both preventive and real searches, is that all the objects and places investigated should be sealed and labelled to avoid time being wasted by repeated searches or, what is worse, not carrying out certain searches.

Given the danger of an explosion, an effort must be made to reduce the effects of one, especially in vital areas. Although there are appropriate containers on the market, the following may be used:

a) Sacks made of soft material which can be packed around the device to insulate it and protect vital areas and material.

b) Padded containers which absorb the shock wave.

c) Special (anti-explosive) blankets that are on the market for dealing with small devices (such as letters, packages, etc.).

d) Materials which tend to fragment or which could produce dangerous fragments should never be used.

If the ship is in the port then it is important to remember that the personnel authorised to touch an explosive device are the State Security Forces and Bodies. These forces must be collaborated with, especially by providing information or by accompanying them as they proceed to secure areas, but crew members should never go beyond these duties.

14.9 Detection of possible suspicious packages

The following measures are known to be efficient: do not smoke, do not throw water on the package or get it wet in any way, do not move it manually, do not open it, do not move metal objects close to it, do not perforate it.

With suspicious packages in areas where there are people, do not take the package away until the people have been evacuated.

Do not play the hero. This area of work corresponds to the professional bomb disposal team of the S.S.F.

When the threat comes in the form of a letter or package, the following clues should be visible: the sender or its country of origin are unclear, it is unbalanced or the contents are not equally distributed, it is excessively heavy in relation to its size, it is bendable at the edges or in the centre but cannot be folded, it is excessively hard or rigid, there are bulges caused by wires in the packaging, it has greasy marks on the outside, it smells of almonds, marzipan or some other strange smell, it is too well sealed with glue or adhesive tape, it has a second layer of packaging which is also perfectly sealed.

In such cases, the measures which should be taken when a device is discovered in a letter or a package are: do not let anyone touch it, do not play with it, handle it carefully, being careful not to force it, evacuate the immediate and surrounding areas if necessary, depending on the size of the package, keep personnel away from the area, during the evacuation open doors and windows, do not try to neutralise it with water, contact the State Security Forces.

If specially trained personnel are available and there is safety equipment aboard, the explosive device can be put in an adequately protected place or covered with an anti-explosive blanket.

14.10 Monitoring vehicles

The monitoring of vehicles is an important link in the security chain on ferry-type passenger ships, as they are ideal for carrying a large amounts of explosives and for reaching vulnerable parts of the ship if access control is insufficient.

Vehicles must be searched prior to boarding in an area of the port chosen so that the farther the parked vehicles are from the passenger boarding area and the vital areas or the ship's superstructure and points of access, the greater the safety aspect.

Regarding the exterior check of the vehicle which must be done when there is a suspicion it may carry an explosive device, it important to point out that one of the best places to hide a device is on the underneath. This makes the inspection of the vehicle rather uncomfortable, especially if the weather is bad, which can lead to a weariness resulting in a dangerous neglect of duty on behalf of the security guard in charge of checking vehicles.

To avoid such a scenario, equipment has been devised in the form of mirrors with a long handle at an angle to make checking the bottom of the vehicle much easier. It is advisable for the equipment to also have some kind of light attachment to help check shadowy areas as this is extremely useful, especially in checks carried out at night.

These vehicle searches should not exclude well-known vehicles as their owners or drivers may be the unwitting carriers of explosive devices.

It is recommended that the person checking the vehicle should be accompanied by its occupant or driver during the process, especially in the case of vehicles carrying merchandise.

The search should be carried out in a methodical and orderly fashion, from the front to the back, first outside and then inside. It should include the engine compartment, the driver and passenger area and the boot. After this the underneath should be checked using the aforementioned equipment if possible. Both the bonnet and boot of the car should be opened by the occupant or driver of the vehicle.

15 Dealing with a crisis

15.1 Introduction

A crisis is the continuation of an emergency situation after this has surpassed a critical threshold.

The critical threshold is very variable and depends on factors of time, place, the sensitivity of the persons involved, and the emphasis and the guidance by third parties, among others.

We must not forget that the word crisis, from the Greek *krinein* (to decide), means "the culminating moment in a serious process".

According to the U.S. Army Time–Sensitive Planning a crisis is an incident or situation which poses a threat and that develops rapidly, creating extraordinary social, economic and operational conditions, etc.

The concept is more clearly defined in the Civil Defence manual. A crisis is a situation created by a momentary or lasting rupture with the prevailing order of life, provoked by internal or external causes which put the relevance of the fundamental values for that order in danger, creating a state of uncertainty with little time available to make pressing decisions and, in some cases, with few resources for intervention.

Regarding business organisations, for a shipping company with the ship as its production centre it is best to use the following definitions of the concept of a crisis:

- a. A change in the normal events which affect an organisation, alter its capacity for action and which demands quick decisions be made.
- b. A chain of events which leads to a breakdown in operations and which definitively influences our capacity for action.

The difference between a crisis and an emergency is that the former is more serious than all predictable emergencies which have been studied and prepared for with resources, feedback, support and insurance.

A breakdown in the normality of a situation can be defined by the following levels of seriousness in ascending order: normality, problems/breakdowns, incident, emergency, crisis.

A *problem* is understood as something which only hinders normality.

An *incident* is something which affects normality and reduces the level of this normality or the scope of it for a short period of time.

An *accident* takes place over a short period of time, but breaks with normality and the level of normality generally falls towards zero with limited scope.

An *emergency* destroys normality altogether and, as a result, the level of normality tends towards, and does reach, zero. All areas are affected. External help is needed. The time it takes to develop is limited and can be calculated, as can the losses produced.

A *crisis* not only destroys normality, but affects the normality of other groups as well. The time it takes to develop cannot be calculated, nor can the consequences and, therefore, neither can the losses it entails. From the very first moment the level of normality drops towards zero, especially as regards the psychological/spiritual aspects, rather than the physical/material ones.

The intervention carried out in an emergency situation is a response to the identification and evaluation of the risks. It follows certain rules and can be planned in detail or very strict procedures may be established.

A crisis, on the other hand, can be provoked by so many exogenous or endogenous factors that it is impossible to follow such strict rules and procedures. This does not mean, however, that a crisis cannot be predicted nor dealt with using a minimum of techniques.

15.2 Planning

Planning for a crisis consists of establishing (after a general planning phase) a crisis system comprising the following subsystems: information, activation, proposal, execution, monitoring, and deactivation.

An accident aboard ship could cause a crisis in its shipping company, and even between countries, but it is very unlikely that a ship will suffer this kind of crisis and its shipping company not. For this reason, a crisis on board ship must be analysed with the shipping company forming a part of the crisis. In an emergency, the command, coordination and execution structure is totally internal with regards to the ship. During a crisis, this structure is external with regards to the ship, but internal as regards the shipping company. The Captain, and the human and technical resources which he has available, form part of a high level operation.

Whilst in an emergency the highest level decisions are made by the Captain, in a crisis they are made by the highest ranking director of the shipping company or the crisis manager.

The organisational structure in a crisis situation consists of the following:

Committees
In a crisis, the committee (also known as the crisis cabinet), is chaired by the director with the participation of the crisis coordinator or manager, and the directors of the different departments within the shipping company who are needed depending on the type of crisis.

The managing director or president of the company will only be involved when there are strategic or important decisions to be made, although they should be kept regularly informed of how the crisis is progressing.

The communication plan
Any official may be delegated the responsibility of putting the information plan into action as far as the passengers on a ship are concerned. This is a plan which directly supports the emergency operation.

Conversely, in a crisis situation the communication plan is directed at the general public and other groups, and is normally broadcast via the media.

The spokesperson, as the face of the communication plan, should be a professional and know techniques for controlling and dealing with tense situations.

A good emergency plan with a bad information plan can be successful. On the other hand, a good crisis management plan with a bad communication plan is sure to be a failure. We could go even further by saying a bad crisis management plan with a good communication plan can be a success.

The recipients of an information plan are limited: the passengers. The recipients of a communication plan are the public in general. However, it is advisable to identify which groups within the general public will be most interested: those affected, relatives of the crew and passengers, shareholders, suppliers, the authorities in general and port authorities, port personnel, future clients, potential clients, auxiliary services, the competition, the staff of the shipping company itself, etc.

15.3 Aspects of crisis situations

Each crisis develops at its own speed and goes in its own direction.

A constant and concerted effort should be made to ascertain where we want, or can get, the situation to go and how long we have available to get information (the more reliable the better), although this will be practically impossible, obliging us, in the majority of cases, to work it out for ourselves or make guesses. Any details we can get will be valuable for this.

All courses of action taken must be aimed at stopping the advance of the crisis and to slow it down. With each course of action taken, a decision must be made about how much it should be publicised or how discreet we should be.

To fight against time and win is that important that it means the command should have all the bodies and means necessary for receiving and providing information and following the courses of action necessary.

The fight against the crisis tends to go two steps forward and three steps back. We will only be losing one step each time. Later on our position will become firmer and we will begin to advance little by little.

Attack, attack, attack, is the basis for resolving a crisis situation. That is, however, easy to say; what is difficult is to know how, when and with what level of discretion we should do it. If we know that, then the next step is to achieve coordination.

Quite often in crisis situations some of the services needed or the people in charge of basic departments are missing or not available. These should be substituted immediately.

An essential characteristic of the crisis team is its ability to work as a team in a disciplined and detailed way, beginning and ending the course of action at the time and place indicated.

When the crisis stems from voluntary action, the director must know how to accept or refuse the demands received, and how to do it calmly, justifying any refusals, standing their ground and negotiating the demands as far as possible.

In these cases the director is, above all, a negotiator and trader. If they believe that someone else in the team would be more successful with the negotiation, then they can delegate.

Information refers to collecting together news items, looking for information, forming opinions, giving information, resolving differences, being connected.

The objective of the information is to follow what is happening and, particularly, to know what will happen.

Attention focuses on the dead and injured, grouping them together/personalising them, increasing quality, predicting needs, seeking recuperation.

The objective of the attention is to recuperate normality, to keep control with surveillance.

Action taken to control the situation will be aimed at all the causes, all the further developments, all people, all movements, all resources, all the ways out of the situation.

The objective of the control will be to create certain levels of safety, to control the attackers.

The principles of *logistics* consist of providing resources, eliminating resources and teams, avoiding damage and loss, starting the recuperation, and preparing support.

The objective of logistics is to recuperate normality, and to provide or withdraw resources.

The board comprises: the president/owner, finance director, personnel director, legal advisor, image consultant, press officer, representatives from the operational teams, and State representatives.

The objective of the board is to direct the action and advise on support.

15.4 Parameters which define and differentiate crisis situations

a)   The instigators: an individual, a team, a group.

b)   The motivation: political, financial, mental imbalance, vandalism, social.

c)   The potential victims: the instigator or instigators themselves, a specific person or group, groups, collectives, crowds.

d)   The final objective: within our reach, possible through negotiation, out of our reach, out of the reach of the government.

e)   The level of vulnerability of the attacker: easy, complex, with possible serious consequences, with serious consequences.

f)   The skill behind the threat: proven/reliable, questionable/possible, doubtful/not reliable.

g)   The determination to carry out the threat: decided/sure, decided/not fully, divided at a decision level.

15.5 Analysis of the level of self-protection

The basis of a safety analysis is the study of the capacity to prevent, dissuade, limit or react when faced with a possible attack.

Prevention
A combination of factors to make sure that they CANNOT attack what we want to protect. This is normally done on the following basis:

It is NOT known that it EXISTS	NO - YES
They know they should not talk about it	
If they talk it cannot reach the "others"	
There are only a few who know about it	

They will NOT be able to GET CLOSE	NO - YES
Only a few know how to	
They know they should not talk about it	
If they talk it cannot reach the "others"	
If they get close we can SEE	
If they get close there is an ALARM	

In this time we have the CAPACITY TO REACT:	NO - YES
If not we have EXTERNAL SUPPORT	
Different types of REACTION HAVE BEEN PRACTISED	
Their EXIT from the place or area is RISKY	
Their ESCAPE will be DIFFICULT	

It is NOT known where IT IS	NO - YES
There are only a few who know about it	
They know they should not talk about it	
If they talk it cannot reach the "others"	

It CANNOT be LOCATED	NO - YES
There are few who know the location	
They know they should not talk about it	
If they talk it cannot reach the "others"	

They will NOT be able to ENTER/ACCESS the place or area because:	NO - YES
Of the control there	
Of its physical resistance	
Of its complexity	
When they try to enter it will be KNOWN	
If they try to enter there is an ALARM SYSTEM	
If they enter, achieving their objective will take TIME	

Dissuasion

This refers to a collection of actions which retain or impede the attack by convincing a person or persons psychologically or physically that they have no chance of succeeding. In other words, to dissuade is to make them not dare to do it.

To know how effective this is, a study is made of the existence and level of:

GENERAL SECURITY measures in the ENVIRONMENT	NO – YES
REGULATIONS AND security MEASURES are greater as you approach certain areas	
Unknown security measures	
THE IMPRESSION is given of PROFESSIONAL AND TOUGH SECURITY	
THE CONVICTION OF REAL DIFFICULTY	
EVERYBODY who is looking out for my well-being and interests IS MONITORING the SUSPECTS OR DANGEROUS INDIVIDUALS	

Limiting

This refers to the process of decision-making, individual actions and the use of resources that has to be followed once the attack has happened to hinder and stop the development of the situation and to control the extent of the damage done.

• Do an analysis of any limitations there may be:

There is protection, at least minimally effective, which prevents a discrete or direct approach being made to the PROPERTY	NO - YES
There are enough security guards to deter or limit intrusions or internal advancement	
There are regulations regarding urgent security information on all incidents considered unjustified or without a clear reason for them	
There is a reserve of link resources and communication channels for emergencies	

There are rules or regulations for the justification and restriction of internal movement	NO - YES
There are adequate resources and trained personnel to control this movement	
There are physical resources in place to hinder intrusion in areas where property and goods are to be protected	
There are resources for visually monitoring the areas that need to be defended or kept under surveillance	
There is an alarm system in addition to, or substituting, the surveillance	
There is protection, at least minimally effective, which prevents a discrete or direct approach being made to the PROPERTY	

15.6 Human behaviour under pressure

Above all, we need to remember that passenger ships have a very different function to any other type of boat. On a passenger ship there is a multitude of people who require assistance and who, in the main, are not familiar with their surroundings. The crew is affected by the need to add passenger service duties to their normal ship's duties. In addition to the behaviour of the passengers and crew, there is the behaviour shown by possible attackers, the secondary intervention forces and the relatives of everybody involved in the crisis on board.

It is important, therefore, not just to look at human behaviour under pressure, but also in daily routine.

The catalyst for many critical situations experienced on board ship is a general lack of prevention, not realising that the people involved in the attacks will be subject to high levels of stress. This fact makes it easier to detect the attackers and can help prevent the crew acting in such a way as to provoke a negative reaction.

The complexity of human behaviour demands we be strict when discussing the many difficulties it provokes. The focus needs to be on the basic aspects of individual and collective behaviour, taking into account that *behaviour* refers to all a person's actions which have some kind of consequence, either for the person themselves and for others, or for their physical surroundings. These actions are based on many determining factors or psychological, environmental, social, biological, educational, perceptional, cognitive factors, etc. In other words it is a unique phenomenon, but with multiple causes.

Individual behaviour

Understanding individual behaviour will help us understand the mechanisms at work in mass behaviour in crisis situations. Spontaneous behaviour does not exist, as there is a catalyst for every action which obliges the person in one way or another to respond, thereby creating an action-reaction chain. It is this very chain and its consequences that modify the behaviour of people in their relationships as well as in their surroundings. In an emergency situation, different people react in different ways. This behaviour can result in these people adapting well to the situation, or not adapting to it at all.

Experience shows us that in the majority of critical events many individual reactions save the situation when the prepared intervention systems failed. What did the people who survived the crisis situations have in common?

Whenever a person, no matter what type they are, is faced with a situation in which they are threatened, if they do not react accordingly they will be put under pressure. This is a situation which produces a certain amount of stress.

There are many factors which influence the results of dealing with stress produced by a crisis situation, and these also vary a lot from person to person. A series of parameters do exist, however, which are common to everybody.

These parameters can be put into a graph which helps us evaluate critical situations and the behaviour of the people involved.

On the one hand, time ticks by a second at a time and can be a precursor to stress if a task is not completed within the set time. There are situations in which time is not an issue and others in which it is the decisive factor.

The other factor to mark on the scale in relation to time is the level of activity the person subject to critical event experiences. This scale of activity comprises different areas which show the stress suffered, as well as the level of normal activity and the disaster line (Fig. 15.1)

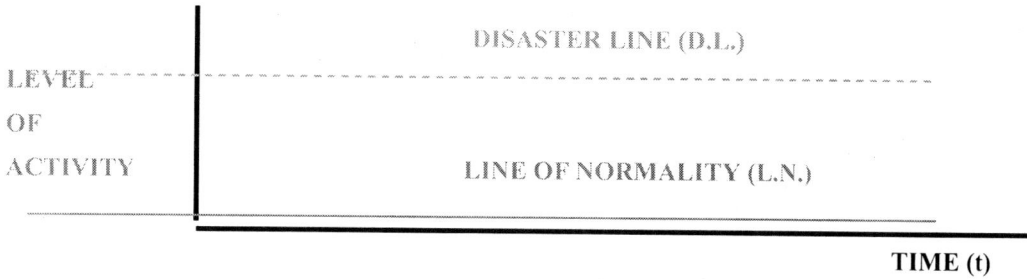

Fig. 15.1

The disaster level is reached daily in all areas of life; things happen that are out of the ordinary and which have no logical explanation, but the analysis from a time perspective gives us an objective view of the event.

One domestic example of this is when one spouse murders the other. The people that knew them do not understand how it can have happened, they were good people, they talked to their neighbours, nobody knew of any particular reason that could have caused it. What happened?

Starting at a normal level of activity (Fig. 15.2), the couple goes through a phase of routine (1-2), then their level of activity goes up a little when their first child is born (2-3). With time the financial problems of the couple are brought under control (3-4). Living together causes small changes in the relationship and they begin to have little arguments (4-5), with time the scale of these arguments increases substantially (5-6). The spouse who is the attacker loses their job and the level of stress increases (6-7) with nothing there to help reduce it. One bad day, a fact of little consequence causes the level of stress of the attacker to pass the disaster line and they murder their spouse by stabbing them thirty times.

The analysis shows that the level of activity increased slowly and steadily over a long period of time and, as it could not be dispelled, the stress accumulated and got nearer and nearer the disaster line until something insignificant caused it to move over that line.

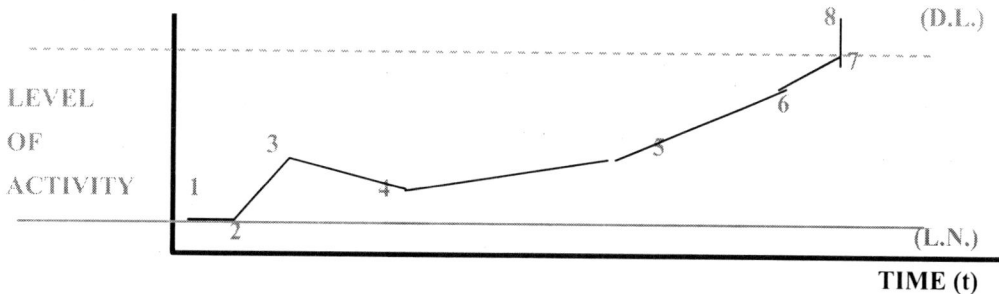

Fig. 15.2

Another case, which covers a much shorter period of time and which involves another unforeseen act, is the case of a student who has to sit an exam. The student knows about the exam three months in advance (Fig 15.3), and plans to start studying for it one month beforehand (1-2). When the student reaches this point and sees exactly how much material there is to study, their level of activity rises sharply (2-3). During the first few days of study they become less anxious as they start to learn the material (3-4), and it stays that way for a few days (4-5) because they think they are in with a chance. However, when there are only a few days left they realise that they will not be able to study all the material required and that they will have to focus on the areas that are more likely to come up, and this increases their feeling of anxiety (5-6), which increases even more two days before the exam (6-7). On the day of the exam, as well as experiencing a physical problem, the student's level of stress crosses the disaster line and their mind goes blank meaning they do not reply to the questions about the subject matter they were familiar with.

The analysis shows phases of stress in the activity levels related to the subjective criteria that the student discovers in the time period leading up to the exam. These take the student closer and closer to the disaster line until they pass it.

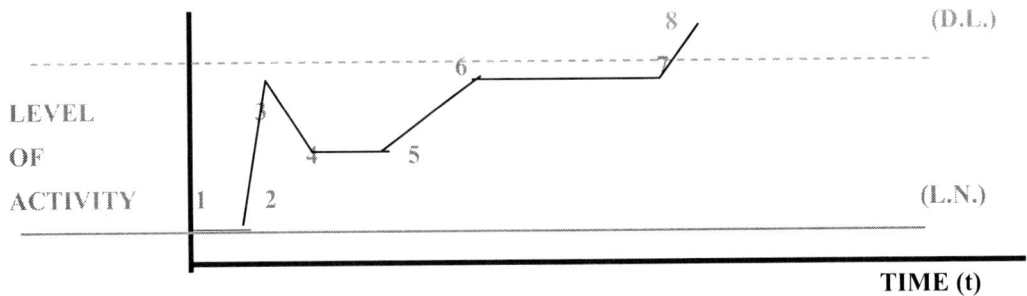

Fig. 15.3

Yet another case is one of a man who needs to board a ferry (Fig. 15.4). He is sleeping (1-2) with his activity levels well below the line of normality, when he wakes up he sees with surprise that the alarm has not gone off and he has just enough amount of time to get to the ship (2-3). He gets washed quickly, goes out into the street and gets a taxi (3-4). Whilst they are driving along his stress level remains the same as he is thinks he will be on time (4-5), suddenly they turn into a street where there is a traffic jam (5-6), when he gets to the ferry port he has a few problems with the boarding pass and checking his luggage in (6-7). When he finally boards and gets to the reception desk the stewardess tells him that the first class cabin he had booked is already occupied and there is not another one available. The passenger becomes furious and verbally attacks the stewardess (7-8).

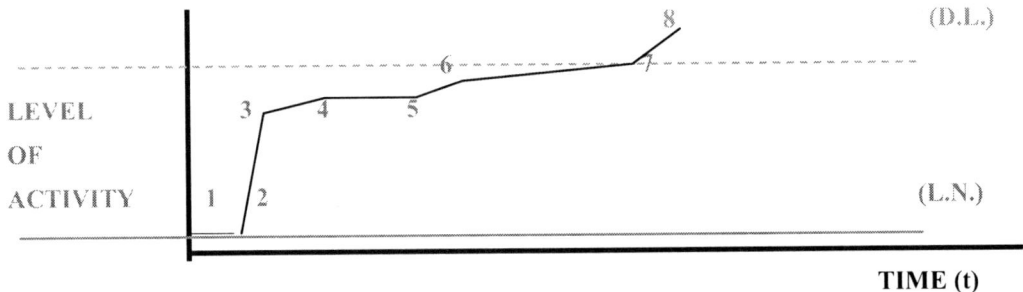

Fig. 15.4

The situations which put pressure on us are all very different from each other and, as can be seen above, all present very different graphs. For example:

a)   Time pressures

Time becomes a priority in the resolving of a crisis. This unbalances a person and their stress levels shoot up in accordance with the requirements of the task in hand and the impossibility of fulfilling them within the given time. The greater the level of imbalance, the greater the loss the person will suffer. There are many types of pressure, but this is one of the most common.

b)   Social pressure (success/fear of failure)

Time does not play an important part in the resolution of this crisis. The pressure is applied by the environment and the loss of family or social support, etc. The pressure accumulates and the disaster line is reached when the person crumbles, mainly because of conflicts in their social role.

c)   Accumulated internal pressure (frustration)

The stress generated by frustration is accumulative and takes quite a long time to saturate the capacity for resolution of a person and to send them over the disaster line.

d)   Pressure from physical fear

The pressure from physical fear creates the need to resolve a situation in the shortest time possible. This, along with the fact they are in actual physical danger, generates a very high stress peak, sending the person right up to the disaster line and often over it.

15.7 Shock and panic reactions

The pressure caused by physical fear is the most useful for controlling public order and for the later understanding of the action taken by groups or masses.

The possible reaction for all people is the same. There is no human being alive who does not comply with this principle, they only differ in the intensity of their reactions. Under pressure, the reaction oscillates between *shock* and *panic* (Fig. 15.5).

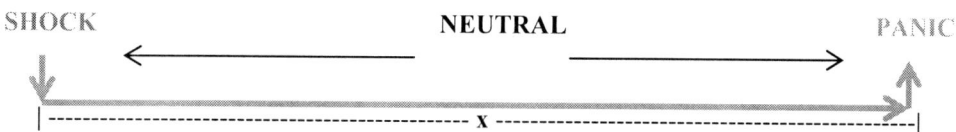

Fig. 15.5

Shock is characterised by slow movements or a lack of them, cold sweats, pallor, silence, body language creating barriers and protection (including the foetal position). They are unable to communicate themselves, but are open to receive communication.

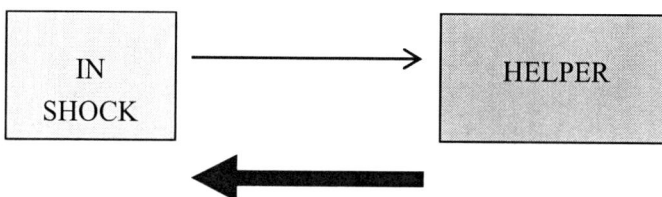

Panic is the opposite of shock. The characteristics of a panicking person are hyperactivity, hot sweats, a flushed face, shrieking or a raised voice, open body language postures.

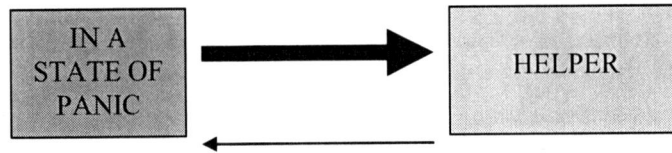

We cannot, therefore, state that everyone goes through a state of shock for a certain length of time, before entering a state of panic to a greater or lesser degree.

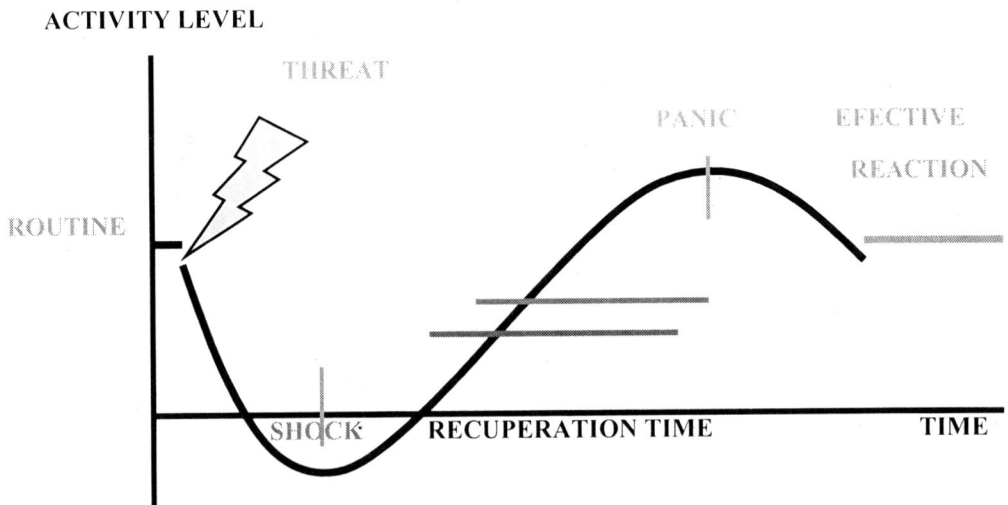

Fig. 15.6

After this the effective reaction phase is reached, which is the state we want as the action needed to resolve the crisis can only be generated in this phase (Fig. 15.6).

The time period between the threat to the effective reaction is known as the *recuperation time*. This is the time we need to shorten to be able to improve our possibility of survival. Among the methods used to achieve this are simulation exercises, which aim to provide us with the experience and knowledge necessary to deal with the extreme situations we are confronted with in a crisis.

In the effective reaction phase, which is considered so important, the courses of action that will prevent the threat being carried out and any unacceptable damage are created, always making sure that the action taken is carried out at the right time, at the right intensity and in the right place.

All effective reaction implies an orderly decision-making process. These decisions will have specific characteristics depending on the thought process used by the people:

    a.   *Conscious*: with slow, thoughtful and easily controllable responses. These people make good decisions.

    b.   *Subconscious*: quick responses made without thinking and learnt from repetition. Good use of protective equipment (hosepipes, extinguishers, mouth to mouth resuscitation and heart massage)

c. *Unconscious*: very quick, thoughtless, involuntary. Hands protecting the face, blinking.

The state of mind of the people with regards to their personal feelings will also contribute to a better and more fitting response. The most obvious example is when an order has to be established for the abandoning of the ship, where the people who have more chance of survival have to have priority over those with less chances.

Finally, in the effective reaction phase a significant amount of the survival, fighting, altruistic and human instincts that everyone has within them must also come out.

15. 8 Simulations

During a well-organised simulation, of a fire for example, everybody develops their own self-protection system which will change their way of behaving in real situations with similar characteristics. This will bring the effective reaction phase closer thereby shortening the recuperation time. What benefits will be drawn from the simulations when the participants are faced with a similar case scenario in the future?

1) They already have a previous experience with fire, which will decrease the negative factor of surprise.
2) After the simulation they will have read more about this type of situation or studied them in more depth.
    They have become more aware of the situation and the reality of it.
3) The more real the simulation was, the more perceptive they will now be when it comes to detecting possible signs and critical clues.
4) They will mentally relive how a situation of this kind progresses, remembering the mistakes they made and saw others make the first time.
5) They will realise or find out about the most effective courses of action to be taken, thus increasing their options.
6) Psychologically they are not in the same position as before, but view things much more realistically.
7) The psychological aspects do not need to be the same. They can be positive or negative, without the simulation affecting the decision-making process.
8) They will reach the effective reaction stage more quickly in each critical event they experience.

15.9 Psychological aspects in stress situations

The intensity of the changes caused by the emergency situation varies from one person to another and depends on:

• the subjective perception of the intensity of the threat
• how close the danger is
• previous experience (in similar situations)
• personality type
• awareness of their own ability to deal with the danger successfully

15.9.1 Phases of effective reaction

When confronted with a threat, the effective reaction depends on many factors which influence each of the following phases in a different way.

a. **Analysis phase**

People tend to react without analysing a situation, and the information in many cases comes from eyewitnesses to the first threat. The eyes of these witnesses do not, however, see the importance of the secondary threats. Analysis takes place in the brain, not in the eyes. An incorrect analysis will cause an inefficient reaction to the situation.

To do a correct analysis we must remember that we have a lot of information stored in our subconscious. This information will help us, although not always to the extent we would like because the knowledge we need cannot be remembered precisely enough, or because we can even be led to believe certain reactions are correct when they are not.

The existence of a previous experience will alter the result of the analysis, as well as the recuperation time. A person may believe that a course of action taken in the past which resolved the crisis can resolve the current situation, but this may not be true.

Meanwhile, a non-treated post-traumatic shock caused by a similar situation, may create a situation where there is no analysis done.

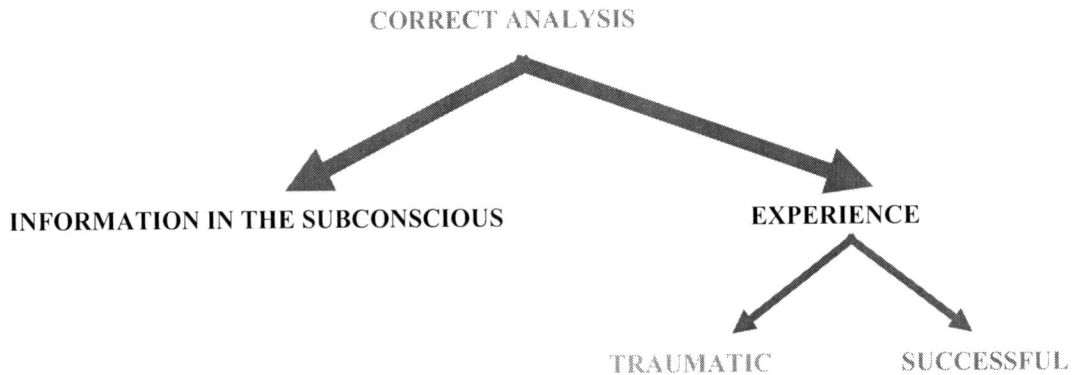

CORRECT ANALYSIS

INFORMATION IN THE SUBCONSCIOUS   **EXPERIENCE**

TRAUMATIC   SUCCESSFUL

The objectives of the analytical phase are:

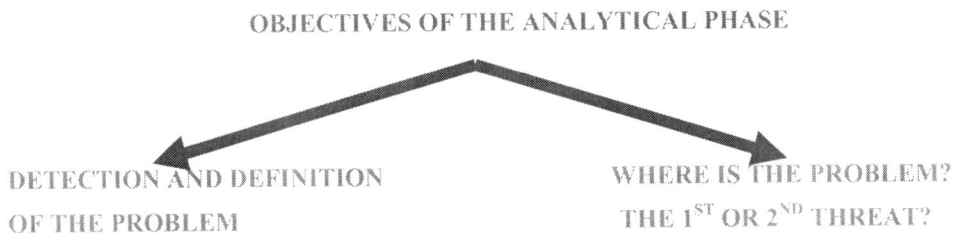

OBJECTIVES OF THE ANALYTICAL PHASE

DETECTION AND DEFINITION   WHERE IS THE PROBLEM?
OF THE PROBLEM   THE 1ST OR 2ND THREAT?

b. Consideration of the options

Depending on the results of the analysis carried out, the options for lessening the effects of the crisis will be considered. There are only two possible reactions: to get oneself together and head towards the danger to fight it head on, or escape and flee the threat.

> A. Towards the threat with the idea of overcoming it
> B. Retreating away from the threat

15.10 Factors which interfere in the consideration of the options

Lack of emotional control
Anger, honour, fear, hate, love, etc. can all seriously interfere with the analysis and even more so in the consideration of options. Being unable to control one's feelings leads to a lack of discipline, impatience, and personal security.

Lack of experience / practice
- Doubts about one's own ability even though it exists.
- Not knowing key elements of the critical event, i.e. where it is happening, technical aspects the person is not aware of.

Excess confidence and previous success
- These do not guarantee a way out of the current situation.
- Undervaluing the situation.

Decision

After the analysis and consideration of the situation, the best option must be chosen and all energy concentrated on it. Indecision regarding other options should be avoided. Achieving this depends on

- the organised and conscious process of analysis and consideration of options
- the operational capacity, previous practice
- the availability of objective data
- the intensity of the threat
- the physical information
- the existence and good condition of support resources

The reaction phase

Although this phase is not often reached without action, there are known cases of people becoming blocked when they come to carry out the action decided on in the consideration of options. The problems encountered in this phase are:

- Quick and wrong analysis
- Reaction without considering the options
- Decisions made without operational capacity

It is important to activate a reaction system which examines the results to be able to re-evaluate the quality of the decision / consideration of options / analysis.

It is clear that all these phases take up precious time which is not available in some crisis situations. If we are to believe that under pressure our judgement and thought processes are altered, then it is obvious that the decisions should be made in a normal, routine situation. All this goes to prove that the work with simulators, the plans of intervention created, and the realism conveyed in the training of crew members will help us achieve shorter and shorter recuperation times. All these things will increase the possibilities of successfully dealing with the crisis situations on board.

15.11 Communication and messages

The ability to resolve emergency situations comes from the level and quality of the information received during the situation itself. The control of the passengers will also be achieved by information shared with them and the degree of understanding they show. It is, therefore, evident that communication and the content of the informative messages sent out are vital in all cases where the human beings play the main role in the emergency.

If any element is identified as distorting the clarity of the messages received then it must be corrected as soon as possible and equipment and procedures must be modified and new organisational aspects added, etc. to ensure everything is done to guarantee the message sent reaches the right destination.

One of the main problems is due to the acoustic characteristics of the areas in which the internal PA system sends out messages. There is usually some distortion in the voice, a lack of clarity and interference which is heard above the message.

The following will be distorting in this case: the presence of stable noise on *various levels, fluctuating* noise with pressure levels over 2 dB, *intermittent* noises with drops in the level in time periods of more than one second, *pulsations* with acoustic energy lasting less than a second, *almost-stable pulsations* of an amplitude comparable to intervals of less than 0.2 seconds between individual pulsations. All these will affect the correct and necessary hearing of the message, and this has to be added to the total noise level which can mask a message broadcast in a noisy area.

On a ship many of these noises are produced, the noise levels are quite high, the PA system is not always calibrated to cope with these factors and, furthermore, in an emergency situation noise levels are even higher, making communication even more difficult.

To give an idea of how difficult it is to hear when noise levels are high, below the distances at which hearing is possible is related to them (Table 13.1).

The appendix to the Recommendation on methods for measuring noise levels at listening posts on ships (Resolution A.343-9 of the 12.11.75) established that background noise levels should not exceed:

    a.   68 dB in the eighth band centred on 250 Hz

    b.   63 dB in the eighth band centred on 500 Hz

As for the dominant frequencies, few studies are made which allow a PA system to be installed at a different frequency to the frequency of the normal dominant noise in the area (during routine working conditions) (Table 13.2).

Table 13.1

LEVEL OF INTERFERENCE WITH THE CONVERSATION (dB)	The maximum distance at which a conversation in a normal tone of voice is considered intelligible (m)	The maximum distance at which a conversation in a raised voice is considered intelligible (m)
35	7.5	15.0
40	4.2	8.4
45	2.3	4.6
50	1.3	2.6
55	0.75	1.5
60	0.42	0.85
65	0.25	0.50
70	0.13	0.26

Table 13.2

TABLE OF ACCEPTABLE NOISE LEVELS IN PASSENGER SHIPS	dB(A)	DETECTED
Luxury cabins	50	> 60
Economy class	55	
Rest areas on the open deck	60	
Restaurant and passenger smoking room	55	
Cinema, shops and infirmary	55	
Gym	60	
Officers lodgings	55	
Crew accommodation	60	
Management office	60	
Bridge ailerons	65	> 70
Kitchen, pantry and games rooms	65	> 70
Control rooms	65	> 75
Workshops	85	
Engine room	90	> 100

For this reason the alarms should sound for only a short amount of time as, once they have alerted or warned the crew and/or passengers either fully or partially, we do not want them to stop people hearing the voice speaking on the internal PA system. The time needed for the warning, plus an extra margin to be on the safe side and cover unforeseen circumstances, will give the total time for an efficient alarm.

Once people are paying attention and the exterior alarms and bells have been silenced, it is time to begin the announcements.

The announcements should be short, concise, direct, and only provide the information we want to give. They should not be open to incorrect interpretation, should not create more unease and should aim to reduce any worries provoked by the emergency itself. To achieve this, the following should be taken into account:

a.   The languages the announcements should be made in. Obviously this should be the minimum number possible but which reach the greatest number of people. On Spanish ships they should be made in Castilian Spanish as other languages spoken in the country are not understood by everybody. Depending on the port of destination, they could also be made in Arabic in the area of the Gibraltar Straits, German for the Balearic Islands and, depending on the season, in French. The announcement should always be made in English after the Spanish version.

b.   The text of the message given should always be studied beforehand to ensure it uses the correct and appropriate words. It may possibly have been written beforehand by a communications expert.

c.   The announcement may be made by a crew member as long as they do so from an isolated area so that the noise and speech of other persons around them does not also go out over the PA system.

   It has to be remembered that the person who is making the announcement may also have the same worries and feeling of nervousness, shock or panic, etc. and that they may, without meaning to, convey this in their message, thereby creating a negative effect on the listeners.

   The problem with live announcements is that they are not always made by experts who can keep the tone, volume and inflections of their voice steady. On the one hand this makes the announcement more personal but, on the other, any variations in the voice may have the opposite effect to the one desired.

   It is also difficult to guarantee that in an emergency this person will stay stoically and permanently in an area where they cannot breathe because of smoke, etc. It is perfectly understandable that this person will run to safety, abandoning the task.

d.   For this reason, it is advisable to have a sufficient number of pre-recorded messages of a general nature for different situations. The direct and personal system should only be used when the situation so requires it because of the circumstances. Of course, not everything can be pre-recorded, especially for the more advanced phases of the emergency when the courses of action taken should be in accordance with the requirements of the situations and the evolution of the emergency.

e.   If the emergency puts the PA system and other internal communications out of action, the announcements should be made aloud by all of the crew members involved in organising and evacuating the passengers. This means, yet again, that each of these people has to know beforehand how to carry out these duties. They need to be taught how to do it, to be shown in practice sessions, to make up their own messages and to speak in public (among crew members), etc. until this becomes almost routine.

16 Management of multitudes and masses

16.1 Conflictive group behaviour

The psychology of the masses joins the complex study of individual human behaviour with the concept of territorialism and interrelations with others.

The mere concentration of people aboard a passenger ship in itself represents a potential danger which may be unleashed at any moment. A collective protest about a delay may trigger a crisis on board if not treated correctly. Of course, an accident such as a collision or a fire, or similarly, an act of terrorism, may demand that the control of the passengers be considered alongside other crucial tasks such as the extinguishing of fires or negotiating with aggressors.

There are a series of myths which should first be eradicated before we can understand how groups react in an environment as little known and as hostile as a boat or ship.

Among the most widespread myths, there are three which should be dismissed in order to understand the reality of human behaviour in emergency situations.

The panic myth

When in a state of nervous tension, hysteria, panic and the impulse to flee prevail. Individuals seek salvation without a fixed criteria, destroying everything in their path and ignoring the presence of others that may need assistance.

This pattern of behaviour is certainly possible if a situation is not dealt with correctly, but by no means emerges from the outset. It is true to say however, that certain individuals enter into a state of grater or lesser agitation provoked by panic. This situation will only constitute a danger if intervening action is not taken, given that the panic may be transmitted to the other passengers which in turn may give rise to highly dangerous group behaviour.

The shock myth

The majority of human beings react by entering a state of shock. In this case passive or senseless behaviour prevails. This type of behaviour does not last long in a group, as the majority of people soon react effectively. Only a minimal group remains in a state of shock for extended periods of time.

The vandalism myth

Many people take advantage of an emergency to steal goods, loot etc.

The truth is that the general attitude in such a case is quite the contrary. Many people offer to assist others, even endangering their own lives by doing so. In such situations it has been observed that negative actions are committed by individuals not involved in the catastrophe and sometimes coming from other areas, as is the case in the looting of cities in the wake of an earthquake. This type of behaviour has even been seen in rescue workers; however it is very rare indeed.

16.2 Groups of people

16.2.1 Crowds

A crowd is not necessarily a mob. It is, however, necessary to distinguish between various types of crowds given that not all crowds require active intervention. A knowledge of when not to intervene and when to make use of authority is indispensable. It is also important to recognise the type of crowd that could easily become an uncontrollable mob if appropriate action is not taken. A crowd can be defined as a large number of people grouped together in a single body without any kind of order. Crowds in general have knowledge of laws and a willingness to respect the principals of public law and order. This is due to people's innate respect for the law. A crowd such as this is more or less disorganised, for the moment has no leader, and is hesitant. It is governed by common sense and reason.

There are several different types of crowd. A *physical crowd* is a group united causally or temporally and is made up of individuals who do not demonstrate group behaviour; this merely indicates a density of human contact. Such a crowd has a common interest for a short time, but has little organisation. This group has no consensus or determination and its members come and go. This type of group will respond easily and directly to an order. "Move along please" or "Get away from here". This group has no psychological unity and as such, requires no further discussion.

Psychological crowds however can be defined as an agglomeration of people who have a continuous common interest, or are emotionally responsive to the same stimulus. For example, a group of people at a football match, a political rally, an accident or similar occurrence.

A *conventional crowd* is one brought together for a concrete reason, such as a group at a football match who have come to the stadium to see the game. The members of the crowd are not interdependent, but are united by a common interest. In this type of crowd, individual behaviour is controlled by well established rules and laws created for these occasions. It is however possible that such a group may become hostile and frenzied, for example, when some spectators start throwing bottles at the referee, or when arguments or fights begin in the crowd. In both cases there is a tendency for aggressive characteristics to develop. These tendencies can be restricted by the rigid and meticulous execution of rules and laws.

The *expressive crowd* is named this way as its members are involved in some kind of expressive conduct, such as a dance, a song or a film session. Such groups are expressing their feelings, releasing their energy through their movements. Such crowds are neither aggressive, nor do they use their energy to cause damage. It is far better that the group continues its activity, and be permitted to express itself, provided that they do not disturb the peace. If this expressive use of energy is interrupted, the latent energy may be diverted towards destructive or aggressive forms of behaviour.

When a crowd is made up of individuals who have not come from a specific place, but have congregated to witness an accident, fight or catastrophe, it is known as a *curious crowd*. It is cooperative and keen to assist. While such a group is forming, the crew must attempt to disperse it, while at the same time, making use of certain individuals' cooperation if necessary.

A non-organised group looking to be led into disorderly behaviour, but at the moment hesitant, lacking organisation, audacity and a common objective is termed a *hostile or aggressive crowd*. The group is made up of determined leaders, active participants and a number of spectators. This group is agitated and threatening; they make fun of and harass the crew. Whilst under control, this group will remain a crowd, if control is lost, however, the same group will become a mob.

Crowd control is absolutely necessary for the crowd to remain as such. Action must be taken to prevent the crowd from becoming a mob, and thus eliminating the resulting safety risks. It is imperative to control a crowd before it becomes a mob.

To achieve this the following steps must be taken:

1. Gather information about the nature and character of the crowd, and all possible information on the matter.
2. Have a definitive plan of action for each eventuality, and inform the bridge about the matter.
3. Have an adequate force ready and available to control the crowd, in addition to other forms of negotiation for immediate use in the case of emergency.
4. Have all PA systems, systems of communication with the bridge etc. ready, functioning and in good order in case of an emergency.
5. Have all crew members ready and in their respective positions before the arrival of the crowd, fully informed and with precise instructions.
6. Establish a real time communication system so that key individuals are kept up to date with the development of events.
7. Establish definite limits for the crowd and maintain them. It is far easier to detain a crowd than to push it back. A rope barrier creates a beneficial psychological barrier when restraining a crowd. People must not be allowed to pass such a barrier or to play with it.
8. Crew members must not contradict each other with regard to the limits established in rules that must be adhered to.
9. Causes of tension such as, hysterical individuals, drunks, disorderly individuals and rule breakers must be separated immediately from the crowd.
10. A constantly moving crowd must be dispersed before it becomes a hysterical and aggressive crowd.
11. Preventative measures. The opportunity to throw objects such as bottles may easily be limited by the use of paper cups. In this way it is possible to eliminate the risk of one excited individual throwing a bottle and others following his example.

One of the tasks of the crew in treating the public during a crisis is to clear the way for the fire extinguishing crew if a fire is reported on board. Quick action is essential in order to clear the way at junctions. Keeping hoses clear is of paramount importance.

Barriers must be used to prevent people from getting to close to the fire, or accessing risk areas.

In the case of fights breaking out on board, or even in case of a homicide a crowd may form which can be dangerous, agitated or hostile. For this reason, it is the small sized crowd which is most difficult to control. The first step is to find out the area in which the disturbance is taking place. If necessary an intervention must be organised to isolate those participants who are disturbing other witnesses. If it is decided that an individual must be separated from the group, this must be done, and the individual removed from the area as quickly as possible. All intervening crew members must take care not to become isolated amid a hostile crowd.

It is imperative that the crime scene remains undisturbed, and that the procedures already stated in the chapter on investigation are followed.

Open areas must be cordoned off and interior areas sealed until the ship arrives at a port and the security forces take charge of the area and initiate an investigation.

16.2.2 Masses

When attempt are made to move the mass from a passive to an active state and the crowd is organised, a collective soul emerges. Conscious individual personalities fade in favour of a common sentiment. The factors which may cause this state are:

- A strong belief in the power of the individual.
- The individual becomes impulsive when protected by the mass.
- Contagion, forming a part of the multitude.
- Suggestibility, individual lose their conscious personality, acquiring a high degree of exaltation.
- The multitude is intellectually inferior to the isolated individual.

The characteristics of the mass are its manageability, impulsiveness, impressionability and credulity.
The sense of reason in multitudes is based on very simple ideas often involving association with similar cases and generalisation of individual cases. Imagination is representative, powerful and active. All of this makes the emergence of a mob or even a riot possible.

16.2.3 Mobs

A mob is a crowd whose members, stimulated by intense excitement, lose all sense of reason and respect for law and order. This group will follow its leaders in committing illegal acts. A mob can be characterised by its clear organisation, it has leaders who direct the group. The group's actions have a common motive, but as there is such a high level of activity, the group is dangerously close to the disaster line. The group is lead by their emotions.

It has been observed that different types of mobs are aggressive. They attack, rebel and terrorise. Their actions are unjust. Their objective is the destruction of persons or of property. However, other groups denominated *escape mobs* have also been observed.

Such a group is fearful and will attempt to escape anywhere. It is the state of panic which creates an escape mob. Individuals completely lose their power of reason and can end up destroying each other if they are not controlled.

1. *Acquisition mob*. This group is motivated by the desire to obtain something. An Acquisition mob may be seeking life saving equipment because no crew member is there to guide them.

2. *Expressive mob*. This group expresses fervour or noisy rejoicing. Examples may bee seen at a religious rite, an athletic event, or a New Year's celebration. These forms of expression can be destructive as a result of their high level of activity and proximity to the disaster line.

The formation of a mob follows a preparatory stage. There are a series of events or a series of vicious rumours that have created a state of tension. This increases the level of activity of each person involved.

The first step in the transformation of a ready prepared and sensitive group into a mob is a circumstantial occurrence. This occurrence may be an accident, an unsatisfied request for information or resentment towards the shipping company as the result of poor service. The group's expression may now be more dramatic than in previous occasions. Attracting attention in an agitated manner is characteristic of this group. An occurrence causes a crowd to form in a determined place, its members begin to walk from here to there like cattle, and this, in turn attracts the curiosity of others.

As the incident attracts more passengers, the group grows and grows. The crowd becomes denser, and strangers begin to talk to each other. The crowd mingles without any sense of reason, and always remains agitated because of the situation; this is how each of the members becomes a part of the situation. As the crowd continues to mingle, it becomes more and more agitated. Some individuals leave to group to advise their friends of the situation, thus recruiting more members for the group. Rumours and hysterical agitation continue.

All of this results in a stimulus spiral. One agitated person stimulates another who in turn stimulates a third person. The third person may further stimulate the first, over exciting him more than before. In this manner, through constant stimulation among individuals a generalised climate of tension and agitation is produced. As tension and excitement mount, individuals act less because of the stimulation they receive from within the group.

This process creates an atmosphere of conformity within the crowd, like a collective hypnosis in which the individual loses control and responds only to the collective reactions of the crowd.

Individuals lose their own conscience. Any demonstration of brutality that occurs will be approved by the mob. The whims and sentiments of the mob dictate the actions of each individual. This is when the mob vents its frustration, discharging its fury on an objective singled out for violent action.

If a mob is not dealt with in time during an on board crisis, it may become a panic stricken mob. Its origin lies in fear and ignorance. It is terror, caused by an irresistible fear that creates a very strong emotional state.

This irresistible fear can make individuals blind to reason, and provoke frenzied attempts to reach security. Panic mobs are violent and difficult to control. This is because the individuals that make up the group are in such an extreme state of agitation that their actions become irrational. Their actions in fact increase their personal risk rather than reduce it.

16.3 Situations that cause panic

1. A perceived threat. It may be physical, psychological or a combination of both. This type of threat is considered so imminent that there is no time to lose, and one must attempt to escape. At this point the mass is still manageable, as it is in search of a solution and a leader.

2. Partial entrapment. There is only one (or a limited number) of escape routes in a situation dominated by a perceived threat.

3. Partial or total elimination of escape route. The escape route may be blocked or simply not known.

4. Breakdown of communication between the head of the group and the rearguard. The false presumption that the exit is open means that the rear of the multitude pushes in an attempt to reach the exit. The resulting pressure causes those at the front of the group to be suffocated, knocked down or trampled.

16.3.1 General causes

Panic is the result of unexpected abnormal circumstances, which occur suddenly and for which people are unprepared. Everybody is taken by surprise and feels the urge to take action, but individuals are unable to adjust quickly to the new situation. Nobody is there to guide them.

Panic may ensue as a result of rumours; the boat will not remain afloat much longer, and will sink...., the area is dangerous due to radioactivity, poisonous gasses or an imminent explosion.

Panic may be caused by real disasters: large fires, explosions caused by rioters or natural causes.

Smoke can create general panic. People, temporarily blinded by the smoke, move towards danger areas, thinking that they are going in the other direction.

16.3.2 Psychological characteristics of the mob

Once a mob has formed, its members display unique psychological characteristics. Recognition and appreciation of these will be of incalculable value in crowd control. Visible characteristics are homogeneity, emotionality, and irrationality.

Homogeneity of mental state. The members of a mob share the same attitudes, opinions, frustration and conflicts. The mob is so united that it appears not to be made up of individuals, rather, its individuals merely represent a part of one single mentality.

Emotionality. In a mob, this refers to the high degree of tension and agitation maintained by the participants. Hostile emotions such as hate and fear dominate over mercy, love and other non-aggressive emotions. While the mob carries out actions, agitation is continually mounting.

This is often referred to as *the stimulus spiral*. Each member of the mob perceives emotional excitement greater than his own, given that the other individuals surrounding him are also in a similar state emotional excitement. This causes further excitement in each individual.

When needs are left unsatisfied, the tension felt by each given individual increases. This state or condition is known as frustration. Liberation of these tensions is referred to as satisfied desires. Emotions invariably accompany any process of increasing or decreasing tension; that is processes of frustrated or of satisfied desires. Rage may accompany frustration or what is obtained, such as when one is not rewarded for having done excellent work.

Fear may accompany the frustrated effort to avoid the threat of bodily damage. Direct treatment of the frustrations and conflicts of the crowd is the clearest means of managing emotional excitement. This is of course more difficult that it may appear given the subconscious frustrations in which members of the crowd are usually enveloped.

It is possible that the rage of a mob projected onto a victim is simply an emotional response paired with the discontentment of the members of the mob, the violation of the body of a victim or the damage of property. However, the real source of frustration may lie in subconscious conflicts among members of the mob, such as the threat of economic losses through competition when the victim is involved in the matter, or unsatisfactory social experiences with the victim's social group (for example, loss of sense of reality). The individual's subconscious demands to be satisfied and that is why violence in a riot or mutiny may last several days.

Irrationality. Two types of irrational behaviour can be observed in a mob. The first is the narrowing of the individual's capacity to comprehend. The mob is panicking, there is a fire in a theatre, the mob collectively comprehends that there is only one course of action to take. This course of action is to rush towards the exit. Given that the chosen exit route is not always the only one available; the mob's behaviour makes the situation more dangerous rather than less.

The irrationality of the mob members is not due to their stupidity, but rather is due to their lack of perception, that is to say that the only option they consider is to make a run for the door. This may be applied to all types of mobs. A lynch mob wants to kill somebody and does not wait to consider other possibilities; it centres only on hanging its victim. The same pattern can be observed in those participating in a riot.

They have one intention and do not wait to consider consequences or other options. They do everything in their power to injure, destroy or damage anything or anyone that stands in their way. The other aspect of the irrationality of mob behaviour is its aggressive character. Like a children, members of a mob get angry and act with violence to relieve their feelings of tension. When an adult, who should seek a more acceptable solution, behaves in this manner, he is said to have a regressive character.

Rioting. The members of a mob have lost their self identity and self consciousness to such an extent that they believe they have attained anonymity. Generally speaking this is the case, given the difficulty in identifying and arresting those provoking the disruption. This sense of anonymity goes hand in hand with the loss of a sense of responsibility, in turn giving rise to a series of antisocial and illegal actions. The members of the mob completely forget their duty to society, and even the well-being of their own families.

Universality. This refers to the impression an individual in the mob gets that other members apparently approve of the actions the mob is taking. The basic idea is that "everybody is doing it". This explains why the mob believes it taking the correct course of action.

16.3.3 The personalities of the mob

Although the members of the mob have lost their sense of individuality, they still show some basic characteristics which once known, will help the crew to know how to control them.

The professional agitator. This person is experienced in participating in and organising disturbances. He doesn't allow himself to get carried away by the spirit of the mass, and maintains full control of his faculties. His actions are deliberate, calculated aimed at the accomplishment of his goals.

The presence of a person detested by the group or someone belonging to a hated social class is enough for the mob to take a violent course of action.

There are certain psychological influences which usually play in the agitators favour. If known and understood, these factors can be used to put into action strategies to disperse the mob.

1. *Novelty.* The new and the unknown holds a unique fascination for the average person. There is no doubt that some individuals might happily yet subconsciously accept a change in the monotonous routine of his daily life, and react enthusiastically to new circumstances.

    In this situation, habits which have formed in the individual will not fully function. There will be an absence of the specific stimuli which usually govern his actions, and the previous experience formerly used to resolve problems will not be applicable.

2. *Investigation.* In a new or unknown situation, an individual who lacks experience will accept the suggestions of someone who is apparently experienced in the matter. In addition, the members of a mob frequently have no prior knowledge of the situation, and it is herein that the problem lies. Because of this lack of any clear knowledge of the situation, individuals within the mob are willing to accept the ideas of the leaders. Ideas spread within the multitude, without individuals giving any thought to their consequences.

3. *Contagion.* People are emotionally stimulated by the actions of others, even though they may not share the grievances causing the incident. It is possible that people share emotional responses out of compassion; but occasionally this becomes rage. People imagine that they have the same problem as others, and as a result they become angry at the mere thought of an insult or damage.

4. *Imitation.* A primitive desire to imitate others is aroused when individuals find themselves in a mob. They fear that the fury of the multitude will be directed towards them if they do not agree with the others. The individual must be in possession of extremely strong convictions in order to resist the desire to imitate.

5. *Anonymity.* When individuals form part of a mob, they may lose self consciousness, and mix with other members of the mob thinking that they will not be recognised. As a consequence, they think they will not be held responsible for their actions.

6. *Liberation of repressed desires.* When forming part of a mob, the generally restricted repressed desires of individuals are released. In this way individuals will feel unimpeded and will participate actively in the actions of the mob. This will give them the opportunity to do things they previously lacked the courage to do.

7. *Sense of power.* The size of a mob gives a person a sense of power and the desire to use it. Most people like this feeling of power, and will use it when they feel they have it at their disposal. This sense of power is increased by the lack of a sense of responsibility, a combination which may manifest itself in a very dangerous manner.

8. *Sense of right.* The common purpose of the mob causes individuals to believe that their courage is justified. This manner of reasoning may be verbally expressed in this way. How can our anger and out actions be wrong, when our companions are also angered and behaving in the same manner as us? This merely serves to convince all members of the mob that their thoughts and actions are justified.

16.3.4 The tactics and violence of the mob

The activities of the mob are limited by the inventiveness and experience of its leaders, and the availability of weapons, supplies, equipment and other materials. The degree of violence will be limited by the people in the group, the characteristics of the area, the cause of the disturbances, weapons, the climate and the ability and prior training of the group's leaders.

The types of violence that may be observed in the mob are as follows:

1. *Verbal abuse,* insults, provocation, jesting and shouting can be expected from a mob. The use of the megaphone system on board by a false leader may intensify the disturbances.

2. *Written abuse,* in the form of notices, fliers, and abuse written on placards can be used to attack those in command.

3. *Noise,* made by shouting or chanting or any other means will invariably be used by the mob. Chants are very effective as the increase the intensity of the disturbances as well as the agitation and aggressive character of the mob.

    It's rhythmic pattern often accompanied by small instruments such as whistles have the tendency to increase the level of excitement and aggression. All of this serves to tire and demoralise the crew.

4. *Throwing objects,* with anything the mob can lay their hands on. These objects may be thrown by members from within the mob or situated in around its exterior.

5. *Hand held weapons.* The members of the mob may have access to various types of hand held weapons. For example, spikes, garrottes, knives or chains. The type of arms used may give some indication of the spontaneity of the mob and the calibre of its leaders.

6. *Firearms,* which in most cases will be used spontaneously having been snatched from the security forces on board ship. Another possibility is that the organisers of the disturbance intended to gain control of the ship from the outset, and smuggled weapons on board for this purpose.

7. *Fire,* used by the mob as a means of attack. Fires may be lit as a form of protest. Prisoners in transport have been known to set fire to mattresses as a means of protest.

8. *Attacks on small groups*, in which the mob is capable of throwing itself onto an individual or a small group to assault or even to kill.

9. *Destruction of private property and looting*, of decorative furniture, chairs, tables etc. which may be upturned, damaged or set fire to. Cabins and vehicles may be looted.

16.3.5 Tactics

The mob's most commonly used tactics are as follows:

A. One tactic is to spread all over the boat in order to impede freedom of movement, especially of crew members.

B. A skilled leader will use tactics to prevent the any intervention from the crew, and to counteract any interventions that may occur. These tactics may include the setting of fires, causing confusion, disruptions and the destruction of property.

C. Leaders may position women and children at the front of the group in the hope of having their demands met.

16.3.6 From mob to riot

A riot is the use of force and violence to disturb the peace, or the threat of the immediate use of force and violence. Of course, two or more people need to be involved, for example, a group of prisoners who have managed to overpower the police forces charged with their transportation.

A riot does not occur suddenly. It is the culmination of tensions which have developed within the given community. It is necessary for the crew to be alert and ready to recognise the signs of these tensions, in order to take preventative measures.

These warning signs are as follows:

A. An increase in the quantity of rumours and protests coupled with an increase in their sensationalist nature.
B. Much more frequent occurrences of resisting the law, and an increase in the number of (true or false) reports or complaints about the brutality used by crew members.
C. An increase in the number of violent threats, as well as acts of violence. One isolated incident is not significant, however when various incidents occur simultaneously in different parts of the boat, or throughout the journey, it is a strong indicator that more serious disturbances will occur.
D. A lack of confidence or resentment towards the law and the rules established on the ship.
E. Booing in public and other reactions at the slightest provocation.
F. Acts of vandalism by members of the minority, especially in busier areas where they will have a greater effect.
G. Appearance of insulting or threatening graffiti on board, in addition to fliers, pamphlets and other menacing literature.
H. Increased antisocial activity in youths, including vandalism among gangs or groups. This has a special tendency to occur when the young people in the minority group are involved.

I. A progressive tendency among demagogical groups and crowd agitators to act openly and brazenly; to use propaganda against the group; to presume a widespread acceptation of their ideas.

J. Protest meetings.

16.3.7 Riot control

When the mob is very numerous, it can be dispersed by dividing it into smaller segments which are then separated and in turn can be dispersed. Only the necessary manpower should be used in carrying out this procedure. Once the groups have been reduced, negotiation and transmission of ideas becomes easier.

When there are a number of smaller groups, dispersed over a larger area, it is far better to group them together and address them as a larger group. If the group has been in constant movement, it is advisable to close off areas that we don't want them to gain access to or to return to, either because this may endanger navigation or in order to reduce their contact with other passengers as far as possible. It is better not to trap the mob; the best course of action is to guide them to the area where their actions will be least detrimental to the security of the ship.

Leaders should be isolated from the mob as son as possible given that the mob needs leaders to remain active. A leaderless mob presents no great problem. For this reason, instigators should be separated from the mob at the first possible opportunity. A professional instigator will operate from a secure location behind the crowd.

This instigator will usually use a leader within the mob to do his dirty work. These instigators and leaders are usually recognisable because of their activities within the crowd.

Any victories achieved by the mob will make subsequent attempts to bring them under control more difficult. Conversely, victories on the part of the authorities on board will demoralise the mob leaders. Once these leaders lose their lead, they will usually fail to recover lost ground, especially if they have lost authority within the group.

16.3.8 Reactions

In emergency situations, cooperative behaviour begins to emerge within the group. Many groups of people know each other, families etc., and if the area is familiar, they will know the way out.

Altruistic behaviour emerges, and conflicts among victims of the accident rarely occur. This problem may occur when an individual wants to re enter the site of an accident after having been evacuated, because a friend or relative hasn't come out yet. For this reason, all evacuations must be guided in one single direction, and nobody must be allowed to access the interior by this route.

When considering the spatial characteristics and structure of a given area, we can see that in open spaces, fewer incidences of mass panic occur. This is because it is far easier to find a way out of the emergency situation, and there are usually fewer obstacles along the escape route, for this reason the influence of territorial aspects is lesser. There is a far lesser chance of a contagion of collective hysteria. The probability of having a large agglomeration of individuals at one single point is low.

However, in a closed space, in a ship for example, where the alternative is an uncomfortable lifeboat, where the possibilities of survival are slim, this situation becomes more complicated, and more conflicts will emerge.

The characteristics of passenger ships make the process of evacuation even more complicated. Escape routes are complicated and unevenly distributed which may produce a sense of disorientation among passengers. If, under normal circumstances, a passenger who is unfamiliar with the ship becomes disorientated, in an emergency, any unguided movements become extremely complicated.

Additionally, on such a ship, there are various decks, each of a different size and layout, all contributing to an even greater sense of disorientation. For this reason, the manner in which stairs are used is of tantamount importance, given that they are the areas where most accidents occur in an emergency situation. This is generally due to lack of visibility because of smoke, toxic fumes which may produce neurological effects, the spreading of heat, lack of illumination, or badly placed illumination.

If the ship is heeling over, stairs may be rendered unusable. In this case there is a need for banisters or handrails which aid spatial orientation on the stairs, and at the same time, provide supports to hold on to in areas which are difficult to pass.

If the accident were to affect parking decks or loading bays when in use during disembarkation, the situation becomes far more dangerous than is often thought. All the above mentioned problems are intensified. Exit routes are too narrow for such a large contingent of people if the bay doors are not opened, and the ramp not lowered. The effects of smoke will be far greater due to poor ventilation in these areas. The vents or air conditioning work as injectors, filling the bays with smoke, increasing the risk of toxic reactions and reducing visibility in the case of fires. The individual will feel a greater sense of entrapment, which increases the possibility of uncontrolled behaviour.

On the parking deck, the vehicle fuel tanks may explode, representing an additional risk which will complicate the situation further, as will the dense black smoke produced almost immediately by burning tyres and plastics. A total reduction of visibility can occur very quickly in such a situation.

In this situation, risk of trampling and death by crushing increases, as a consequence of irrational escape behaviour. Action must be taken immediately to control the passengers' behaviour, and to correctly organise the evacuation.

In addition, the time of day in which the accident occurs can also be important. During the day, people feel more secure, they know there are people prepared to assist them and visibility is better. Also their biological rhythms are increased, which aids their alertness.

Conversely, during the night people feel deserted and less alert. Their biological rhythms are lower even in ideal circumstances. If we add to this the complication that some people may take some kind of tranquillisers or barbiturates at night, we will see that levels of attention and alertness will be markedly reduced.

The probable consumption of alcohol, with its corresponding toxic effects will result in inappropriate reactions that further complicate the situation, and the negative effects of alcohol will only be intensified by smoke.

On board entertainment and leisure facilities, such as the cinema or disco, are also problematic areas. When an accident occurs, it does so unexpectedly and any information regarding the accident is unclear. Individuals are distracted and in a state of absolute relaxation, and for this reason their feelings of disconcertion are greater, tending to produce behavioural reactions which are more instinctive and primary than rational. This produces an extraordinary increase in the appearance of ineffective reactions.

At this moment the person thinks he is caught in a lethal trap, and will try to escape in an organised and is some way logical manner. However he may find obstacles in his path, blocked doors for example which frustrate the escape attempt, which will begin to produce aggressive behaviour. If we add to this the invasion of personal space, it is possible that even brutal behaviour may appear. Additionally, on board ship, the individual is usually accompanied by friends or family, this will contribute to an increased sense of disconcertion and cause behaviour inappropriate for the situation. In the case of having become separated from a relative or friend in the chaos occurring at the beginning of the situation, and in an attempt to locate this person amongst the fray and prevailing shouting, the individual is likely to react even more irrationally.

If we add to this the probable presence of elderly or infirm people aboard, risk of a delayed evacuation and also incidences of crushing will be further increased. This is because these individuals or their personal circumstances (use of crutches, wheelchairs, walking sticks etc.) will become obstacles impeding smooth flow of passengers along the escape route. It is these individuals who are likely to become the first victims of the emergency.

For this reason, when organizing or channelling escape routes, faster individuals should go first, while those with impediments of any kind should go last aided by crew members or other passengers.

Another factor to consider is that, although only one escape route may be available, people will unconsciously tend to try to get out the same way they came in. If this exit is blocked or closed, once again the evacuation time will be lengthened unnecessarily.

Only the broadcasting of evacuation messages and clear signalling of the exits will effectively aid the secure carrying out of an evacuation. If this is not done, it will lead to confusion (from lack of visibility for example).

16.4 Factors in successful evacuations

There are several positive factors which require consideration in order to attain an organised and controlled evacuation in all its stages. Among other points, the following should be considered.

- The level or preparation and training and command of the people making up the crew of the ship, especially those who will be in contact with passengers, and who will be responsible for their safety.

- The level of prior planning and preparation, that is to say, the experience attained in emergency simulations and emergency or intervention planning exercises, the degree of realism and the in depth treatment of the different stages, phases and developments and the participation of everybody involved. The reliability of emergency procedures lies in the modifications and changes made following the carrying out of partial and general emergency practice drills.

- The number, positioning and effectiveness of both protective and preventative technical equipment installed in the ship, in addition to the level of aptitude in their usage and their level of maintenance and conservation. The renewal and updating of emergency equipment, as technology advances, before they become considered obsolete and ineffective.

- The verification of the condition and functioning of all types detection systems, for example, fire or smoke detectors in terms of safety and intrusion detectors in terms of security. Additionally, when considering the working condition and usage of equipment, the audibility of PA and other sound systems over and above the noise level in each area under consideration must be verified. The call must be identifiable and the message must be clearly audible over and above other noises of audible frequencies.

- Clear and unmistakeable signalling in the direction of evacuation flow, in all routes, emergency exits and accesses to established security areas, procuring also that these routes remain clear of obstacles which may be displaced and create a blockage in the orderly circulation of guided passengers.

- Knowledge, on the part of all crew members involved, of the location of electric controls, both for the initialisation and disconnection of all electric circuits related to lighting, air conditioning, lifts, electrical locking systems etc. the use of which, in one sense or another, may mean an improvement in the conditions of the area through which the evacuation is guided.

- There is no doubt that, whatever the origin of the emergency; all crew members must know how to locate fire extinguishing and personal protection equipment quickly and without hesitation, enabling quick intervention in such circumstances.

16.5 Order and priority in evacuation

Although difficult to accept, an order of priority must be established from the outset. The evacuations carried out must be those which can be carried out quickly and do not hinder rescue efforts.

Saving the greatest number of lives is the objective of any rescue operation. The speed and efficiency of the procedure are fundamental in achieving this objective. For this reason it would be an error to position injured or incapacitated people at the front of the crowd. The total passenger extraction time is the length of time taken to move the last passenger to an area designated as safe, and the speed will be that of the individual in the worst condition, that is if other if objective criteria are not adopted.

The desired objective would be to see in the newspapers and other media following the tragedy that the number of deaths was minimal or zero. Unfortunately, the efficiency of an organised evacuation may rely upon some very difficult decisions such as the selection of those with more possibilities for survival. Nobody should be left without the opportunity for salvation, but those with greater possibilities for survival should be dealt with first.

16.5.1 Psychological factors in the behaviour of victims

Once the above analysis has been carried out, the following factors must be listed:

- Spatial disorientation
- Loss of sense of time
- Distortion of perception
- Motor agitation
- Liberation of primary instincts
- Exasperated egocentrism
- Compulsive attitudes
- Mental confusion
- Disconcertion
- Distortion of attention and willpower
- Overwhelming emotional responses
- Noise
- Level of suggestibility

This last point is of utmost importance as it is the cause of mental contagion. Those with more overly dramatic personality traits will demonstrate this effect to a greater degree. They will be more susceptible or sensitive to its effects, which is of great importance in the phenomenon of *mass panic*.

16.5.2 Phases of action for passengers and crew

In a critical situation two types of behaviour will usually emerge. It is important to know and recognise these behaviour patterns in order to plan the tasks involved in an evacuation.

First Phase

Initially there will be a period of commotion. All those involved will be flooded with emotions and other stimulus, and will feel unable to react to the situation and will freeze. The crew will quickly initiate, thanks to their training, the tasks recommended in the emergency guidelines, and any others the captain may order.

In the first phase of the commotion the passengers will seek a leader and a solution to save themselves. These are this first moments of alarm, where a good observer or trained individual will be able to read the signals that allow him to predict how an individual will react in the coming moments. This process occurs in fractions of a second. There is a time limit within which leadership must be consolidated. If this time passes it will become much more difficult to control the group. The passengers find themselves paralysed, but fortunately, their input communication channel remains open. Emotions are so strong that the individual is unable to process intellectually the avalanche of stimuli and emotions experienced. The individual freezes and is unable to carry out any activity, but the entering information from the leader manages to give the support that the group requires.

The passengers' cognitive system may also freeze, increasing under this circumstance, their level of suggestibility. From this moment they will require someone to direct their actions. Their autonomy disappears, and their individuality will fade until it disappears creating a need for mass crowd control.

Once evacuated and in a safe location, the individual who formally became depersonalised at the moment of the accident, gradually recuperates his individuality and begins to use his sense of reason once again.

Second phase

During the second phase the individual suffers such agitation that his sympathetic nervous system fires causing uncontrollable physiological reactions. Evidently, all of this directly related to the individual's personality, as was indicated when looking at individual behaviour. At this moment, the group begins to activate its fighting system, and has the whole organism at its disposal for carrying out appropriate activities for this state of alert. This system has a feedback relationship with the individual's psychological state, and if this relationship is perfectly balanced, the responses carried out by the organism will be appropriate, however if this is not the case, inappropriate responses to the situation may appear.

In this phase the group will become mobilised, demonstrating motor responses appropriate to the situation. This will depend on their self control capacity, security, ability to rationalise and psychological balance, in addition to physical capacities. Conversely, senseless and irresponsible motor responses may appear, due to the opposite of the above mentioned reasons.

Fortunately, the majority of passengers react within a logical time frame. Only a small percentage of the passengers will go into critical states of shock or panic.

Group members will react once they have begun to take action and receive feedback on the effects of this action on the situation, in a rational and intellectual manner using solution strategies and making reference to relevant information they have in their memories. Self help reactions are very frequent, but it is much better to channel them in an organised system. Passengers who have reacted and have the physical capacity could assist in the evacuation if part of the crew is occupied with other tasks.

16.6 The psychology of masses

The reactions of people in non structured groups follow very similar patterns to the initial reactions of individuals. The difference lies in that, as time passes, the group acquires its own identity, which cancels out individual reactions sometimes to the extent that behaviour will be opposite to that of isolated individuals. On board ship there are numerous situations which can lead to forming of masses which require treatment. A group of passengers who are not satisfied with the service provided, rival football teams on board the same ship, extradited immigrants who attempt to take the ship by force, either partially or totally. These are some of the situations which require the correct intervention of the crew.

In the midst of the mass, people become automated, and allows themselves to be carried away by the current in which they is immersed. The makes the multitude impulsive, unstable, and extremely credulous. The manifestation of maximum expression may change from one sense to its opposite. Intelligence is minimised, the capacity to reason almost disappears, credibility reaches infantile extremes, and any unfounded rumours which spread will be taken on board by the mass with an incontrovertible force of truth. False news, as absurd and incredible as they may be, spread through the multitude with uncommon speed.

The mass is conscious of its strength, and in many cases will try to impose its point of view through violent action. Individually as a result of the protection of the group, the option of committing a crime is seen as an act that can be carried out with impunity. The guarantee of impunity will be greater in relation to the size of the multitude, and causes individuals to commits acts that in isolation they would reproach from the depth of their hearts.

The multitude is characterised by an accidental unity of thought. Each individual's own personality is replaced by a collective personality as a result of a strong suggestibility effect. Violent sentiments in the mass are even stronger because of the absence of responsibility.

The mass which vigorously demands a lack of effective authority, displaying the weight of their number, will not maintain their demands for long, given that they are incapable of maintaining a long lasting desire in the form of a constant thought.

The mass does not dominate its reactions, nothing is pre meditated. Because of its unreasoned brutality, and the unexpected aspect of its reactions, it constitutes a very dangerous weapon in the hands of those with the knowledge to use it. For this reason, the aims and goals of these individuals, in addition to their capacity for action are aspects which must be considered at all times, by means of effective, detailed and opportune information.

There are various sociological rules and laws and a series of countermeasures for channelling the threat of an uncontrollable mass.

The number of individuals in the group is proportional to the problems that it may generate. The number of individuals will suppress individual conscience and aid acquisition of a sense of security in the face of punishment if the group undertakes any illegal actions.

Any meeting not directed by crew members must be avoided. Crew members however, may be able to intervene in meetings that do occur and channel behaviour in a positive manner. Individuals directing the crowd will be identified and isolated with the maximum possible discretion using any excuse. This type of passenger may become a false leader of the mass, and should be discredited at the first opportunity.

Suggestibility leads the group to accept the ideas of certain individuals, without making rational judgements about them. It is necessary to convince passengers to desist in their actions by means of messages broadcast over the PA system or related face to face by crewmembers. Prevent any psychological action on the part of false leaders that may emerge by isolating them.

Contagion contributes to the progressive attraction of more people to the group, and to the fast transmission of ideas from one person to another. For this reason the causes of contagion must be quickly eliminated. By isolating and treating individuals in a sate of panic for example.

16.7 Control of peaceful multitudes

Multitudes may form for many different reasons and may have various different aims. The multitude may form in accordance with prior planning or may emerge spontaneously and unexpectedly. In most circumstances the multitudes we come across on board will not be violent, however, the agglomeration of a large number of individuals run the risk of becoming a danger to themselves, and provoking, in cases of disorderly behaviour and unexpected reactions, accidents, aggressive behaviour an damage to people and things. A situation which produces a certain fear or worry, in the multitude may degenerate to become a strong sense of fear that spreads like gunpowder and may escalate to become a generalised panic with fatal consequences. It is fundamental to be prepared for this situation.

Another consideration is that, even the most peaceful human concentration acquires, when moving in a given direction, a terrible force that is capable of overcoming and crushing a group of crew members positioned at that point, if the reaction is not previously predicted, or the stimulus provoking the incident is not avoided.

All of the above creates a necessity to predict in all cases, the possible reactions of a multitude, irrespective of how peaceful they may be, to prevent the crew from becoming overwhelmed by them. Additionally, the larger the group of people, the more diligently these predictions must be made, evaluating in each case all circumstances which may occur. It is not the same to have a ship 20% occupied as it is to have 100% of the places on board taken.

16.7.1 The manner in which multitudes move when trapped

Escape from a fire in a space with two exits. If we compare the behaviour of the multitude with the movement of water, it is logical to assume that the group will divide themselves between both doors to make the evacuation easier. However in real simulations it has been shown that the group crowd around one door, blocking it, while only a few individuals are able to take the initiative and escape through the other door. (Fig. 16.1).

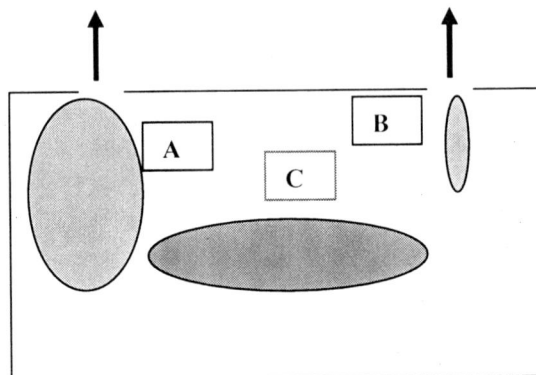

Fig. 16.1

16.7.2 Exit from a closed space with only one door

Running is the best way to become trapped. The differing speeds of individuals in a group provoke pressures of such force that they are able bend steel girders. The injured become simply another obstacle. In the simulation of a case with only one exit, an agglomeration of people is produced, blocking the door and forming a fan shape around it, when speed of movement becomes greater than 1,5 m/s. (Fig. 16.2)

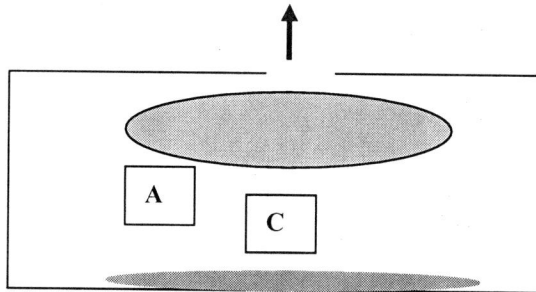

Fig. 16.2

Looking for an unseen exit. When panic arises, the mass tends to form a flock that follow each other without giving any consideration to alternative exits. This gregarious form of behaviour minimises the possibility of finding the exit. If the individuals making up the mass were able to avoid the panic reaction and think routinely, they would spread out to be able to find the exit as quickly as possible. However, in figure 16.3 we can see groups of people (in green circles), immersed in a smoke (H) filled atmosphere, spread all over the area, without any plan of action, and no efficiency in finding the exit.

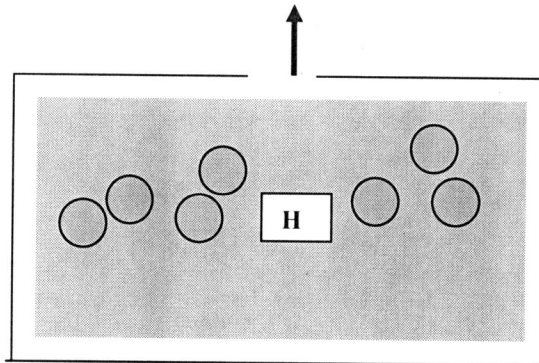

Fig.. 16.3

In these circumstances a large number of passengers would be expected to be affected by inhalation of toxic gasses produced by the combustion (in red).

16.7.3 Escaping through a passage with a wider intermediate area

The simulated corridor (Figure 16.4), is three meters wide along its narrowest parts, and six meters wide along its widest part which must be traversed in order to guide the evacuation from point A to B. When the people who are escaping (1) arrive at this part (2) they will attempt to overtake each other. The problem arises when the passage becomes narrower again, and the different speeds of the mass produce an agglomeration at the exit (3)

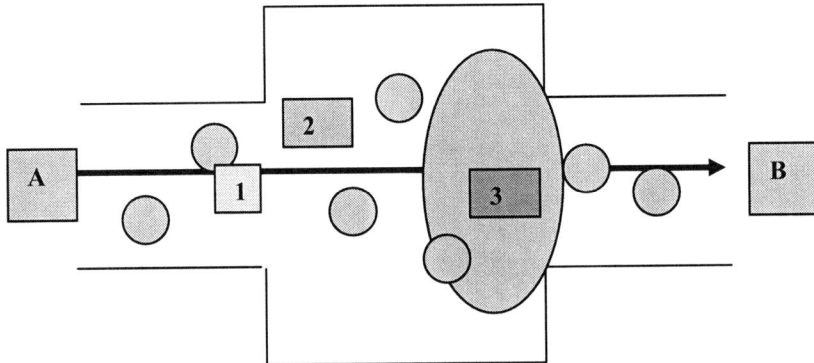

Fig.. 16.4

16.8 Controlled evacuation

The following terms must be differentiated:

1. *Evacuation*. Movement of public from a possible danger area, to another area with a greater degree of security than the first. The possible materialisation of a danger constitutes the threat. A bomb threat for example.

2. *Rescue*. Movement of public from an active danger area to a secure area. This occurs when the threat is real, but hasn't yet reached its full potential or has passed. There is a high probability of harm. For example, a passenger who is drunk and armed threatening the public in the area.

3. *Abandon*. Only applicable to boats or ships, this constitutes the last possible alternative in order to save passengers, when there is no possibility of reaching safety on board. This will occur when the threat has very high possibility of causing numerous negative consequences and all possible solutions have been attempted unsuccessfully.

The abandon phase is very well planned and is well known by all those involved in seafaring, as it is the action most commonly taken in the case of extreme emergency. The emergency guidelines of all ships organise and distribute the roles of each member of the crew from A to Z from a little written but tried and tested manual. The efficiency of the abandon ship phase may be at risk if not preceded by an excellent evacuation phase.

During the rescue phase, the partially effected passenger is alive and understands the threat, and may have already been affected by it. There is a greater feeling of tension and the probability of sporadic episodes of panic is high. Good leaders are required in the crew in order to control the public and remove them from the area.

Finally, the common denominator in all cases where guiding the public is necessary, is that under no circumstances can the evacuation be allowed to fail. That is the aim of this chapter.

In the case of emergency, the concentration of people generates in itself a *second threat* and in the majority of cases it actually becomes the principal threat. The danger of the initial threat creates the necessity for evacuation, while the dangers that develop as a consequence of behaviour of the individuals under threat constitute in themselves a second threat. There are numerous cases which demonstrate the above, among them are:

- 27.12.2000. In Henan (China). 309 youths lost their lives and 60 more were injured in a fire that occurred at a Christmas celebration in the Dong Du disco. The security mechanisms proved to be insufficient and the emergency exits became blocked.

- 30.10.2000. Stockholm (Sweden). At least 60 adolescents died after a fire was declared in an immigrant's cultural centre. A further hundred people were injured.

- 23.12.95. New Delhi (India). A fire caused by a short circuit at a graduation ceremony cost the lives of 400 people, the majority of whom were minors. The fleeing of the terrified multitude causes hundreds of injuries.

- 30.10.90. Zaragoza (Spain). An overload in an electrical system provoked a fire which spread rapidly due to the plastics, carpets and curtains decorating the Flying 43 disco. 43 people lost their lives.

- 29.05.85. Brussels (Belgium) In Heysel stadium 39 fans of the Italian football team Juventus died. They had travelled to the Belgian capital where their team was to play the English team, Liverpool. Hooligans provoked a human avalanche, leaving a further 500 people injured.

When the public feel threatened, they seek a leader or a solution to regain the feeling of safety they have lost, be it real or fictitious. In general, when a mass of people see something they do not understand, for example, seeing others running without knowing where they are running from or why etc., a leader is required to inform them so that they may make a decision, such as whether to run or not, or to direct them in a convenient direction. This information or guidance must be given in such a manner that what is said appears coherent, offers the sense of security that has been lost, and represents a solution to the problem of comprehension in which they are immersed and feel intensely.

On board a boat of ship, this leader cannot emerge from among the mass of passengers, given that they are unfamiliar with the environment. Opportunist or cynical leaders offer nothing positive to the safety of the passengers, however it is evident that they will achieve their desired role if nobody from the crew who seems at ease in the situation, has the correct image (use of uniform) and knowledge (preparation) comes to their aid, and is able to control the mass.

Any delay in the imposition of correct leadership on the part of an adequate crew member will mean that there is a higher probability of not attaining this leadership with the effectiveness required for the guidance and management of the passengers, always in line with the characteristics of the present threat. The time which transpires from the identification of the danger, the moment that the passengers become aware of it and become restless, until the leader appears, is referred to as *critical time.*

All actions which follow may be well directed and accomplished if the mass follow this one leader. This true leader is necessary because of their knowledge of the ship and their possession of the means of getting the passengers to safety. Any sporadic leaders that may appear from among the passengers should be stopped, and convinced to accept the crew member as leader in agreement with the majority of passengers.

Often it is sufficient for crewmembers to state that they are *speaking on behalf of the captain*, or that *the captain has said* something, or that as a member of the crew they *know the ship and what is happening and have real information a their disposal,* etc.   These phrases give veracity, confidence and are deserving of the passengers' attention.

The importance acquired by a leader coming from the crew is understandable, perhaps because of their responsibility for the area where the accident has occurred, perhaps because the have arrived at the scene of the incident, or simply for being chance spectator of some conflictive occurrences.

In all cases, the leader must take action in view of the principal threat, but at no time must they cease to carry out preventative activities in relation to the secondary threat.   Should this secondary threat emerge the leader must analyse the situation, evaluate the alternatives, decide on one course of action and act according to this decision.

16.9 Basic principle in a controlled evacuation

Given the single objective of guiding a group of people from point A to B, and the complimentary objectives of evacuation the greatest number of passengers in the least possible time, it is indispensable to adhere to the following principles.

1. *Single direction of the evacuation.* The definition of the objective in itself excludes movement of individuals from B to A.

2. *One way circulation.* To reiterate the previous point, nobody must be allowed to turn back once the evacuation has begun.   There are no excuses, no matter how strongly or emotionally they are presented, that will convince those responsible for the evacuation.   In order to remain firm on this matter, lies or previously rehearsed justification may be used.

3. *Immobility of the crew.* Previous analysis under routine conditions of an escape route will determine the number of crew members necessary to conduct the evacuation with guarantees of success.   Once situated in the section they are responsible for, no crew member can be permitted to accompany any passenger.   Their mission is to direct the people so that they may follow the established flow and direction.   To move, accompanying somebody, means that this crewmember would then have to turn back, breaking the basic principles previously stated, and at the same time, running the risk of being followed and as such increasing confusion in this section.

4. *Keeping assigned sections free of obstacles.* If any person being evacuated cannot continue due to injuries, tiredness etc., they must be kept near to the crewmember in the most convenient place and position in order not to obstruct the flow of passengers using this escape route.   This individual must wait for help to arrive, or take advantage of passenger collaboration to help the individual towards the safety area.

5. *Use of messages gestures and resources.*   Phrases such as: *move along, keep moving, continue, go towards my colleague* accompanied with a swinging arm pointing in the direction of the exit may be sufficient.   If visibility is reduced or zero along the escape route, then the gesture should be made with a torch in the hand.   The passengers will continue in the indicated direction, given that they will be able to see another crewmember there with the same gestures, words and manifestations (light).

6. *Extraction priorities.* In order to guide the maximum number of people in the minimum time, the first people to be evacuated must be those without any apparent problems in their emotional state, the most willing and those with greater possibilities of reaching the safety area where they are directed. Following them will be those affected by panic, given that they will be provided with a solution, and in this way will enter into their affective phase. Their evacuation will also reduce the risk of contagion among the remaining passengers. Following them will be the passengers in a state of shock, they will see how people are leaving the area and will hear encouraging phrases with emphasis on *for your security, passengers must obey instructions and move towards the security area, follow them to safety.* These messages will pass easily through their input channel, which is fully open when the individual is in a state of shock.

7. *Evacuation of the injured.* Those responsible for the evacuation will finish by taking the injured passengers along the escape route where they will find the static crewmembers responsible for each section. These crewmembers will provide assistance, and attempt to maintain the speed of the escape at acceptable levels while making sure that nobody has been left behind both in the space that has been evacuated and along each section of the escape route that has been used. The evacuation will end when those responsible for the evacuation join the reception crew in the security area or meeting point.

16.10 Procedure for evacuating people to a distant area

Two conditions may arise in the guiding of people from one space in the ship to another:

A. The people who must be evacuated are able to see at all times the beginning and end of the route, on one deck. (horizontal level, Fig. 16. 5).

In these cases evacuation from one space to another entails little difficulty. In this case it will only be necessary to locate one assistant/guide at the in the extraction area (E) and another in the reception area (R), represented by the larger green circles. If the route distance was long, in order to gain a better fluidity of movement and a guarantee of the strength of the evacuation, it may be necessary to position a member of the crew at an intermediate point along the escape route, represented by the smaller green circle in the diagram

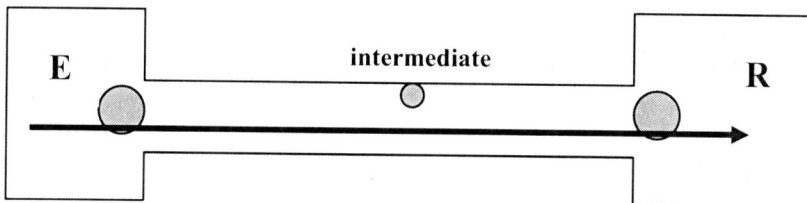

Fig. 16.5

B. The route that must be followed in intricate and may involve more than one deck, meaning access to different levels of circulation. (stairs, Fig. 16.6).

In these cases, evacuation guides, always taking into account those responsible for extraction (E) in the threat area, and those responsible for reception (R) in the area considered safe, will be distributed along the escape route in such a way that they can see each other, and be seen by the people being evacuated. At any confluence in the passage, it will be necessary to position a crew member to avoid confusion and to keep directing people in the correct and secure direction of the evacuation.

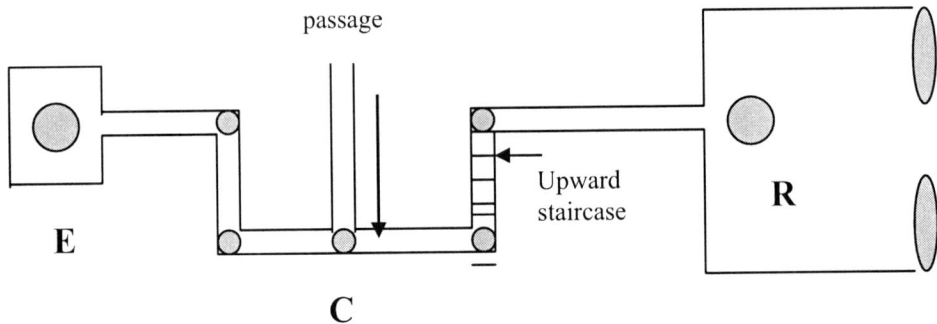

Fig. 16.6

16.11 Attention for those evacuated and rescued in an emergency

Following an emergency, all those affected will require psychological treatment according to the gravity of the threat suffered:

- Proximity. Attention must be given in places near the accident in order to prevent the situation from worsening, taking those affected to further away areas.
- Urgency. It is necessary to act with utmost urgency, intervening as soon as possible to avoid the emergence of certain symptoms or avoiding that other symptoms become chronic.
- Expectations. The transmission of positive information to those affected is fundamental in improving their capacity to deal with the situation. The victim demonstrates normal reactions in a traumatic situation. Positive expectations must be created with regard to a quick return to the lives lead prior to the incident. These strategies attempt to improve self esteem and the capacity to affront the situation.
- Simplicity. Given the emotional weakness suffered by the victim, specialists recur to brief and simple methods of treatment.
- Unity. Chaos and the fracturing of personality will take control of the feelings and perceptions those affected have of the accident. One of the principal tasks of the psychologist is to help these individuals to structure these experiences and re-establish cognitive control of the situation.

"The non existence or inappropriateness of personalised treatment cause in 60% of both direct and indirect victims, a danger of suffering some psychological disturbance throughout their lives, leading to an increase in self medication, consumption of toxic substances or absenteeism form work[1]."

---

[1] Words of Dr. Zahava Salomón of the University of Tel Aviv (Israel) during the I International Meeting of Victimology, held in Madrid in 1998.

17 Intervention in crisis situations

Intervention in any type of incident, accident and emergency on land, regardless of the final outcome, is often straightforward, as much for employees involved in industrial activity (working) as for those affected (citizens unrelated to the activity). A simple call to the appropriate emergency services (ambulance, fire brigade, civil defence, etc) and the situation can be viewed safely from close quarters, as mere spectators of the event. On the whole, once the most basic intervention has been carried out, and the emergency services have arrived, neither party has anything left to do except maybe offer their help, and this is generally not accepted as it is considered unnecessary and would put unqualified people in danger.

Aboard a passenger ship at sea, the crew has numerous obligations to ensure general safety and, more specifically, the safety of passengers. Collaboration from the latter group is expected, as they must follow the instructions received from the ship's personnel.

Furthermore, it is important to remember that all vessels are independent units, remote from external help centres (S.S.F and others related to *safety*) and that the incident/emergency/crisis takes place on an unstable base which often complicates the possibilities, if they are any, of allowing adequate access to direct and efficient intervention in order to minimize the cause or origin of the crisis. This does not mean however that external support is unnecessary or inappropriate and therefore should not be called. Intervention at sea can be complicated by difficulties in reaching the vessel caused by sea conditions, by the safety of the boat, ship or vessel itself, or by the dimensions and accessibility of the type of vessel.

In a similar way, assistance from the air can also be difficult due to obstacles, such as high aerials, chimneystacks, superstructures etc., which impede the manoeuvres of external resources. The limitations of the helicopter, such as its range or its performance in strong winds, create a huge added difficulty to that already on board during a crisis situation, even though it has been known for a helicopter to intervene in gusts of wind of 50 kph (~ 28 knots).

To compensate for the impossibilities of receiving external help, such as that included in *safety,* in terms of the required reaction times for certain interventions (fire, flooding etc), as well as the necessary equipment (large quantities of foam-forming agents, extinguishing agents etc), the idiosyncrasies of maritime activity collected over centuries of navigation and similar situations, and especially the consequent ratification of regulations, have allowed extensive documentation and procedures to be established which take into account many escalating crisis situations.

If then, the crew's knowledge is so superior, in regards to other activities on land, how is it possible that accidents on board ships cause such a high number of fatalities? (Obviously this does not include those caused by survival tactics on board lifeboats or by extended submersion in the water). It seems evident then that something does not coincide with the reality experienced on board during such crisis situations.

All intervention, in the wide field of safety and security, requires meditated and deep consideration of the numerous variables that intervene, according to the case model within the category of possibilities.

The ideal form of intervention under real conditions will coincide with response actions that have:
a) been previously analysed and executed in sequence within the programmed exercise schedule,
b) undergone a subsequent discussion (*debriefing*),
c) undergone the pertinent modifications in all of the aspects that were seen to be inadequate or inappropriate,
d) been transcribed onto paper, and have been carried out with new approaches and have been sufficiently satisfactory to qualify for the norms of emergency intervention.

Such procedures have been given many names, such as *intervention plans, attack plans*, etc. and thanks to the similitude achieved when offered via computer programmes, with the simplicity of being able to manipulate all the variables in order to create the most credible reality, they are also known as *simulators*, and each action, as simulations.

17.1 Current situation

Industrial activity, both processes and services, carry with them a potential risk of incidents and accidents which have the scope to be extremely serious and which can affect individual elements of the system (accidents) or the activity as a whole (emergency). With this in mind, companies design and establish preventive measures of protection and attack to best meet the response needs according to the intrinsic risk analysis. The document, consensual and ratified by the appropriate body, which brings together the actions to control the malfunctions in a generalized way, is known as the safety plan/s.

The safety plan creates an outline of the tasks assigned to the crew, specific to post and position aboard the ship. In theory it should form the basis for the correct execution of the details of the intervention plan, however, inexplicably, it never seems to.

17.2 Safety plans

The analysis of ships' emergency plans, as described in the documents known as *organisation profiles* (official documents), reveals great organisational gaps in determining the real situations during which they should be carried out in accordance with the instructions given (table 1).

The specific example for a chemical tanker is:

Table 1

EMERGENCY	Nº 1 1st OFFICER	Nº 2 1st ENGINEER OFFICER	Nº 3 3rd OFFICER	Nº 4 MECHANIC	Nº 5 FIRE MARSHALL	Nº 6 BOATS-WAIN	Nº 7 – 8 – 9 OTHERS
LEAKS AND SPILLS	Lead: 1st Stop emanation. 2nd Prevent ignition.	1st Assist nº 1. 2nd PBE 3rd Protective clothing.	PBE Protective clothing.	Assist nº 5 Protective clothing.	Responsible for detecting the leak. PBE	Lead nº 7, 8 and 9	Water, extra protective equipment.
FIRE IN THE HOLD	Lead: 1st Stop influx. 2nd Control the fire 3rd Rescue staff	1st Assist nº 1. 2nd PBE 3rd Protective clothing.	PBE Protective clothing.	Assist nº 5 Protective clothing.	Responsible for detecting loss. PBE	Lead nº 7, 8 and 9	Water protection for nº 1, 2, 3, 4, 5.
TOXIC GAS LEAKS	Sea: Boats, PBE and evacuation. Port: Indicate safe evacuation route for personnel.	PBE	PBE	Assist nº 1	Assist nº 1	Under orders of nº 1	Under orders of nº 6
FIRE IN THE CABINS	Lead: 1st Evaluate situation. 2nd Inform the bridge.	1st PBE 2nd Fire fighting hoses	Search and Rescue team	Assist nº 2	Secure pumps and hold valves.	Lead nº 7, 8 and 9	Provide hoses for nº 2 and 4
FIRE IN ENGINE ROOM	1st Prepare extra equip. 2nd Fire not to leave engine room. 3rd Rescue.	Lead	Remain outside engine room Assist nº1	Assist nº 2	Assist nº 2	Lead nº 7, 8 and 9	Provide hoses and equipment.
RESCUES	Lead: 1st PBE 2nd No part.	PBE and related issues	Substitutes nº 1 or nº 2, if delayed. Hoist team	Assist nº 2	Levels of gas and oxygen.	Under orders of nº 1	Hoist and rescue
MAN OVER BOARD	Boats and their functions	Responsible for engine.	VHF Board boat	Lowering	Lowering	Lowering and crew	Member of the boat
RUN AGROUND	1st Breakdown control. 2nd Investigation.	If the impact is on engines, in charge of room.	Assist nº 1	Assist nº 2	Secure cargo.	Under orders of nº 1	Under orders of nº 6

When carried out in perfect conditions (in the absence of a real emergency), during prescribed periodic exercises, these missions are executed at the start of action (physical presence of the crew members assigned to the tasks, presentation of equipment, activation of some equipment such as fire fighting, etc.), in some cases even the actual use of equipment (water jets, setting off alarms, practice with PBA and other equipment, etc.), and specifically those related to nautical training (operations with boats and lifeboats, operations with cargo, etc.). Due to the difficulties of recreating realism in some instances, such as the rescue of crew members involved in extreme conditions involving twisted iron bars or in places with difficult access, the exercises can be purely testimonial.

Everyone can read about the type of emergencies that can afflict their ship in the organisation profiles, however, beyond that the immense majority will depend on the knowledge of just a few experts, without extending the boundaries to detail the circumstances and conditions that constitute the determining factors of a real emergency. Such factors could be; the intervention in an emergency related to the lateral or central tanks, involving products of differing hazard levels of classification (distances, protection, methods); the possibility of combining and distributing interventions with more than one intervention team and command (the loss of the 1st Officer upon whom all the responsibility for action falls, the intervention of the 2nd Officer who is not cited at any moment), in the event of rescue, it may be that the third officer substitutes numbers 1 and 2 if they are delayed (delayed, by how long? Is it possible to refrain from executing rescue actions when life is at stake?, etc.). Other duties, on the other hand, such as those indicated for the first officer in event of fire in the cabins, to evaluate the situation and inform the bridge, constitute an unavoidable obligation (in the majority of cases) that nobody must ignore. This, however, is only applicable in the case mentioned.

With regards to the case presented, it can be concluded that:

a) the simplicity of the document is not a positive factor for the general content of the assignments and duties established in the organisation profile.
b) it constitutes a document whose periodic reading by crew members does not enrich their knowledge nor does it put them in the real situation of a possible emergency.
c) improvisation will be the logical and anticipated result of any type of intervention in a real emergency.
d) the probability of success in the control of the emergency will be low.

17.3 Nautical emergencies considered in the organisation profile

If we analyse the content of the organisation profile for a passenger ship, which is often defined as a profile of obligations and instructions in event of emergency, it is worth commenting that the demands will be much higher depending on the number of passengers aboard and the number of crew members manning the ship. In this example, the ship has 50 crew members on board and can transport 950 passengers. In order to simplify the analysis of the duties as described in the organisation profile, reference will only be made to the most significant parameters.

It is also worth noting that the procedures, missions and duties of each and every member of the crew, without exception, are normally well defined, especially in relation to the phases of abandoning ship, running aground, collision, man overboard and operations involving special lifesaving equipment.

Strict and simple instructions are given to each crew member with respect to the places they should go to, who they report to, which actions should be carried out on fixed installations of the ship (close valves, water tight doors, portholes and skylights, fire fighting equipment, ventilation), and the carrying of portable devices and other types of equipment for survival in lifeboats.

The emergency warning procedure, situation control, duties of the chain of command and the objectives to achieve are described in depth and can be executed in perfect circumstances and conditions under ideal weather and sea conditions, during daylight, with cooperative, emotionally stable passengers who are happy in the knowledge that there are few or no passengers aboard (declared or not) who are in need of special assistance or care. Also, when the ship shows no obvious signs of listing or sinking, when there is sufficient and constant illumination within the superstructure and when the ship has the correct signposting to avoid mistakes, doubts or leading people towards undesired areas (destroyed meeting points or rendered unusable as a result of the emergency).

In the event of fire, there are instructions such as:

a) The fire-fighting teams will converge and the leaders will inform the bridge of their readiness.
b) Once the extent of the disaster is known, the Captain will order the evacuation of the passengers to the meeting points.
c) The Captain will sound the general emergency alarm.

Although valid, such premises can be considered incomplete, or at the least, subject to the viability of internal communications by fixed systems (they can be damaged or rendered useless) or by mobile systems (zones that are out of range, defective or missing equipment, etc.). One or another will end up without objective criteria or a team to carry out the task, faced with the lack of receiving and managing the necessary information in the crucial moments of the emergency, when actions must be carried out without delay in order maintain control.

It is, however, the cases that make reference to the rescue of passengers that show discrepancies and doubts in the real performance of courses of action for control. Even today, techniques for crowd control and control of the phenomena that appear in human responses and behaviour in emergency situations and social environments have neither been considered nor incorporated into the system, and leave a vast gap in terms of *security*.

17.4 Aspects of *security* considered in the Organisation Profile

These are some examples of instructions given to passengers and teams in the hypothetical organisation profile:

> *a)It is important to remain calm and follow the instructions given by the crew.*
> *   When there are a certain number of passengers, maintaining the calm will be not possible by simply showing intention and willingness; people do not understand the situation that is developing around them, the reason why it is occurring, signs of smoke, flames, injuries, cries for help, people running with no clear direction, pronounced heeling, etc.

b) If appropriate, the Captain will order the passengers to move to the meeting points.

- If the Captain maintains constant communication with the different teams, he will receive objective, truthful and sufficient information to be able to establish an exact idea of each detail of information, and will be more likely to make consequent commands. If this is not the situation, how can decisions be made? A different situation is that of the decision to abandon ship. This is always subject to quantifiable variables regarding the ship's ability to withstand attacks on its structural elements (water pipes, flooding or progressive listing, uncontrollable fire, etc.)

c) The passengers must make their way to meeting points in the event of emergency.

- This is not always the case. Emergencies (fire, flooding, etc.) and crisis situations (bomb threats, hostage taking, arguments, etc.) can make it impossible for certain groups of passengers to follow the instructions outlined in pre-established, ideal conditions.

d) Signs will indicate the route to meeting points.

- The same may apply here as in the previous point. How can there be fixed signs or indications when the real needs of the evacuation flow may not be in the direction indicated?

e) Meticulously study the safety information found in the cabins.

- The reality of the situation is that few people read the instructions beforehand, remember where they are or what they should do. It should be expected that many passengers will not be in their cabins or on exterior decks and therefore will not have the possibility to refresh their memories of what they have previously read.

f) The crew members in charge of the evacuation will begin to vacate the cabins and communal places, directing the passengers to the meeting points.

- The instruction itself is adequate; however the procedures create doubt and must be followed precisely for greater reliability.

g) The passageways and stairs will be monitored to maintain order and oversee the movement of the passengers.

- Here the instruction is also adequate, but presents certain unknown factors affecting efficiency when involving the treatment of people in different emotional states (shock, panic), interior environmental and adverse exterior conditions (darkness, tilting floors), and when the number of those involved (crew members) and each group of passengers who must be evacuated from a specific area is not proportionate.

h) Special attention will be paid to those persons who have been identified as needing special care.

- A first reading of this will give the impression that there will be others who have not been identified as needing special care, but they will need it as they are no longer self-sufficient as a result of the emergency.

With regards to the specific duties assigned to the members of the crew in the event of evacuation:

a) *Attention will be given to the ship's passenger list and the register of those showing the need for assistance and special care.*
   - The same comments can be made as outlined in point h) of the previous section.

b) *There will be a staff member responsible for directing each area.*
   - The instruction is good, but the reality is doubtful. During an evacuation, when the passengers represent a large number of people, few crew members will be able to pay sufficient attention to their subordinates in the action, but will rather play an active role in the action.

c) *Order must be maintained at the meeting points.*
   - This is a complicated objective to achieve, keeping in mind that the evacuated group will meet up with other groups from different areas, bearing different information, presenting persons with differing emotional and physical states, aggravated by overcrowding in a reduced space and from seeing the situation from a new perspective which may be very different from that which was expected, looking for a currently non-existent saviour.

d) *"...leading the passengers up the stairs preferably on the port/starboard side".*
   - The most delicate aspect of an evacuation is to keep to the pre-designated routes, regardless of the real situation of the moment. If there is constant and objective communication/information, those in charge will be able vary the access routes to determined places, but the circumstances can change from one moment to another during an emergency, and as there is continual evaluation of the event, the procedure should allow for alternatives to be adopted, avoiding doubts and routes taken in vain.

e) *"...the evacuation will be led towards the meeting point, informing the person there in charge".*
   - An evacuation is not precisely like driving a herd, where there is obedience and nobody questions the instructions. An evacuation is nearly always chaotic, complex, with people trying to return to the point from where they were evacuated, people who cannot keep up with the rhythm of the group they are in, due to their physical conditions, age or state (injuries), and an endless number of possibilities correlating to the variability of the human response to critical situations, which always require an organised approach and the follow through of a strict and demonstrated methodology.

The crew carry out periodic exercises by religiously following the content of the organization profile. These are included in the section concerning maritime accidents. They constitute a routine and knowledge that has been accumulated over many years, regardless of the success of these actions in real situations. Yet all the crew understands and has come to terms with this. However, what would be a training exercise on other types of ships, on a passenger ship the approach is radically changed due to the presence of the passengers, which become the principal and unique objective. Exercises on board passenger ships, with their intervention, are reduced to merely driving a reduced number of passengers from one point to a meeting point, executed in the best conditions and circumstances with minimum disruption and nuisance, and without the realism which would undoubtedly exist during a real evacuation, with disorientated people, nervous states, agitated conduct, injuries, physical handicaps, etc.

In the conditions mentioned, the exercises serve merely to practise the use and handling of safety equipment, to identify the position of available places (lifeboats, hoses, extinguishers, alarms). Although these exercises form an operative practice, they have little to do with reality as they are carried out at predetermined times (no element of surprise), in the best conditions (the exercises are postponed in bad weather, they are always done during the day), and never with a mass of uncontrolled people.

For this reason, unlike exercises, simulations are formalised starting from an erratic arrangement and layout of people (crew and passengers) to which aspects and circumstances of reality (scenario) are added, with maximum surprise, giving a global vision of the situation thanks to interaction with the rest of the ship and its distinctive characteristics, and with the inclusion of the necessary human factor of all those aboard. Special attention is paid to the knowledge possessed by the components of the intervention teams (individual and group), the average ages, their limitations (claustrophobia, vertigo, obesity, health problems) and the inherent individual skills (strength, leadership, negotiation skills).

Another factor that must be taken into account with simulations (as a method of approximating the recreation of reality) is the elevated conviction that the crew members will give more than is expected in relation to their role and responsibility, therefore a well-trained crew will have higher possibilities of providing a much more efficient response. However, the effects and signs of an emergency have a tendency to surpass the sum of the interventions team's human strength, and in these circumstances it is often desirable to obtain the collaboration of the passengers in simple, concrete tasks, which can be undertaken without endangering lives. In all emergencies there will be those who step forward to help and, even if they are not all required, some will meet the needs and be of assistance (used as reference points during the evacuation, helping other passengers to follow the evacuation routes).

The negative aspect to bear in mind is the emotional state of the crew (occupational stress) provoked by ruling situations inside the ship (bad coexistence and living together of the crew members, lack of communication), or by the company (lack of support, seasonal factors of higher occupancy and longer routes), lack of safety (high accident rate), personal factors (the degree of involvement and inhibition of each post on board). All of this will translate into a mental (and sometimes physical) state outside the normal levels of routine and stability, which will unintentionally impact on the execution (as a precedent) of the response diagram for emergency situations.

17.5 Intervention in a crisis situation

In the event that a crisis situation is detected or declared, the recommendation is to follow a conduct procedure that does not leave gaps in information or any aspects to chance. The most appropriate would be:

1. *Study the situation in the most detail possible.* Time dedicated to analysis not only allows *understanding*, but also provides a first time for reflection that prevents hasty and inappropriate actions being executed.

2. *Type of crisis underway.* Focus the attention on the incident and relate the possible consequences.
3. *The point of origin of the incident.* Clarify the scope of the crisis, providing it with spatial and physical aspects, which will also help relate the crisis in terms of time progress.
4. *The severity of the incident, based on the intensity and magnitude.* This is the result of summing up the factors obtained in the previous points, which allow the first intervention forces and their deployment to be specified.
5. *Known secondary threats.* Starting with the immediate surroundings expand it in a circular manner to include other spaces and people that could be affected if the incident continues or progresses.

The initial response could be the result of various courses of action carried out simultaneously by more than one person. The objective is to neutralise the crisis. Obviously the action applied may result in success or failure (Diagram 17.1).

Diagram 17.1

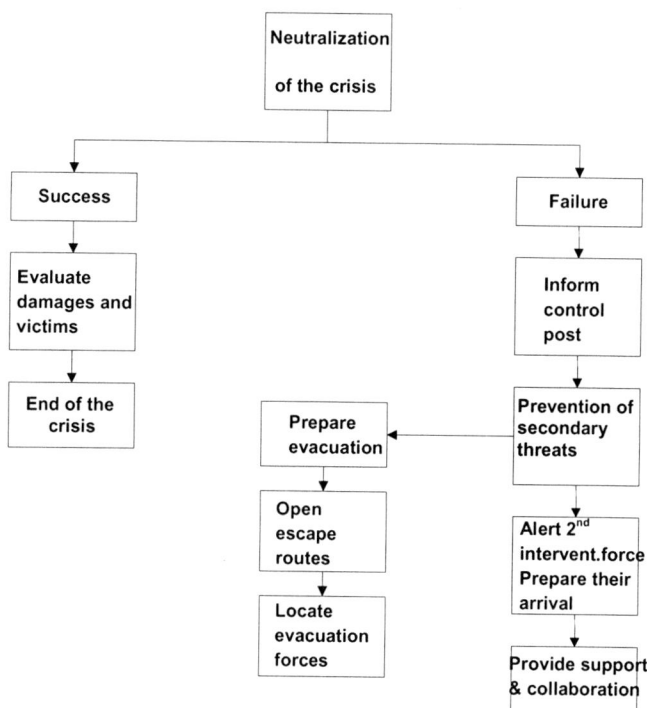

The teams on board will always be the first intervention, although not always acting simultaneously. There are no more crew members waiting to be called into action if the first to intervene do not gain control of the emergency. For this reason the second intervention teams are those expected to be on the ship if it is in port just within the time it takes them to reach the ship. In the aspects of *security*, the second intervention teams will also consist of the State Security Forces which may reach the ship via helicopter or naval vessels.

It is evident that the spatial and structural layout of the ship will be unknown to the second intervention forces, and for this reason the support and collaboration provided by the crew will be gladly received. The success of the intervention will depend on the mobility of said forces inside the ship and knowing that they will receive the best information to aid them in their courses of action (fire-fighters and State Security Forces).

In general, the commanders of the second intervention forces will assume the command of the operation once on board.

17.6 The human factor in the intervention

The objective is the availability of adequate people to execute the safety plans, in routine as well as emergency situations. Three groups of forces will be considered:

- Preventive; on board, this group will stand out as being made up of officers and crew. Its tasks involve constant attention to the detection and identification of risks inherent to the activity being carried out, and attempting to eliminate said risks. This control can only be achieved if all involved know the safety procedures as well as the relevant norms established. The control will be heightened if the exact whereabouts of each crew member during each activity is known, and if all safety rules are adhered to.

  Preventive measures will be taken: not providing information regarding on board procedures to strangers, the location of control elements, personal details of the passengers, and especially of the crew.

  The responsible officer must immediately be made aware of any transgression of the established safety rules or of any abnormal situation which could affect the safety of the ship and those aboard, such as an obstruction of the evacuation routes, objects out of their assigned place, suspicious behaviour of a passenger, etc.

  For these duties, the crew must receive the adequate training.

  As regards the human factor, the duties that the passengers and the security forces on board may be assigned should also be included. When docked, the preventive measures provided by the security teams responsible for the ship, the ground staff, the harbour security and the State security forces will be invaluable.

- First intervention. This will consist entirely of crew members and the possible security teams found on board, those on official service as well as those who are amongst the passengers. It is this group who will follow and implement the intervention procedures from the start, who will suffer the surprise of the emergency and its effects of shock and panic, who will, according to their technical preparation, return quickly to an effective reaction to understand and execute the orders they receive, and who can efficiently apply personal initiative in the best conditions.

- Second intervention. Those who respond to the ship's or the responsible authority's call. They will consist, according to the type and severity of the emergency, of fire-fighters, emergency medical service, state security corps, armed forces, maritime rescue service, civil defence, harbour security, tugboats, ships located nearby.

The more complex the number and origin of the second intervention forces, the more difficult the coordination. Someone should take charge of the group, as the person responsible for control of the emergency and should be accepted and recognised as such by the rest. If this coordination does not exist, is set up late or is carried out inefficiently, the final result could be a resounding disaster. Here is where a strong layout comes in, to manage an efficient crisis cabinet.

If the human element during the routine phases was well established and defined, during the emergency phase, once normality is disrupted, the creation of *activity under pressure* will condition all those involved, or rather, the aggressors (*security*), the crew and passengers (in all circumstances) and the second intervention forces who were called or alerted.

Concerning the effect on the crew, the rupture of routine will cause great difficulties in decision making during the activity under pressure phase, hence the importance of simulations, exercises or intervention plans, that are carried out prior to the appearance of a critical incident. (Diagram 17.1)

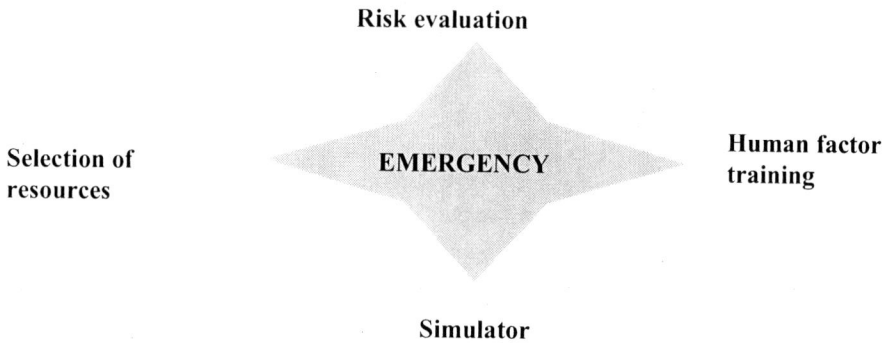

Fig.. 17.1

17.7 Content and operational design of an intervention plan

Every intervention plan should contain the following aspects in its basic design:

1. Correct determination of the type and initial scope of the emergency (damages, distances)

2. Aggravating circumstances in the close surroundings of the initial scene (stores, fuel)

3. Time of the incident, location of the ship, weather and sea conditions and their impact on the ship

4. Number of passengers aboard, their distribution per area, and specifically those located near the emergency zone

5. Distinctive features of extreme seriousness, such as victims, persons declared missing

6. Typical location and distribution of the ship's crew according to the time of the incident

7. If occurring in special areas, such as the parking deck, engine room, the bridge, etc., any known or assumed detail that is worth including in the case.

The setting out of the case requires precise follow-up on the plans of the ship and the charts, in order that all crew members who must intervene in the simulation have an exact idea of the supposed reality (possible). The objective is that everyone understands that the emergency point or zone is not independent from its surroundings and will, therefore, be conditioned by other spaces which have distinctive features, that are occupied, for example, by people (number), and that the area will have some equipment, to a certain extent, that will provide protection, defence and resources against the cause of the emergency.

It is vital that once the 7 aspects of the content have been established that they do not undergo change, as they constitute the scenario and the action that will be represented. If an aspect is modified, it will create a new scenario with possible conclusions that differ from the original. Only the evolutionary aspects of the emergency (propagation of the fire to adjoining areas) and the consequent phenomena (propagation of smoke, other groups of people affected) that must be incorporated at the appropriate moments, with the most realism possible in terms of appearance and magnitude, and depending on the type of emergency and its known physical signs (temperature, timing, movement, deflagration).

The more scrupulous and rigorous the distribution of the people within the bulk of the ship (on the decks, in the cabins, the dining rooms, the games rooms), the more intense the intervention planning by the crew and its brigades needs to be.

The first course of action of every simulated exercise must be adapted to the norms established in the organisation profile, in which each individual (every crew member, without exception) must check that they can execute their task in the circumstances shown in the simulation (access routes, distance to cover, time estimated to reach the envisaged important points, and those which allow access to the site of the emergency if necessary).

This first phase will demonstrate the benefits of the interaction between the theory and the reality. No amount of consideration can predict certain access routes being rendered useless (destroyed), the dispersion and isolation of a significant number of the crew (communication breakdown), or crew members that have been affected (injured) in the emergency. There will also be the first certain realisation of added complications (number of passengers affected and their logical emotional state, impediments in the use of fitted protective facilities).

Special attention will be paid to, and times measured (better if done during the simulation), of the calls to the crew and the manner in which they are conducted, general and one-off alarms, areas out of range and no coverage for portable equipment, availability of each crew member from their initial location (cabin, work post, other), the influence of the time of the incident on the crew's response and the effect on the passengers.

Following the first phase (initial response) it is advisable to use this moment to question, identify and discuss the protection systems installed on the ship in the conflictive area (this will be done *in situ*), its effects and manifestations, activation boxes and valves (especially the manual types), water-tight and fire door locks, opening and closing procedures, obstacles preventing correct activation in harsh conditions (flooding by extinguishing agents), limitations of use in special circumstances (injuries and rescue operations), alternatives and resources to control the situation under the effects of risk agents (water, extinguishing powder, gases). This is an important phase of the simulation as it is vital to remember that not all the crew members are familiar either with the entire ship or its characteristics, and yet they could find themselves, by coincidence, close to the site of the emergency, and unable to refuse to help.

The third phase is the simulation of the presential intervention of the crew in the midst of the general elements (the emergency itself) and the passengers, who they must constantly assist, protect, maintain informed and lead towards the safe areas of the ship. During this phase these two interventions should be carried out in parallel (simultaneously). Equal attention must be paid to both, so neither the courses of action designed to control the emergency nor the control of the passengers suffer any consequences. If, the emergency zone allows, and if the presence of the intervention teams is complete and well organised, the action may be carried out by means of logical coordination between the participants. However, if the access to the emergency zone presents difficulties for access and mobility, leaving the presence of the participants incomplete, this latter group should divide their efforts to cover, as far as possible, the greatest number of the tasks they are able to, of those that are expected if the group was complete.

During this phase, the person in charge of the simulation may introduce variations that, according to the type of simulation, fit in with the logic, experience and behaviour of such an emergency.

There will come a time during the simulation, especially when the emergency is complex and with many implications, that it is necessary to interrupt the process in order to avoid creating too much confusion, to allow the participants to take in the information, and to achieve an outcome, which even if only partial, will help to create a secure base to resume the process at another time. The approach to the simulation after the interruption will be simpler, given that the previous stages will have been discussed and accepted as a good possible response, in which case it will only be necessary to consider the new phases, the new information and the corrections that have been considered.

Once the beginning of the emergency has been determined (definition and operational procedures of each stage, the characteristics and incidents to be recreated in the simulation), and also the moment in which it will be brought to an end, then all questions will be answered and doubts clarified so that the simulation can pass from the preparation stage to the execution stage, following the design precisely, ensuring that this simulation, and no other, will be carried out.

All detected incidents will be noted, as well as start times and duration of all the actions and the response of each crew member, each group or team. There should be no hesitations in terms of response, nor unexpected interruption along the way, except those applied according to the planned evolution. Once the simulation is complete, all participants in the exercise must reconvene to revise the entire intervention, commenting and discussing the solutions to all incidents, delays, mistakes or problems that arose that were not taken into account in the original case.

If carried out in this way, the simulation, with its resulting modification derived from applied reason and logic, will be complete and ready for execution in the future, and for its final approval as the most suitable procedure in terms of efficiency and effectiveness.

The numerous simulations carried out, discussed and approved, which contemplate a variety of causes, situations and persons involved and affected, endow the ship and it's crew with a feeling of security that is hard to reach by other methods, and even more so when they do not play a part in its creation due to the involvement of specialists. This could be the only possibility when the ship, due to its line and route, does not have enough time to follow the procedure or when its members do not possess sufficient knowledge to execute the simulations.

17.8 Tactical design of an intervention plan (example)

00:30 hours on a January day, a drunken passenger, having assaulted the barman and leaving him unconscious, obtains various bottles of alcohol and then pours the contents over the armchairs and curtains of the bow bar (B Deck) (Diag.17.5), proceeding to set light to them.

At this time, the ship is 50 miles from the closest point of land, sailing north at 18 knots, under weather conditions of heavy squalls, with an easterly wind of 30 knots (Diag. 17.2), and heavy seas, exerting rolling and pitching of 15° and 5° respectively.

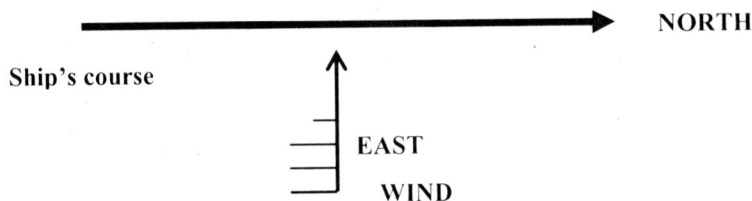

Ship's course → **NORTH**

EAST

WIND

Diag.17.2

The area affected by the fire is equipped with smoke detectors, which alert the bridge, and a fitted water-based extinction system, with pressure lines and fuse-obturated water sprinklers.

The passengers are distributed as follows; 150 passengers seated in armchairs in the affected salon (bow deck B) of which 6 are suffering third-degree burns, 450 passengers in the cabin areas immediately below the initially affected deck (C deck), and 150 passengers arbitrarily distributed between seating in passageways, rest areas and cabins located on other decks (poop deck B, centre deck C, poop deck A)

The crew consists of 60 members; 10 officers with cabins located on the deck directly above the fire (A deck); 10 crew members of the deck department, of whose berths 5 are located in central C deck and 5 poop deck C; 8 are from the engine department and are split up in a similar way to the deck crew, and the remaining 32 are from the housekeeping department, with 12 berths in central C deck and 20 on the same C deck, 10 at the bow and 10 at the stern.

The crew on duty at the time of the incident consists of the following:
    a.   On the bridge, the 2nd officer, 1 helmsman-lookout, and a student.
    b.   In the engine room, the 2nd engineer officer, 1 greaser and a student.
    c.   A watchman on his rounds, which at that moment finds him on poop deck C.
    d.   The barman of the bow bar (injured) and another barman in the nightclub on poop deck A.

Variations due to the evolution of the emergency will be the following:

    a.   Propagation of smoke to A deck, 6 minutes after the alarm is sounded.
    b.   Outbreak of panic amongst the passengers located in the seating area of B deck, 8 minutes into the incident.
    c.   Notification of smoke intoxication in the cafeteria on poop deck A, 10 minutes into the incident.

d.   Failure of the ship's main generator, 12 minutes into the incident.

The ship does not have a medical officer or a nurse on board, only 10% of the crew, other than the officers, has first aid training; amongst the passengers there are three members of the State Security Forces.

The distribution of the passengers and the crew, in terms of their localization and numbers, are shown in the sketches set out below: 17.3, 17.4, 17.5, 17.6.

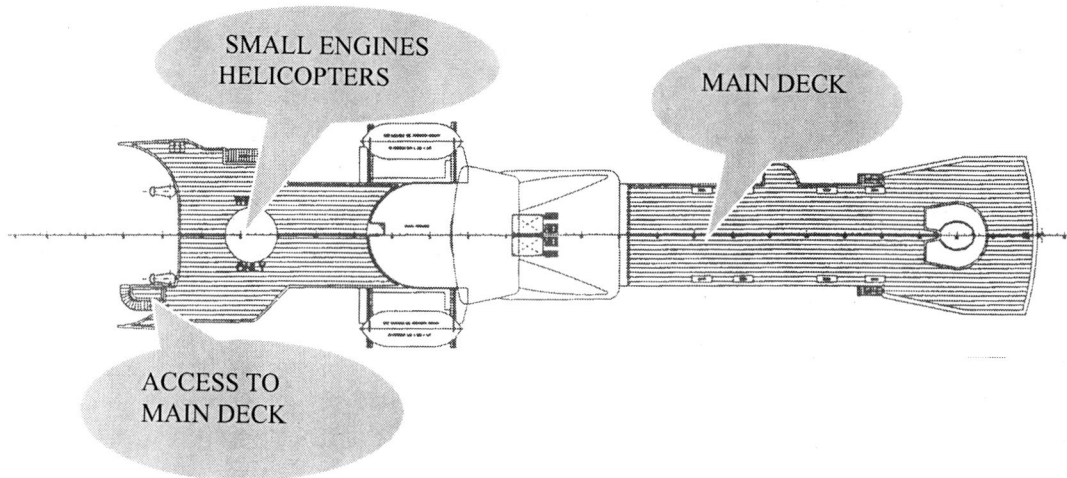

Fig. 17.3 Main Deck

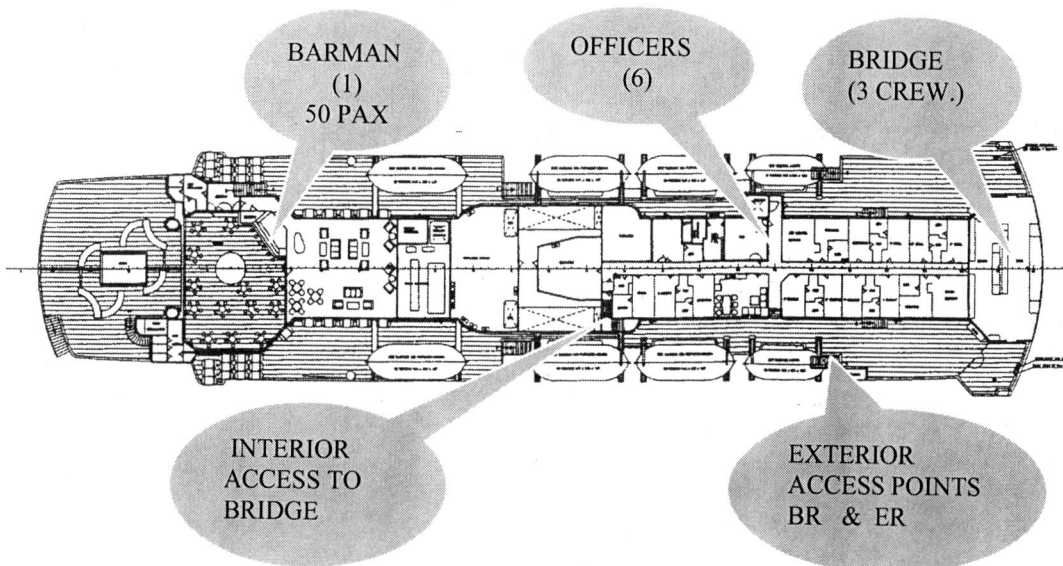

Diagram 17.4. A Deck

RANGE OF SMOKE
DUE TO FIREDOOR

AREA AFFECTED BY
THE FIRE

50 PAX
SEATED

ACCESS POINTS
BR-ER TO LOWER
DECK

150 PAX
1 BARMAN + 6
INJURED

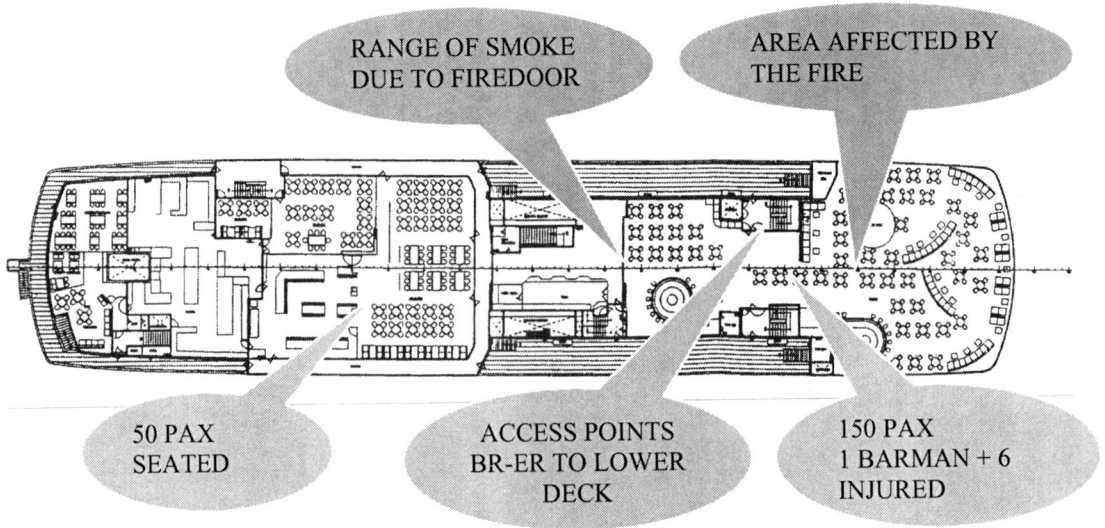

Diagram 17.5. B Deck

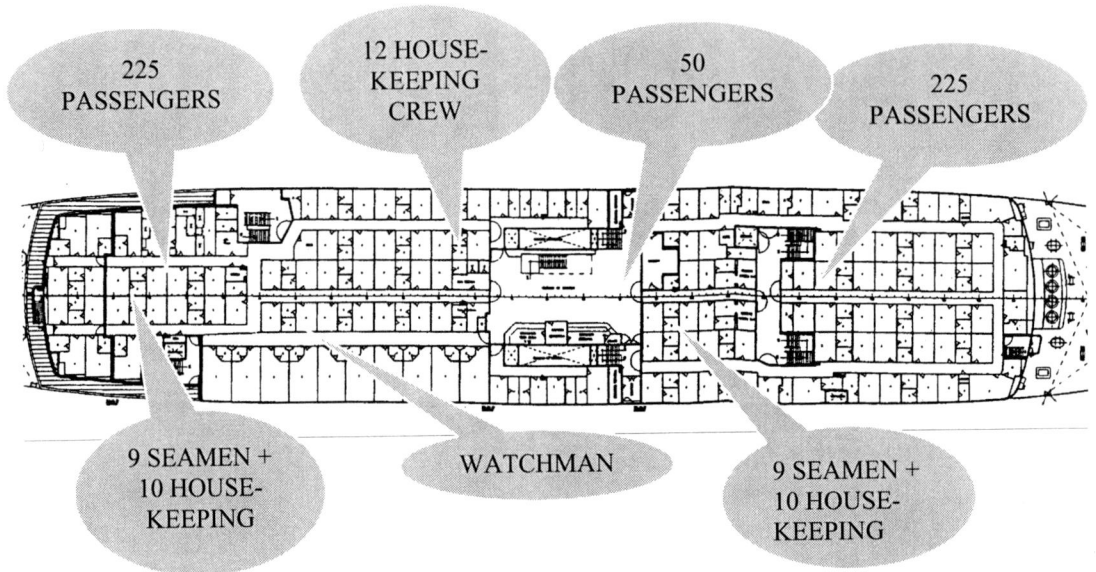

225
PASSENGERS

12 HOUSE-
KEEPING
CREW

50
PASSENGERS

225
PASSENGERS

9 SEAMEN +
10 HOUSE-
KEEPING

WATCHMAN

9 SEAMEN +
10 HOUSE-
KEEPING

Diagram 17.6. C Deck

17.8.1 Intervention phases, order of occurrences and responses.

A. Detection phase, information gathering, first courses of action.

1. Detection of the emergency. Produced by the smoke alarm in the panel situated on the Bridge. The 2nd officer hears the smoke alarm, approaches the indicator, locates and identifies the place, decision making (Diag.17.7).

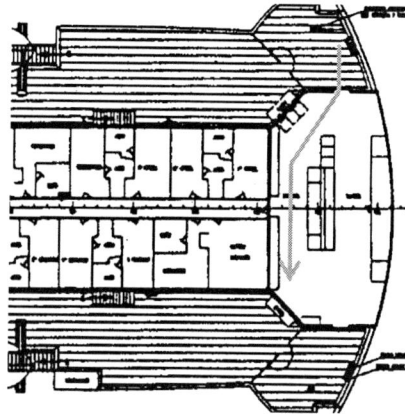

Fig. 17.7

The action carried out by the 2nd officer requires approximately 1 minute.

2. The 2nd officer, instructs the student to notify the Captain and inform him of the alarm and location (Diag.17.8). Consequently, the Captain comes to the bridge and takes command.

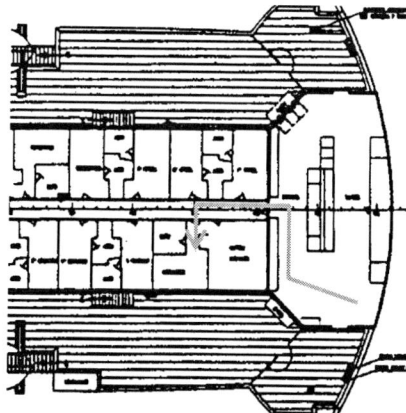

Fig.. 17.8

Whilst the student notifies the Captain, the 2nd officer contacts the watchman on his rounds via walkie-talkie to instruct him to go immediately to the area indicated (bow bar B deck). The watchman arrives at the stairwell on B deck, having taken a route via C deck to the main staircase, climbing the stairs and stopping at the fire doors (Diag. 17.9).

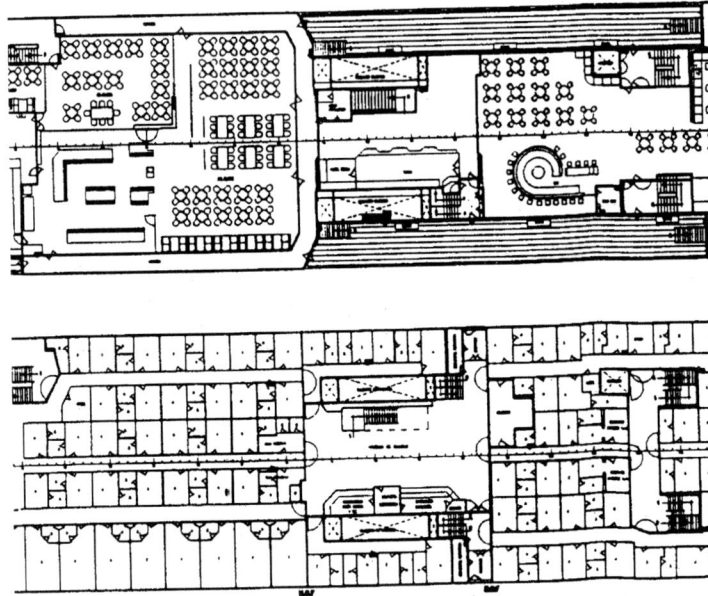

Diag. 17.9

The calls and the time it takes to reach their destinations, both the Captain and the watchman have taken a total of 1 minute.

3. The watchman informs the bridge that there is a large amount of smoke increasing by the minute, coughing passengers exiting the affected bar and others shouting that there are injured inside (Diag. 17.10). Some head towards the stern on the same deck and others set off towards the stairs heading to the lower deck, where the cabins and possible guests, luggage, etc are located.

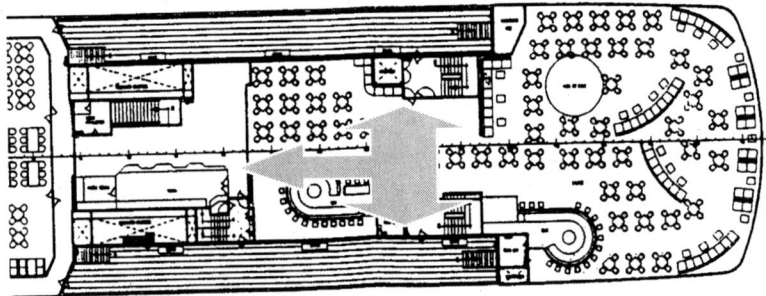

Diag.17.10

At the same time, the first sprinkler activates in the area of most heat created by flames which are increasing in intensity and volume.

The 2nd officer informs the engine room of the occurrences and proposes that all the fire-fighting equipment (pumps, auxiliary pumps) be activated. He then proceeds to shut off the ventilation in the area of the fire, isolating and sectioning it off.

The Captain, who has just arrived on the bridge, analyses in a few moments the certainty of a fire, by the activation of the smoke alarm and the sprinkler, and orders the fire doors to be shut. He instructs the bridge officer to go and help the watchman (Diag.17.11) and the 2nd officer to sound the fire alarm to the crew (not the passengers). In this manner he has activated the emergency plan. The wind as far as the ship's course is concerned is favourable, as, if flames were to be produced, they would be projected towards the port side where they would not affect any further structural elements or equipment.

When the seaman who had initiated his route through the interior (1) attempts to open the door to the access stairs to B deck, he notices a large amount of smoke has entered into the central staircase before the fire doors were shut, so he must retrace his steps and head on through the port wing (2), the exterior stairwell to B deck, enter inside by the poop door of the bound-house and enter the stairwell where the watchman is located. This is filled with smoke and arriving at his level, the air is almost unbreathable.

All the actions at this point have been executed in a time of 2 minutes, except the seaman who has taken 4 minutes.

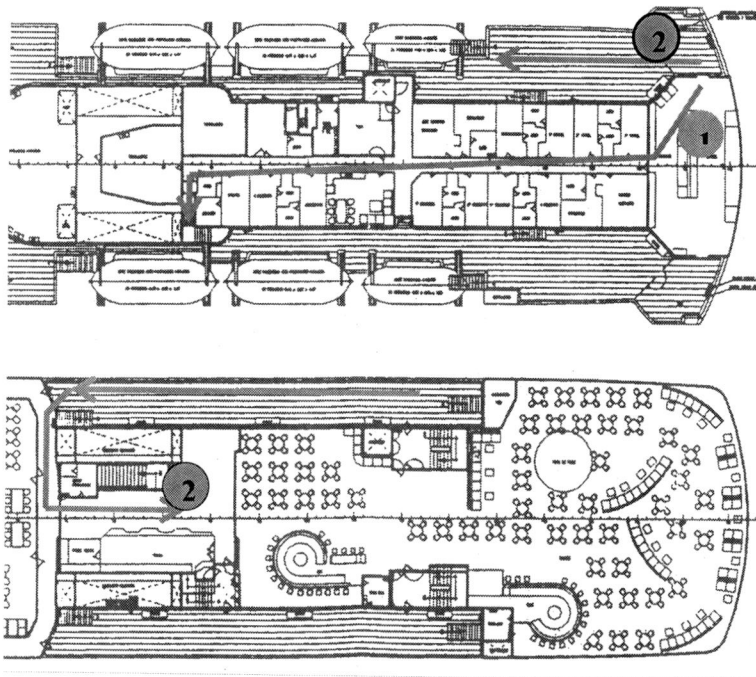

Diag.17.11

The Captain's analysis of the situation, according to the information received, together with assisting 2nd officer, is that the fire is being combated by the automatically activated fitted extinction systems in the affected area. The localisation and control appears to be stable although the smoke is filling the lower (C) deck via the lateral stairwells. An aggravating element is the onset of panic amongst the passengers (150) and especially the certainty of injuries amongst a still undetermined number who are surrounded by smoke from the fire. On the other hand, the crew has been alerted, and can be expected to be operative in between 5 and 7 minutes from the call, the time generally considered realistic, and which has also been confirmed through periodic exercises executed on the ship.

The bad weather has prevented the passengers from exiting on to the lateral decks, which would have provoked a feed of oxygen and possibly the flaring up of the fire.

B. Securing positions and starting courses of action to control the situation

4. From minute 2 of the emergency when he informed the bridge, until minute 4 when the seaman from the bridge joined him, the watchman had been attempting to conduct a controlled evacuation of the passengers towards the stern away from the staircase and towards the seating area on the same B deck. Some of the passengers, as they were close, used the interior staircases which connect along the side of the ship with the lower C deck, whose open doors allow the smoke to pass to the lower deck. During this time, two of the injured are able to leave the area of the fire on foot and they collapse the other side of fire doors.

   The 2nd officer informs the poop bar barman on A deck of the current situation by telephone, and instructs him to control the passengers in his area.

5. With the arrival of the seaman in minute 4, the injured are removed from the passageway, a crew member stays to provide medical attention and another continues with the evacuation towards the stern on the deck.

   Meanwhile, the passengers who descended to lower C deck are vocally alerting (some shouting) a large number of the passengers who are located inside the cabins (225 pax.) and almost all the passengers who are seated on sofas in the stairwells, towards the stern, according to the passenger distribution described in diagram, which generates certain confusion, nervousness, and leaves questions unanswered which would calm them down, etc.

   The occupation of the passageways coincides with the progressive arrival of the crew (flows 3) who, without knowing exactly what is occurring, are accosted by passengers (flows 4), obstructing their paths, slowing down their progress to reach their designated posts (Diag. 17.12)

   Something similar is happening to the 50 passengers in the seating zone where some of the passengers from the initial emergency area are now arriving. They are distressed to see some coughing, some nervous, and understand that something serious is happening but they do not have any precise information.

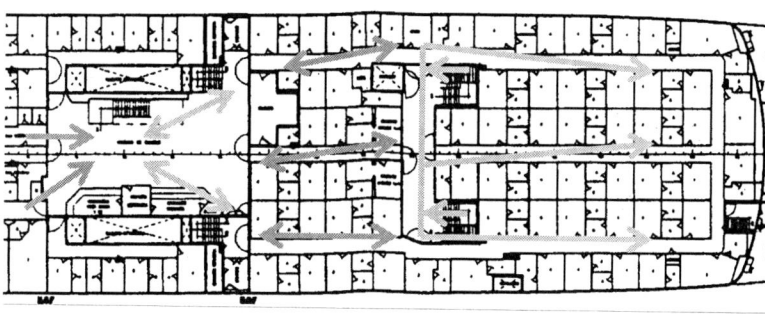

Fig. 17.12

By minute 6, the First Officer and 2 waiters from the starboard C deck have made their way to the B deck staircase. As they are equipped with PBE, they form the first line of fire-hose protection and are able to make a primary analysis of the main fire zone (Diag. 17.13).

That leaves the crew member coordinating the passenger evacuation from the fire zone who, as soon as he is joined by other crew members, forms another line of hoses to intervene in their support.

It has taken 4 minutes to set out the hoses, advance with personal protection and reach the pockets still in flames.

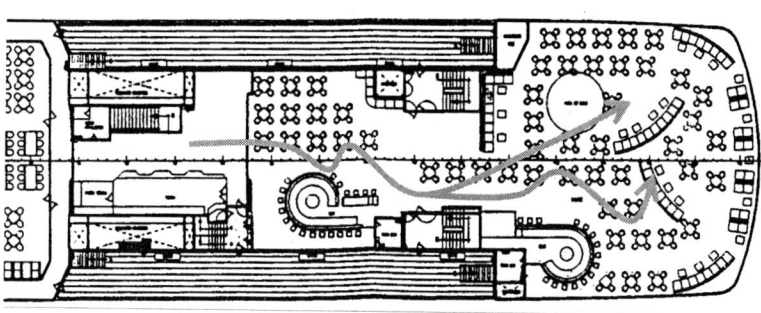

Fig. 17.13

By minute 8 other equipped crew members are joining in, in accordance to the instructions of the organisation profile, and by minute 10 of the emergency their incorporation is complete.

It is important to remember, however, that in minute 6 unrest is spreading due to the appearance of smoke in the bar at the stern on A deck, and that in minute 8 bouts of panic emerge amongst the passengers seated in the armchairs on B deck at the stern, and that in minute 10 there are signs of smoke inhalation amongst those in the cafeteria on A deck.

In terms of the situation, the Captain can conclude that, up until minute 10, when all the crew members are present to carry out the actions in an organized manner, the fire appears to be under control, or rather, that it is confined to its point of origin, but that the smoke is invading other zones of the ship and affecting passengers, and that there is still no creditable information concerning the number of injured or the severity of their injuries.

C. Crisis control phase

6. Once all the crew members are present in their assigned positions, the Captain begins to receive real and objective information from all areas of the ship. In each hub of crisis he orders the most appropriate actions to control the passengers and the atmospheres of each area in agreement with the known circumstances. He instructs the crew members with first aid knowledge (6 crew members) to B deck bow bar to help the injured, as well as the off-duty officers. The 3 members of the State Security Corp have made themselves known to the crew members in their respective areas and are actively collaborating in the control of the passengers.

    The time dedicated to the communications could have been approximately 4 minutes, but half way through this time the main generator cuts out, leading to a failure of all systems, which, however do start to come back on after one minute, thanks to emergency power. The ship loses propulsion and progressively loses speed.

7. This new situation creates general panic amongst the passengers. In the areas where there is thick smoke, visibility is almost zero despite the emergency lighting, which does not provide sufficient light because of its location just below the ceiling and high up. The actions being carried out by the crew members in these areas are now detained, as they do not have torches or other equipment for indicating and lighting. Some of the passengers who had begun to evacuate calmly, now find themselves in practical darkness, and return to their cabins and shut themselves in. The two engine officers who had come to the rescue now abandon their actions and head towards the engine room to help regain normal operations as quickly as possible. The action taken to control the passengers has not only been interrupted but has also worsened.

8. In minute 15 of the emergency, with nearly all the operational conditions of the ship back up and running, the Captain announces a calming message over the loud speaker, saying that everything is under control and that actions to ventilate are being carried out to dissipate the smoke remaining inside the ship, and with that, the emergency is officially over.

9. During this interval, the remaining pockets of fire are controlled and extinguished, assisted by the three sprinklers that have sprung into action, preventing the temperatures from rising to unbearable levels in the area. As control of the situation is regained, the doors leading to outside are opened to expel the smoke created by the fire. The injured are receiving assistance outside the area, amongst them the passenger who provoked the fire.

10. Following the 2 minutes of maximum tension coinciding with the general power cut, and the comforting words from the Captain, the crew resume actions to control the passengers with gradual success.

D. Return to normality phase

11. The elimination of smoke from inside the ship, the reduced stress amongst the passengers as they see that the situation is returning to normal, the soothing words from crew and the evidence that everything is under control, even if not immediately, can all be controlled in the following 5 minutes.

12. New informative messages from the Captain help to ensure normality. Contact is made on land to arrange the relevant medical assistance as soon as the ship docks.

13. The used hoses and extinguishers are removed, they are replaced with others to guarantee safety in the area, water is baled out from inside the ship, air fresheners are places in the areas most smelling of smoke, the cabins most affected by smoke are cleaned. The cafeteria and bar are opened. In all the action takes a total of 60 minutes.

14. The passengers return to their cabins or the areas allocated according to their tickets. The remainder of the journey is carried out in the same weather and oceanographic conditions, with relative normality.

The emergency, with its crisis situations has lasted 75 minutes; the 6 injured were attended to until arrival on land when they were handed over to professionals, the damage was localised and limited to furniture in the B deck bow bar, the smoke damage was minimal, the main generator failure was a chance occurrence and the rapid return to normality prevented major crisis amongst the passengers, who were able to be controlled (not without certain difficulties).

Nevertheless, the following aspects of the analysis are worthy of comment:

1. There was no direct and general action taken with the passengers until minute 15, when the emergency was already practically under control, even if there had been panic amongst certain groups.
2. It is not understood how the smoke passed from one area to another located so far away, it is possibly due to ventilation ducts and vents.
3. In any emergency aboard a passenger ship, when one of the principal actions is the control of passengers, the crew must be equipped with torches or similar equipment that can compensate for structural deficiencies in critical moments.
4. All the possible escape routes, including the most efficient, must be planned in advance for all the different emergency scenarios possible on board.
5. It remains to be seen if the power cut led to loss of pressure in the fire-fighting lines and the fitted sprinkler systems, as well as the communications via telephone and loud speaker, as it was not possible to ascertain the efficiency of the portable communication methods in all the necessary areas of the ship.
6. No comparison has been made between the time taken and the level of training of the crew, although it is possible that 10% of the crew, that is to say 6 crew members, is a deficient number for the number of courses of action that may have been necessary, taking into account the presence of smoke, falls, etc.

18 Bibliography

ALLPORT, G. W. Psicología de la personalidad. Barcelona: Paidós, 1965.

BANDURA, Albert. Aprendizaje social y desarrollo de la personalidad. Madrid: Alianza. 4ª ed., 1985.

BERKOWITZ, Leonard. Agresión: causas, consecuencias y control. Bilbao: Desclée de Brouwer, 1996.

ERIKSON, E. H. Dimensions of a New Identity. New York: Norton, 1974.

EYSENCK, H. J. El estudio científico de la personalidad. Buenos Aires: Paidós, 1971.

HAWKES, Kenneth Gale. Maritime security. Maryland, USA. Cornell Maritime Press, 1989.

International Maritime Bureau. Violence at sea. A review of terrorism, acts of war and piracy, and countermeasures to prevent terrorism. 2ª ed. Paris. ICC Publishing S.A., 1987.

International Maritime Bureau. Piracy at sea. Paris: ICC Publishing S.A., 1989.

LOMBROSO, Cesare. El delito, sus causas y remedios. Madrid: Librería General de Victoriano Suárez, 1902.

MASLOW, Abraham. Motivation and personality. New York: Harper & Row, cop., 1987.

OCNE. Los grandes grupos organizados. Tráfico de hachís en España. Mº Interior, 1998

PARRIT, Brian A. H. Security at sea. Terrorism, piracy and drugs. The Nautical Institute, 1991.

PASTOR RIDRUEJO, José A. Curso de Derecho Internacional Público y organizaciones internacionales. Tecnos, 1992.

PERVIN, L. y JOHN, O. P. Handbook of personality: Theory and research, 2nd edition. New York: Guilford, 1999.

ROGERS, C. La psicoterapia centrada en el cliente. Buenos Aires: Paidós, 1969.

SCOVAZZI, Tullio. Elementos del Derecho Internacional del Mar. Tecnos, 1955.

SHELDON, B. Cognitive-behavioural therapy: Research, practice and philosophy. New York: Routledge, 1995.

WRIGHT, Derek Psicología de la conducta moral. Barcelona: Planeta, 1974.

Magazines and journals

American Society for Industrial security. Subcomité sobre puertos fluviales y marítimos. "La seguridad en los puertos marítimos. SECURITY MANAGEMENT. December, 1992, pages. 25 to 28.

"Piracy and others crimes". IMO News, nº 1, 1993, pages. 9 to 16.

Hinz, Earl R. "Piracy Problems. Theft at sea remains a worldwide concern". OCEAN NAVIGATOR, 1995, pages. 75 to 77.

Prescott, John. "Action plan to fight ferry terror". Lloyd's List, 14.02.96.

Shuker, Liz. "Piracy centre saved by P&I clubs' cash". Lloyd's List.

Hindell, Keith. "Securing for piracy". Safety at Sea International, March 1993, pages. 17 to 18.

"Saga of the Arma Sierra. Planned Piracy". Fairplay, 30.11.95, pages. 18 to 20.

Other documents

DEPARTMENT OF TRANSPORT (UK) MERCHANT SHIPPING NOTICE nº M1517 Piracy and armed robbery. 1993.

Souter Shipping Ltd. Shipboard Safety Management Manual. Security, 1995.

IBM Regional Piracy Centre. Piracy update (01.01 to 30.09.95)

Kluwer-Harrap Handbooks. Security of shipping against potential terrorism. Handbook of security (supplement 7).

ITF. Alcohol and drug abuse: UTF directives. December 1992.

Criminal Statistics. Police Head Office. Home Office.

Document on the Regulations for filling in forms on common delinquency.

Legal and jurisprudence texts

Convention of the High Seas, 1958. Articles 14-23. Genoa, 1958.

United Nations Agreement on the Law of the Sea, 1982. articles 100-107 and 110-111. 1982.

IMO. Res. A. 545 (13) Measures to prevent acts of piracy and armed robbery against ships. London, 1983.

IMO. Res. A. 584 (14) Measures To Prevent Unlawful Acts Which Threaten the Safety Of Ships And Security Of Passengers and crew. London, 1985.

IMO. Res. A. 683 (17) Prevention and suppression of acts of piracy and armed robbery against ships. London, 1991.

IMO. Res. A. 738 (18) Measures to prevent and suppress acts of piracy and armed robbery against ships. London, 1993.

Instrument to ratify the United Nations convention on the law of the sea, made in Montego Bay on 10.12.92. BOE n° 39 on 14.02.97.

MSC 53/24, Annexe 14. Measures approved by the IMO Maritime Safety Committee to prevent illegal acts against passengers and crew on ships.

Royal Decree 1119/89 of the 15 September, regulating special high-speed vessels in Spanish waters. BOE n° 224 dated 19.09.89.

Order dated 18.01.90, determining identification requirements for special high-speed vessels. BOE n° 29 dated 02.02.90

Organic Law 4/97 dated 4th August, regulating the use of video cameras by the security forces and bodies in public areas.

Organic Law 12/95r dated 12th December, regarding the repression of contraband.

Royal Decree 1649/98 dated 24th July, a development of Title II of Organic Law 12/95 on the repression of cpntraband.

Organic Law 10/95 dated 23rd November, of the Penal Code. Crimes against public health.

Sentence n° 1088/97 dated 1st December, on regulations regarding the trafficking of drugs and contraband. Proportionality principle. Supreme Court. Penal Court.

Supreme Court Sentence, Penal Court, dated 20.11.97, through which the right of continual persecution is analysed.

Supreme Court Sentence, Court 3 Section 3, dated 09.02.96, the part which considers Royal Decree 1119/89 a merely organisational regulation.

Law 27/92 dated 24th November, on State Ports and the Merchant Navy.

Royal Decree 1027/89 dated 28th July, on flags, ship registration and maritime registration.

Order dated 12.11.98, regulating the locating of ships by satellite in Spain.

By-law 1987, for the monitoring of speedboats in Gibraltar.

EMBARCAÇÔES DE ALTA VELOCIDADES. Law Decree n° 249/90 dated 1st August (Portuguese law).

Information from web pages

- http://www.un.org/depts/los/unclos/
- http://www.un.org/depts/los/losconv
- http://www.imo.org/assembly/
- http://www.imo.org/meetings/fal/25/
- http://europa.eu.int/scadplus/leg/en/lvb/
- http://escher.upc.es/sts/bbdd/aranzadi.htm

MAGAZINES

- *Guardia civil*. Centro de Publicaciones del Ministerio del Interior.
- *Mar*. Instituto Social de la Marina. España
- *Intersec*. The Journal of International Security. England.
- *Seguritecnia*. Editorial Borrmart S.A. España.
- *Security management*. American Society for Industrial Security. USA.
- *Cuadernos de seguridad*. Estudios Técnicos, S.A. España.
- *Tierra, mar y aire*. Órgano de la Hermandad de Veteranos de las Fuerzas Armadas. España.
- *Formación de seguridad*. Editorial Borrmart, S.A. España.
- *Police*. Hare Publications. USA.
- *Marina civil*. Dirección General de la Marina Mercante. España.
- *Manuales del centro de formación de seguridad can padró*, S.A. España.
- *ISR*. International Security Review. England.
- *Gazeta securitas*. Revista de empresas de Seguridad. España.
- *Prosegur*. Revista de empresa de Seguridad. España.
- *Securitas técnica*. Revista de empresa de seguridad. España.
- *Face au risque*. Francia.

9 788498 803730